MODERN LEATHER DESIGN

WATSON-GUPTILL PUBLICATIONS / New York

MODERN LEATHER DESIGN

Donald Willcox

to the memory of S. Barbara Johnstone

Acknowledgments

Your author did wear holes in his boots and peck typewriter keys, but many other people helped in making this book possible. I loudly thank them all, some by name: Don Holden, Susan Meyer, and Margit Malmstrom, my editors; Dave Congalton, Bob Estrin, Larry Hyman, and Chuck Askren for photography; Phil Homes, Irwin Tuttie, Karen Shillington, Betti Nordstrom, and the students and staff at Goddard College for patience and advice; Sandy Willcox for her keen eye and pen; and the following leather craftsmen and leather shops for instruction, insight, friendship, and hospitality—Justis Taylor, Ted St. Germaine, Roger Rello, Leathercrafters, the Om Leather and Sandal Shop, Tom Tisdell, Bort Carleton, The Crafty Seaman, Poor Richard's, Button's Buckskins, Luella Schroeder, Bill Wilson, and "smiling toes" Walter Dyer. I would also like to thank the Berman Leather Company, the Tandy Leather Company, the Omega Chemical Company, the Osborne Tool Company, the New England Tanners Club, and the authors and publishers of *How to Sew Leather, Suede, Fur*.

Contents

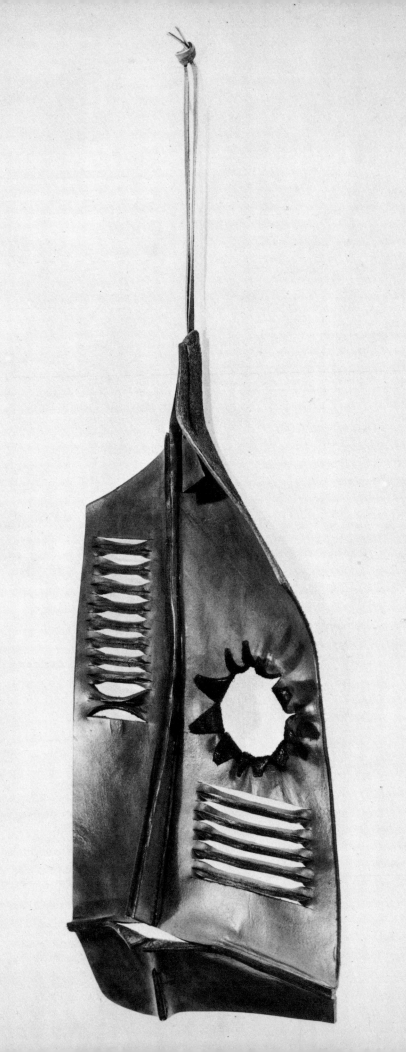

CHAPTER ONE

Working with leather

This book covers two subjects; leather and the craftsman. On the one hand, there's the material, the raw fabricating material called leather. On the other hand, there's the craftsman; an individual who, by using his own hands and mind, transforms this raw fabricating material into new forms.

Leather is sensuous. It has a texture, a color, and a smell; to feel it, to see it, to smell it, is to excite the senses. Of all the raw fabricating materials known to man, leather is perhaps the most sensuous. A fabric that can, of its own, stimulate the senses has an exciting potential for hand craftsmanship.

But what about you? How do you rate with leather? Does leather do anything to your senses? Do you feel any affinity with the material? It's one thing for me to tell you in print that leather is an exciting fabric, and quite another thing for you to experience this excitement for yourself. I can't impose the properties of leather upon you by merely printing black letters on a white page; you must experience this personally for yourself by actually confronting the fabric.

In compiling this book, I've found that leather craftsmen border on considering their craft to be almost a cult; they're protective, and some of them are very secretive about their technical and design involvement with the material. Finding leather has been a personal discovery for them, and they intimately respond to its qualities. These craftsmen have a special rapport with the fabric, and many of them are reserved about giving away trade secrets. It's a bit like knowing where Paradise Island is, but not daring to risk renting the boat to sail there for fear someone else will steal your secret and arrive ahead of you. I hope this book will represent the rental of that boat for you.

Before you start your journey, however, I've a suggestion to make. If you've never before worked with leather, let me suggest that you pop down to the nearest leather or sandal shop and just browse; feel the fabric, and make a point of inhaling a few deep swells as you walk in the door. From that experience, if the richness and excitement of the fabric doesn't captivate you, then my suggestion is to try working in stone; it's you, not the fabric, that's cold.

Alright, so maybe you'll say that everybody doesn't respond to the same thing. I agree. You've got a point. But I still insist that you test your own sensory responses to leather. If you don't respond to leather, then you'll have a real problem working with it. If leather says nothing to you, if it leaves you cold as being simply a pile of dead animal material heaped upon a table top, then the chances are that you've got nothing serious to offer it as a material for your own design exploration.

What I'm getting at is communication. Communication is a form of personal conversation; in this case, an intimate conversation between fabric and craftsman. The whole purpose of design is to communicate, the craftsman working with his mind and hands to produce a design or a product from a particular fabric, *leather*. This intimacy is a continuous give and take between craftsman and fabric. The fabric, its smell, color, texture, and inherent physical properties, challenges the craftsman to explore ideas in design. In a sense, the fabric suggests clues; the craftsman is receptive to, and absorbs, these clues. He interprets them, and develops them into something visual as an end result, or product. This visual end, whether it's a leather handbag, or a piece of leather sculpture, is a direct result of fabric–craftsman communication. And if this communication is strong enough, it will spill over onto the consumer.

Let me try and explain it in another way. The Greek word for design means poetry. In a sense, a leather designer is a leather poet; he gives visual order to raw material. A poet is a word designer; he establishes order with words; he makes words work. They develop meter, rhyme, sound, visual patterns, and when organized into a whole, these words say something; they develop content. In the same sense, a leather designer, by imposing visual order on a fabric makes that fabric work. By means of careful technique, he transforms that fabric into a product, or a work of art. As the poet is married to his words, so the leather craftsman is married to his fabric; and this marriage between craftsman and fabric is now only in its infancy. Communication again is the key word. If you

---

Leather wall hanging/mobile, combining many of the techniques that are discussed in this book: cutting, bending, bonding, sewing, edge-dressing, and finishing. This piece illustrates the versatility of leather as a plastic medium and shows just how fresh and unpredictable a leatherwork project can be. Made by Mrs. R. W. Koegler. Photo, courtesy of the American Craftsman's Council.

can communicate with leather, can carry on a conversation, an intimate visual exchange with it, then leather is all yours to discover.

Leather as a Medium for Exploration

Leather is in; tooling is out. For many years, like an outmoded hemline, leathercraft suffered from the stereotype of being a craft devoted to the stamping and tooling of floral and cowboy surface embellishments. The contemporary leather designer has dramatically transformed this image; his new explorations have grown beyond the stereotype of surface gimcracks and doodads. Leather is now speaking for itself as a pure design material without surface embellishment. The contemporary tanner has produced an endless spectrum of exploratory material which is a legitimate fabricating material in its own right, without falling victim to being only a means toward an end.

Historically, leather has been a product material. What this means is that the eventual end use to which leather has been applied, has, for the most part, been functionally oriented; a billfold, a handbag, a pair of sandals—something one can *use*. But leather shouldn't be restricted to being exclusively a product material. This text will introduce you to avenues of exploration in which leather is used nonfunctionally, in which it can be explored solely as a material for visual form, through sculpture for example, or as a dye canvas, or as a material for making relief decorations.

Format

No precedent or pattern has yet been established as to how one should compile a text on leather design. This is the first book of its kind. The book shoots off into unknown territory, and of course the author flys with it; it's a kind of exploration in its own right. Part of the book will deal with the techniques involved in producing various leather projects. Hopefully, the book includes "secrets" and helpful hints, but it doesn't tell all. I haven't yet discovered all there is to know on the subject. There's room for you to make discoveries of your own, and I hope you will.

Every book must be selective, the book in your hand included. What you see and read in this text falls way short of the whole story on leather. Leather is a vast subject. There are literally hundreds of items that can be produced from this single fabricating material; this book selects only a few dozen. This is partly my fault, and partly the book's fault. The book has a back cover; it must end. It can include only so much. As its author, I've made the choice literally and visually of what the book would say before it reached the back cover. It doesn't say all. It's only a toe in a very large shoe.

I do feel confident, however, that what the book does say, at least visually, through the selection of photographs, is pretty much what's happening in the world of contemporary leather design. Compiling this book has taken me into leather and sandal shops from Maine to Florida, from under the shadow of college campuses, to the surfers of Miami Beach, across the Midwest, and even into the fussy little boutiques on New York's Madison Avenue. Styles and fads burst quickly and have a habit of dying just as quickly. If anything, leather design is ahead of the book; but it's definitely and emphatically not behind the book.

The text excludes the techniques of tooling and stamping leather, because there are already enough pamphlets on that subject without duplicating them here. Finally, and at long last, I think that leather, in terms of the old Victorian West, with its cowboys and flowers, is beginning to grow up. I hope this text can help extricate leather from its craft stereotype of the past.

This book breaks itself down into specific areas and projects, with a reading and suppliers list included at the back. First I cover the materials and workshop; then I deal with tools and techniques; finally, I give examples of specific leather projects, from sandals to sculpture, with a final chapter on how to sell your leathergoods.

Becoming a Leather Craftsman

How does one become a leather craftsman? One becomes a leather craftsman by becoming a doer. This book isn't a novel. What it introduces you to requires action; it requires being a doer. When you've finished with the rhetoric, get off the page and get busy.

You'll be interested to know that most of the craftsmen whose work is illustrated in this text are relatively new to leather design; I mean new since about 1965. Before that time most of them didn't know one end of a cow from the other. Oh, they knew that leather didn't grow on the bark of a tree, but the point is that they dove in head first, experimented, and tried everything and anything. Nothing in leather is too bold or too difficult to at least try. And don't give up the first time. Go ahead and make mistakes. Trial and error in any craft makes for an excellent personal professor. Leather is a relatively quick and spontaneous craft to learn. The second time around on the same project you'll notice definite improvement in your ability, and by the fourth time around you'll begin to know what it is to be a leather craftsman. The whole process comes from being a doer.

What Can You Do with Leather?

What can you do with leather? That question is more accurate if turned around in the negative; what can't you do with leather? And frankly, I can't answer it in the negative. I've been so involved in discovering all of the many things that can be done with leather that I haven't yet found time to consider what can't be done with it.

Did you get the point yet that leather is a medium for discovery? I'll give you one additional shove for security. Sit down and write up a list of everything you can think of that can be, or already has been, made out of leather. Begin with things you're wearing, or what you can see around the house. The list grows long doesn't it? Now compare your list with my "idea" list at the end of this chapter. Maybe, if we were to double that list, we'd be a bit closer to its real potential. In case you hadn't noticed, this introduction has a message. I'm trying to build a fire under you; to get you soaring with your own ideas.

The following list of project ideas is included to stimulate your imagination, your involvement in design, and to give you vivid proof of the potentials of leather. This list is by no means complete. It represents only a strong beginning. I hope you can at least double the list with the addition of your own ideas. All of the items mentioned have been, or can be, made out of leather. A careful reading of this list should be ample proof that leather is one of the broadest design materials known to man.

Handbags: clutch bags, evening bags, shoulder saddlebags, shoulder strap bags, and hand, arm, or belt bags.

Billfolds: regular folding billfolds, and pocket secretary billfolds.

Handwear: gloves, mittens, and muffs.

Earwear: earmuffs.

Footwear: sandals (regular, Roman, and soleless), shoes, boots, slippers, moccasins, moc boots, Apache boots, shoe spats, bush leggings, and footwear ornaments (buckles and bows).

Head coverings: hats, head scraves, and headbands.

Garments: vests, shorts (*lederhosen*), peddle pushers, trousers, culottes, jerkins, jumpers, skirts, dresses, suits, sports coats, hunting coats, capes, and halter tops.

Garment patches: elbow patches, knee patches, and shoulder patches for reinforcing hunting jackets.

Eyewear: leather glasses frames, glasses cases, and headband eye shades.

Leather lacing: shoe and garment lacing, and lacing used as hair ribbon.

Animal equipment: collars, halters, leashes, saddles, and saddlebags.

Neckwear: regular neckties, string ties, neck scarves, collars, necklace pendants, neck pins, and leather string beads.

Belts: regular waist belts, safety belts, kidney belts, shell belts, tool belts, and game-carrying hunting belts.

Hair ornaments: hair pieces, and pig and pony-tail fasteners.

Rings: earrings, and finger rings both single piece and laminated and carved.

Leather as a slip cover and upholstery fabric.

Leather watchbands and bracelets.

Leather cases: knife sheaths, brief cases, suitcases, attaché cases, suitcase name holder frames, bowling ball cases, golfbags, golf club head covers, gadget cases, tool cases, manicure cases, comb cases, change purse cases, pocket–saver pencil and pen cases, compact cases, binocular cases, photography equipment and camera cases, key cases, musical instrument cases, toilet article cases, knapsacks, and leather envelopes and shopping bags.

Leather boxes: punched and laminated for jewelry and stationery.

Leather beads: door beads, room divider beads, leather beads as room screens.

Christmas tree ornaments.

Leather wall paneling.

Leather riding chaps.

Leather as a strip material for hand and loom weaving.

Leather as a strip material for weaving baskets.

Leather as an accessory handle material on ceramics.

Leather baskets: solid baskets (waste, storage, sewing, serving, bread, and picnic).

Archery quivers and arm guards.

Webbed leather suspended furniture: chairs, hammocks, and cradles.

Book and notebook covering material, and leather bookmarks.

Leather as a fabric for lamp shades.

Leather riding crops and whips.

Leather buckles, buttons, keepers, emblems, and crests.

Leather as a negative for abstract wall reliefs, and room dividers.

Leather as furniture veneer: table tops, chest and dresser tops and facings (either in relief, incised, or tooled.)

Chairs: sling chairs, sling stools, and leather webbed chairs.

Bar accessories: wine and liquor bottle racks, wineskins, and glass, cup, and tumbler holders.

Smoking accessories: pipe cases, cigarette cases, pipe racks, and tobacco pouches.

Desk accessories: blotter frames, and pencil and pen holders.

Kitchen accessories: knife holders, napkin rings, and place mats both solid and woven.

Bath accessories: towel bar holders, and brush and comb holders.

Auto accessories: seatbelts, litter bags, map holders, and visor cases.

Fireplace accessories: Bellows covering, wood totes, and fireplace tool holders.

Interior shop signs and display signs.

Leather as a framing material for photos, prints, and paintings.

Leather as clock facing.

Leather as a drum covering.

Leather as a material for sculptural form: kinetic mobiles, incised sculpture, laminated and carved sculpture, wet and bent sculpture, wall relief, leather as a sculptural skin covering, both natural and bleached, geometric leather solids, leather as plane sculpture, leather as an artist's dye canvas, and leather as a material for collage.

CHAPTER TWO

What is leather?

Before beginning this chapter on leather, the author would like to acknowledge and thank both the New England Tanners Club, and the Tandy Leather Company for assistance given me in preparing sections of this chapter. The New England Tanners Club published a small pamphlet entitled *Leather Facts*, in which they did a great deal of research on the history of leather and on the physical make-up of the material. The Tanners Club has granted me permission to use sections of their pamphlet in preparing this chapter, and I'm grateful for their help.

Leather: A Brief Historical Survey

The early history of leather is recorded only in bits and pieces, much of it from deductions linked with art history. We know, for example, that as early as Old Kingdom Egypt, about 2500 B.C., the practice of preserving pelts was already well established. Stone carvings from this period not only depict tanners at work, but record pharaohs wearing sandals obviously made of leather. Early uses of leather included footwear, apparel, forms of protective armor, tent shelters, canoes, water flagons, writing material, and as a window covering in lieu of glass.

By implication, one gets the feeling that preserving leather must have been tied in with preserving the human body through mummification for the life hereafter. Early Egyptians were masters of the art of preserving the human body. It stands to reason that at some point they must have applied the principles of mummification to animal skins. The formulæ used to preserve these skins aren't known; my assumption is that the Egyptians must have used certain preservative properties found in plants indigenous to the Nile Valley.

By the year 500 B.C., the Greeks had developed leatherworking into a well-established trade. The Greeks were definitely using preservative properties

Leather hanging lamp, an example of the degree of sophistication that it's possible to attain in hand leathercraft. The lamp is suspended from a braided leather strap which conceals the cord. When making lamps of this kind, it's a good idea to allow for plenty of ventilation (as was done here), in order to allow the heat from the bulb to escape the cylinder. Made by Mrs. R. W. Koegler. Photo, courtesy of the American Craftsman's Council.

derived from bark and leaves found in the area and soaked in water to produce a tan.

As far as we now know, the Hebrews were the first to develop the use of oak-bark tanning, a process that was widely used all around the world until the discovery of modern tanning in the United States around 1800. Oak-bark tanning was the process of preserving pelts whereby specific derivatives of the oak tree, when absorbed into the fibers of a pelt, would preserve the pelt indefinitely.

Early settlers in this country were quick to discover that the preservation of buckskin was nothing new to the Indians, and Marco Polo wrote detailed descriptions of the uses made of leather by the Chinese. It would appear that the preservation of leather was developed independently by various cultures, and that it must have been almost intuitive to man's drive for survival.

Around the beginning of the nineteenth century, Sir Humphrey Davy discovered that tanning agents could be obtained from trees other than the oak. His early experiments eventually led to the discovery of basic chromium sulfate as a tanning agent—now referred to as chrome tanning.

Modern tanning methods were triggered by the development of two relatively simple instruments, the thermometer and the hydrometer. With the use of these two instruments, the tanner could now accurately determine the temperature of his tanning solutions and the density, or strength, of the solution additives. In more recent years, the development of the electronic pH meter—used to determine the acidity or alkalinity of a solution—has given the tanner still another valuable tool in controlling the rate at which various chemical reactions take place. Along with these tools came the development of the leather–splitting machine and other tanning machines which have now increased the output of leather to staggering proportions.

The contemporary tanner is still making new discoveries. If anything, he's way ahead of the designer and the consumer. Every day he's able to come up with new tannage combinations, with new finishes, new grain patterns, and new "fatliquoring" properties to produce an infinite spectrum of leather from which the designer may choose. In the future, the tanner will, hopefully, be challenged to experiment with tannage combinations designed specifically for sculpture, furniture, and other new uses still to be explored.

Leather as Raw Material

Leather is a flexible sheet material—a material suitable for fabrication. Other materials which fall within this broad definition include textiles, paper, sheet rubber, and certain plastics. In order to define leather accurately, one must see it as an end product of several processes. It's appropriate to begin by looking at these processes before defining leather.

Leather begins with the birth of an animal. This animal is born with a skin covering; a covering of inherited characteristics. This skin covering has an internal structure of interwoven fibers arranged in a completely random pattern. Millions of coil-like molecules develop into tiny fibrous strands. These fibrous strands are woven into each other to form random bundles of fibrous strands, and in turn, the bundles of strands are interlocked with each other in a three-dimensional manner. What results is literally a whole network of molecules, fibers, strands, and bundles of strands all interlocked with each other in a completely random maze.

No two animals, even within the same species, have the same molecular skin structure. Therefore, from birth, no two animal skin coverings are ever identical. Each has its own unique and random internal structure. This is equally true of human beings. No two human fingerprints are exactly identical; each has its own unique characteristics.

What happens to that animal after birth? What kind of care does its mother give it? What are its feeding habits? Does it eat a balanced diet, or must it become a scavenger in order to survive? And what happens to the animal in relation to the natural elements?

All of us are familiar with the way in which salt spray and wind can effect the hands and face of a seacoast lobsterman; his skin develops deep creases, peaks and valleys almost like a topographical map. His exposure to natural elements affects the condition and appearance of his skin. The same is true for an animal; climate and exposure play vital parts in the development and condition of the skin.

What happens to that animal during its lifetime? Is it involved in fights with other animals? Does it get scratched by barbed wire? What type of scar patterns develop on its skin covering? Does a deer hunter drag his buck two miles out of the woods, with the animal's spine bumping along over rocks and branches? What kind of care does the animal receive after it's "natural" life has ended? All of these questions—separately or when lumped together—directly affect the raw material of the pelt even before it's a candidate for leather.

Thus, leather begins its metamorphosis into an end product—a flexible sheet material—at the very inception of the animal's life. This animal skin covering becomes a candidate for leather once the animal's life is terminated. The random molecular structure of this skin covering varies, even within the same species; the animal's diet, its care by the mother, its exposure to natural elements, its encounter with the hazards of life, and the immediate care given to it after its death all affect its future as a candidate for leather. The sum total of all of these elements constitutes the raw material that eventually will produce a given piece of leather. This is why no two finished pieces of leather are ever identical.

Once the life of an animal is terminated, its skin covering is referred to as a pelt. A pelt is an untanned animal skin with the hair still on it. This covering, or pelt, is removed or cut away from the animal's carcass immediately after the animal's death. In this natural pelt state, the skin, if not immediately cared for, will rapidly deteriorate and decompose.

Curing

The first step in the creation of leather after the skin covering has been removed from the animal is that of curing, which usually takes place at a slaughter house. The pelt is placed in an environment in which protein-destroying organisms cannot function. In a sense, the pelt is made neutral by the curing process; the pelt is still not tanned, it's still not leather, but yet it's not decomposing either. It's in a frozen, neutral state where nothing happens to it at all.

There are several methods by which pelts can be cured; the most common of these is the use of salt (sodium chloride). Salt curing can be accomplished in either of two ways; wet salting, or brine curing. In the case of wet salting, the pelt is first washed, and then salted. The pelt is placed hair down on a flat surface of concrete, washed, and then sprinkled with a generous coating of granular salt. Enough salt is applied so that there is a thorough penetration of salt into all parts of the pelt fibers.

Brine curing is a much faster method and is used by commercial firms using large vats called raceways. The pelts are soaked in these vats after the vats have been filled with a brine solution of salt crystals. They're allowed to soak in this solution until they're completely saturated. At this point, the protein destroying organisms are no longer active.

When a pelt is removed from an animal it has two sides; a hair side and a flesh side. After the pelt has been transformed into leather, the hair side is called the grain side. The flesh side always remains the flesh side for identification purposes.

At this point in curing, a pelt is still a pelt—it's not yet leather. The cured pelt is transported from the slaughter house to the tannery, along with hundreds of other pelts, where it will begin its final metamorphosis into leather.

Trimming and Sorting

Upon arrival at the tannery, pelts are first prepared for processing by trimming and sorting; the heads, long shanks, and other perimeter areas of the pelt are trimmed off so as not to interfere with the tannery equipment through which the pelts will be processed. The pelts are also cut lengthwise along the backbone, head to tail, to produce two sides. This is the origin of the term "side leather," or in other words, leather that's processed as two separate sides rather than as one whole hide.

Soaking

The pelts are next soaked in paddle vats filled with water, to which chemical wetting agents have been added in order to restore some of the natural moisture lost in the curing process. This initial soaking not only restores lost natural moisture, but additionally washes and further disinfects the pelts.

Fleshing

The next step is called fleshing. Here, a mechanical process removes excess flesh, fat, and muscle found on the inside (flesh side) of the pelts. A fleshing machine equipped with rollers and cutting blades scrapes away this excess material.

De-hairing

De-hairing is the removal of pelt hair by a combination of chemical and mechanical processes. Dipilatory chemical agents (a lime solution) destroy the hair or attack the hair roots so that it will come free of the pelt; these agents loosen the epidermis (the hard outer layer of skin covering the grain), and remove certain soluble skin proteins that lie deeply embedded within the pelt. The pelts are soaked in the de-hairing solution, again in the paddle vats, and then removed to a de-hairing machine which generates a rubbing action to finally remove all hair.

Bating

Bating is the process of removing all of the residual dipilatory chemical agents left in the pelt after de-hairing. Bating is a three-step process in which the pelts are first washed in a de-liming solution, then soaked in a solution to absorb bates (enzymes similar to those found in the digestive systems of animals that are used to destroy all remaining undesirable constituents in the pelt), and finally re-washed thoroughly to remove all substances used in all of the separate processes up to this time.

Pickling

The pickling of a pelt places it in a condition to receive and absorb the actual tanning agents. Pickling is accomplished with a variety of acids, the most common of which is sulfuric acid, mixed with common salt. The pickling process is a form of preservation in itself and is the final step before the actual tanning.

Tanning

Tanning is the process of converting the pelt into a stable, non-putrescible, or rot-resisting, material. The raw collagen fibers of the pelt are transformed into a stable material that will not rot. The tanning procedure also significantly improves many of the pelt's natural properties; for example, its dimensional stability, abrasion resistance, resistance to chemicals and to heat, the ability to flex, and the ability to endure repeated cycles of wetting and drying.

Chrome tanning is the method in the widest use today. Briefly, this method consists of soaking the pelts in large revolving drums filled with soluble chromium salts, primarily basic chromium sulfate.

A second tanning method is called vegetable, or bark, tanning. This is a tanning process where the pelts are soaked in vegetable materials which are derived from certain kinds of wood and plants. A third tanning process is known as mineral tanning, in which the pelts are soaked in one of several mineral substances, primarily the salts of chromium, aluminum, and zirconium. Still a fourth process of tanning is called oil tanning. With this process, the pelts are soaked in certain fish oils which tend to produce very soft, pliable leather such as chamois. And then there's a combination tanning process where the pelts may be first chrome tanned and then later re-tanned with vegetable materials in an effort to absorb the best of both processes. The process used by the tanner is completely dependent upon the use that the finished leather will be put to—whether it will become sole material, garment leather, lining leather, or perhaps even leather for industrial belting. Each separate method produces special results for special uses, but all processes convert the pelt into a stable, non-putrescible material.

Wringing

After the pelt is tanned, it's fed between two large rollers which squeeze out excess moisture to prepare the pelt for the process of splitting and shaving. The wringing process works on the same principle as an ordinary clothes wringer.

Splitting and Shaving

A leather-splitting machine is similar to an ordinary band saw turned on its side so that the rapidly moving blade edge is horizontal. After wringing, the leather is fed into the splitting machine which adjusts the thickness of the leather into uniformity throughout the entire pelt. A splitting machine literally splits the thickness of a pelt in half, producing two separate pieces of fabric. This is the origin of the term *split*, used in leather buying. A split is the underneath layer of side leather which has been split off the whole pelt; it's devoid of a natural grain. This split becomes a by-product of the original pelt; another whole piece of fabric. After splitting, the pelt is then fed into a shaving machine which further adjusts the uniformity of the pelt's thickness.

Re-tanning

Re-tanning to combine the desirable properties of more than one tanning agent has already been mentioned. This procedural step is optional and is performed after the splitting and shaving of a pelt.

Coloring

There are hundreds of dyestuffs and auxiliary products available to today's tanner for coloring; the tanner can produce a myriad of appealing shades with excellent resistance to fading, perspiration bleed, and to the effects of dry cleaning and washing. Penetration of the dyestuff into the pelt fibers is one of the most important considerations that the tanner faces. The most commonly used dyestuffs and their chief characteristics include:

Acid dyes (penetrate readily, make bright and lively shades).

Metallized dyes (level dyeing, for subdued pastel shades).

Direct dyes (surface dyeing, produces deep shades).

Basic dyes (surface dyeing, making brilliant shades).

Fatliquoring

Fatliquoring is the final wet chemical operation in the tanning process. This is a process in which the fibers are lubricated so that after drying they will be capable of sliding over one another. In addition to regulating the pliability of the leather, the fatliquor contributes greatly to its tensile strength. The basic ingredients in fatliquoring consist of oil and related fatty substances which represent products of the animal, vegetable, and mineral kingdoms.

Setting Out

The first step in preparing the pelts for drying is to set them out. This is a machine process which smoothes and stretches the pelt, while compressing and squeezing excess moisture from it. After being set out, the pelts still contain about 60% moisture.

Drying

Drying is the removal of all but equilibrium moisture from the pelt. Drying is done in one of three ways. The simplest method is called hanging, in which the pelt is draped over a horizontal shaft, as on a clothesline, and allowed to dry. Another method is toggling; the pelts are stretched over frames and held in place by toggle hooks and then dried on the frames in a drying oven. The third process is known as pasting; the pelt is literally pasted onto large plates, scrubbed, wiped, and then dried in a drying oven while the plate moves on a monorail. Normal leather, dry to the touch, still contains 10% to 12% moisture.

Conditioning

Conditioning is the process of re-wetting the pelt with a fine spray mist of water to raise the moisture content to about 25%. The drying process renders the pelt too hard and unworkable for most consumer use, and the proper pelt moisture content must be reestablished.

Staking

Staking is the process of mechanically softening the pelt by both pulling and rolling it to make it pliable.

In combination with the correct fatliquoring treatment, staking governs the final firmness or softness of the pelt.

Buffing

Buffing is a mechanical sanding process that reduces the visual appearance of surface blemishes on the grain side of the pelt. Leather that's not buffed is called full grain leather.

Finishing

Finishing is the process of applying a thin film of several available finishing substances over the grain side of the pelt. A finish film enhances the color, and increases the pelt's resistance to stain and abrasion.

An almost infinite variety of finishes are available to produce special characteristics in leather. Usually, several coats of finish are applied with intermediate drying between coats in order to achieve the desired end properties.

Plating

Plating smooths the finished grain surface and can be used to induce artificial embossed grains. The plating fixes the finishing film and smooths the grain. If the tanner wishes to induce an artificial grain pattern into the pelt, he does it during this process. It's possible to emboss a wide variety of textured effects on the surface of leather, including the simulation of another animal's grain characteristics. While on the subject of embossed grains, I'd like to add one word of caution about exploring the use of embossed grains on specific design projects. It's been my experience in working with embossed grains that somehow the embossing process with some tanners seems to squeeze the leather to the point where the dye penetration is often very close to the surface. If the particular piece of leather is to be bent under stress, it wouldn't be uncommon for an embossed grain to end up with a mottled color effect; the embossed bend area exposes undyed fibers. In other words, when you bend an embossed grain, you're likely to be able to see the undyed fibers deep in the bend area.

Measuring

No two pelts have exactly the same surface area. The tanner buys pelts by weight and sells them to the consumer by area. A measuring machine—a planimeter—is used to determine the square feet in each pelt side. The footage is written or stamped on the flesh side of the pelt before it leaves the tannery.

Grading

Grading is done by eye and hand; it generally refers to the total area of imperfection present on a given hide, the temper of the leather, and the uniformity of color and thickness. Commercial leather grading is based on either a numerical (1, 2, 3, 4, etc.) or a letter

(A, B, C, D, etc.) scale. As a rule of thumb, a #1, or A grade, refers to an almost perfect piece of leather (imperfections smaller than the size of the human hand). A #2, or B grade, refers to imperfections equal to the size of the human hand. A #3, or C grade, refers to imperfections equal to the size of two hands —and so forth. The grade of a given piece of leather is not related to its quality. A #4, or D grade, piece of leather is tanned exactly in the same manner as a #1, or A grade; it's largely the surface area of imperfections (scar tissue, holes, brand marks) that determine the grade.

Definition of Leather

Having traced the life of a pelt from the birth of the animal to the completion of the tanning process, it's now possible to define leather. Leather is the pelt of an animal which has been transformed by tanning into a stable, non-putrescible, flexible sheet material.

The Physical Properties of Leather

What are the physical properties of leather that make it such a versatile and challenging material for design? I will briefly summarize most of these physical properties in the hope that the reader will gain both a technical and emotional feeling for leather. I would again like to thank the New England Tanners Club for allowing me to quote and paraphrase from their pamphlet *Leather Facts.*

Tensile Strength

Tensile strength, by definition within the trade, is the greatest longitudinal stress to which a substance can be subjected without tearing apart. Leather has an extremely high tensile strength; it's one of the strongest flexible sheet materials known to man. The internal fiber structure of leather, as we have already seen, accounts for this high tensile strength. Shoes, belts, gloves, straps, and industrial leather belting, to name only a few of the practical uses of leather, are all subjected to a constant tugging and pulling. Leather's excellent tensile strength permits it to meet maximum stress requirements with ease because each tiny leather fiber joins with other fibers to communally accept an equal share of the stress load.

Tear Strength

Leather has an extremely high resistance to tearing. We have already seen how the molecular structure of leather is completely random—erratic in its make-up. In comparison, many other fabricating materials, for example textiles, are developed around a weave. This weave is induced by man and machine into a more or less orderly uniformity. Leather is exactly the opposite in its core structure; there's no path of least resistance. This absence of weave, or uniformity in the molecular structure of leather accounts for its high resistance to tearing. This gives the leather designer a material that can withstand maximum abuse.

Elongation

Elongation refers to a substance's ability to lengthen, or stretch, when stress is applied to it. Elongation in leather can be directly controlled by the particular tanning process. It can therefore be tanned for machinery belting where a minimum stretch is a necessity, or it can be tanned for gloves where a maximum stretch is a requirement. Leather is unsurpassed as a flexible sheet material in meeting the demands of elongation in a great variety of uses.

Flexibility

Flexibility is one of the inherent, rather than special, properties of leather. There are no weak links in the internal core structure of leather; it can be flexed top to bottom, side to side, grain in, or grain out. A piece of leather can literally be bent in half in any direction without damage to the fabric core. This ability to flex is of prime importance to the designer.

The amount of flexibility in leather can be controlled through the tanning process to adapt itself to opposite extremes of either hot or cold, or wet or dry. For example, leather can be tanned especially for boots worn in the Arctic, the tropics, or the desert.

Puncture Resistance

Leather is highly resistant to puncture. All one has to do to prove this is to try and run a needle through even a thin scrap. Again, the random molecular structure allows for no holes, or weak links in the fabric. This property of puncture–resistance makes leather extremely durable and resistant to wear and abrasion.

Ability to Absorb and Transmit Moisture

We have seen in the tanning process just how many times leather is subjected to soaking and drying without damage to the material; its ability to absorb and transmit moisture repeatedly seems almost infinite. This physical property of leather is extremely valuable to the shoe and garment manufacturer, as well as to the shoe and garment consumer. This is a tough and durable fabric; one that does not have to be pampered. To the leather sculptor, the ability to absorb and transmit moisture is one of leather's most exciting features. Being able to repeat the wetting and drying process *ad infinitum*, the leather sculptor is able to experiment with his visual forms; if he doesn't like what he's come up with in a given bent form, he can re–soak the leather and begin his form exploration all over again. And leather's ability to absorb and transmit moisture gives it an exciting potential for smell. It can be continually treated with oils, waxes, and other finishes which will transmit an environment of rich smells. This ability to absorb moisture also makes it an ideal material for liquid coloring agents; still another bonus for the leather sculptor.

Breathing and Insulating Qualities

No other material affords such universal comfort regardless of the season. Whether you're spending a summer evening on the patio or tramping through a cold winter snowstorm, a leather jacket helps to maintain the air next to your body at a comfortable temperature. Remember that leather was originally the skin covering of an animal; the animal's only outer garment. It's so constructed that it combines both breathing and insulating properties. And in addition, leather's dense fiber structure also acts to keep sharp winds from penetrating through the fabric.

Conclusion

The photographs in this text are visual proof of leather's unparalleled combination of physical properties as a flexible sheet material. No other flexible sheet material can be cut and fabricated into such a wide variety of uses. It can be molded or bent into an endless variety of shapes, and no matter what new shape it's in, leather maintains all of its physical properties. Leather is truly the sleeping giant of design materials.

CHAPTER THREE

Selecting, buying, and storing leather

Leather is commercially available from alligator to zebra; practically the whole spectrum of the animal kingdom. And, within each species, pelts can be tanned into an endless variety of induced physical characteristics (textures, colors, oil bases, finishes, and thicknesses). For example, a cowhide pelt can either be left with the hair intact, given an artificially embossed grain, or left as a smooth, natural grain; it can be dyed one of many colors, left natural, or bleached; it can be treated with fish oils, minerals, or vegetable materials; it can be finished with waxes, or aniline finishes; it can be left intact up to between 14 and 16 ounces thick, or it can be spilt into as thin as 1 or 2 ounces thick. The varieties of tannage combinations for cowhide are equally applicable to most other animal pelts.

Cowhide is the most widely used leather in the world today and the production of leather is an enormous world-wide industry. The approximate number of cattle is presently over one billion head, with the United States producing over one hundred million head.

List of Commercially Available Hides

The following list, with definitions, uses, and in some cases average square feet per hide, will give you some idea of what's available on the market. The list is by no means complete. It reflects only the most common and readily available leathers. The author would like to thank the New England Tanners Club for help in preparing this list.

Alligator: Alligator, crocodile, and related types. Shoe uppers, billfolds, small cases, bags, and belts.

Back: A side with the belly cut off, usually 22-26 square feet per side.

Belly: The lower part of a side, usually 6-10 square feet per skin.

Belting: Available in round and flat, usually comes on a roll, and is used in industry, and for handbag straps.

Buckskin: Deer and elk skins having the outer grain removed. 7-12 square foot skins. Infinite uses.

Bullhide: Hide from a male bovine capable of reproduction. Infinite uses.

Cabretta: A hair-type sheepskin; specifically those from Brazil, used in garments; skins average 7-9 square feet.

Calfskin: Skin from a young bovine, male or female, generally weighing less than 15 pounds. Infinite uses. Skins average 8-12 square feet.

Capeskin: From a sheep raised in South Africa. Used in coats, jackets, hats, and bags. Skins average 6-9 square feet.

Carpincho: A water rodent native tc South America; like pigskin. Same uses as pigskin.

Cattlehide: General term for hides from a bovine of any breed or sex, but usually mature and over 25 pounds.

Cordovan: From a section of horsehide called the shell.

Cowhide: Hide from a mature female bovine that has produced a calf. Infinite uses.

Deerskin: Deer and elk skins having the grain intact. Used for garments, gloves, hats, slippers, and moccasins. Skins average 7-12 square feet.

Extreme: A side just larger than kip, but smaller than cow or steer sides; usually 17-20 square feet in size. Infinite uses.

Flesher: The underneath (flesh side) layer of a sheepskin which has been split off. Used to make chamois.

Glove horse: A supple horsehide used for outdoor garments; skins average 15-20 square feet to a side.

Goatskin: Skin from a mature goat. Skins average 5-7 square feet. Used for billfolds, and handbags.

Goatskin rawhide: A leather tanned for drum tops. Skins average 5-7 square feet.

Hair calf: The skin of a calf with the hair intact. Sometimes used in novelty garments. Skins average 8-10 square feet.

Hair calf clipped: Calfskin with the hair clipped short. Used for novelty garments. Skins average 8-10 square feet.

Hair sheep: Sheep from several species whose wool is hair like.

Harness backs: Heavy cowhide backs for work harness, heavy belts, and sculpture.

Heifer: A female bovine, under three years of age, that has not produced a calf.

Hide: The whole pelt from large animals (cattle, horses, etc.).

Horsehide: Hide from a horse or colt. Skins average 15-20 square feet per side. Infinite uses, especially used in garments and belting.

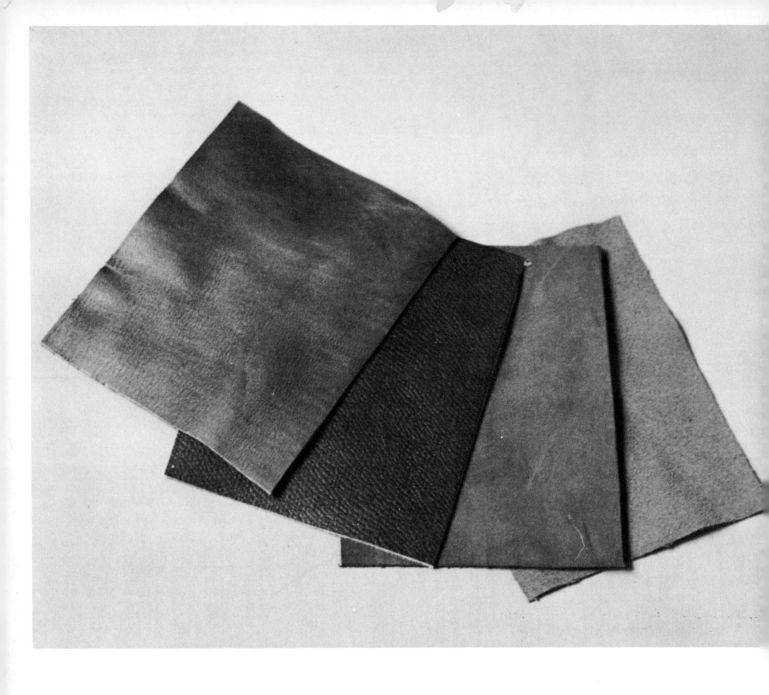

Swatches of leather, showing differences in texture; left to right: grained cowhide, embossed cowhide, suede cowhide, and split cowhide. Photo, Phil Grey.

Kangaroo: From the Australian kangaroo or wallaby. Very dense and tough.

Kidskin: Skin from a kid or young goat; soft and pliable. Often sueded.

Kipskin: Skin from a bovine, male or female, intermediate in size between a calf and mature animal. Infinite uses. Skins average 9-17 square feet per side.

Lambskin: Skin from a lamb or young sheep. Used in billfolds, and small cases. Skins average 8-10 square feet.

Latigo: Cowhide sides specially oil tanned for saddle strings, lacing, etc. Latigo is buff yellow in color and is likely to stretch.

Lizard: Any of a great number of the lizard family.

Live oak: A tanning process on cowhide, especially clear and even grained. It has infinite uses, but is especially good for sculpture, and tooling.

Mocha: Middle East hair sheep, usually with the grain removed.

Ostrich: From the two-legged animal native to North Africa. Used for elegance in small articles.

Peccary: From a wild boar native to Central and South America, similar to pigskin. Skins average 5-7 square feet. Used in billfolds, cases, gloves, and undersoles.

Pelt: An untanned hide or skin with the hair still on it.

Pigskin: Skin from pigs and hogs. Skins average 5-8 square feet. Used in gloves, luggage, cases, and linings.

Rawstock: General term for hides or skins that a tanner has received in a preserved state, preparatory to tanning; a tanner's inventory of raw material.

Saddle skirting: Very heavy cowhide sides tanned for saddles. Also excellent for sculpture.

Sharkskin: From certain of the shark species; distinctive grain and unusual wearing qualities.

Shearlings: Wooled sheep and lambskins, tanned with the wool intact; this leather is available with a nap of either ¼" or ¾". The skins average 6-10 square feet. Used for cold weather garments, and liner pads for gun cases, moccasins, and saddles.

Sheepskin: Skin from mature sheep; used for slippers, handbags, hat bands, and chamois.

Short–hair calf: Small calfskin with the hair left intact. Used for novelty handbags, belts, and upholstered furniture.

Skin: The pelt from small animals (calf, sheep, goat, etc.).

Skiver: The thin grain layer split from a sheepskin.

Side: One half skin or hide usually 22-26 square feet on cowhide.

Slunk: The skin of an unborn or prematurely born calf, tanned with the hair left intact. Used on novelty billfolds, and small items.

Snake: Any of a number of the snake species; novelty grains. Is usually used after being cemented to a backing.

Snake, cobra: The skin of a cobra snake; 4"-5" wide and 4'-5' long. Used for novelty vests, belts, buttons, collars and trim.

Steerhide: Hide from a mature male bovine, incapable of reproduction, having been raised for beef.

Suede: A leather-finishing process where the flesh side is buffed to produce a nap. Term refers to the napping process and is unrelated to the type of pelt used. Very often used in garments, handbags, belts, and shoe uppers.

Walrus: Skin from a walrus, also sometimes sealskin. Exceptionally thick and tough leather.

Water buffalo: Flat-horned buffalo, primarily from the tropics; very commonly used on sandals.

The Subdivisions of a Hide

In processing most hides from large animals, it's customary to cut them into two or more smaller sections for easier handling. The nomenclature of the various visual subdivisions of the hide are shown on the following chart, along with the approximate number of square feet per section for an average large cowhide. The chart is reproduced here with permission of the New England Tanners Club.

Shoulder:	JIHGFE,	10-15 sq. ft.
Side:	ABCD,	22-26 sq. ft.
Back:	ABHQ,	15-18 sq. ft.
Belly:	EKLM,	6-10 sq. ft.
Belly Center:	NFRO,	3-5 sq. ft.
Single Bend:	AKFP,	8-12 sq. ft.

The way in which leather is described and sold varies; the tanner sells in one way, and the wholesaler or retailer may sell it another way (depending upon what he actually has in inventory at the time). If a given piece of leather is described as a bend, or shoulder, the preceding diagram will help you to visually grasp this description in terms of which sections of the hide are included.

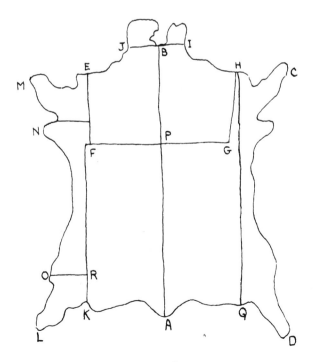

Figure 1. *The sections of a pelt.*

How is Leather Usually Sold?

Usually leather is priced by the square foot, or by the pound. The whole buying process of leather is somewhat complicated by a trade language. The most common designation of leather, at least in retail buying, is according to ounces. Leather is readily available in thicknesses from 1 to 12 ounces thick. It can be purchased thicker than 12 ounces, but only a few retailers stock it over 12 ounces, and very often heavy leather must be specially ordered. The ounce designation indicates the number of ounces per square foot on a given piece of leather. For example, 1 ounce leather weighs 1 ounce per square foot; 4 ounce leather weighs 4 ounces per square foot, and so on. The following chart is a visual representation of the actual thickness of leather according to its ounces per square foot. Generally, leather under 10 ounces in thickness is priced by the square foot; leather over 10 ounces in thickness is priced by the pound.

SCALE FOR DETERMINING THE THICKNESS OF LEATHER

Black solid lines represent leather.

1 2 3 4 5 6 7 8 9 10
ounces

Within the trade, leather is also designated by additional weight and thickness scales. The Tanners Council of America, Inc., has standardized these weight and thickness designations. If, in purchasing leather from a given supplier, the reader should happen to run onto these trade designations, the following charts are included for enlightenment.

STANDARD WEIGHT DESIGNATIONS
Side Upper Leather

HHH	5½ to 6	ounces
HH	5 to 5½	ounces
H	4½ to 5	ounces
HM	4 to 4½	ounces
M	3½ to 4	ounces
LM	3 to 3½	ounces
L	2½ to 3	ounces
LL	2 to 2½	ounces

For plumps of any given weight, place the letter "P" in front of the weight and add ¼ of an ounce. The above weight designations represent general practice in the Side Upper Leather Division of the United States tanning industry. Weights are gauged in the bend area, along the backbone, and approximately 6" in.

Leather Conversion Chart: Thickness/Weight

Within the trade, leather is very often referred to in thickness designations other than ounces. Again, if a reader of this book runs into these designations when purchasing leather, the following leather thickness conversion chart will clarify the language problem.

OUNCES	MILLIMETERS	IRONS	FRACTIONAL INCHES	DECIMAL INCHES
1	.40	.75	1/64	.016
2	.79	1.50	1/32	.031
3	1.19	2.25	3/64	.047
4	1.59	3.00	1/16	.063
5	1.99	3.75	5/64	.078
6	2.39	4.50	3/32	.094
7	2.78	5.25	7/64	.109
8	3.18	6.00	1/8	.125
9	3.58	6.75	9/64	.141
10	3.96	7.50	5/32	.156
11	4.37	8.25	11/64	.172
12	4.78	9.00	3/16	.188

FOR QUICK MENTAL CONVERSION

1 ounce equals .4 millimeters
¼ ounce equals .1 millimeters
2½ ounces equals 1.0 millimeters

1 ounce equals ¾ iron
1 and ⅓ ounces equals 1 iron

1/48" equals 1 iron
1/64" equals 1 ounce

How Do You Purchase Leather?

If you're buying small quantities of leather, you may be restricted in your volume buying to purchasing only from retail outlets. There are 108 Tandy Leather Company retail stores throughout the country, and all of them provide generous discounts on volume buying. If you're able to buy wholesale, the list at the back of the book will provide the names and addresses of a number of suppliers. The sales policy of the individual leather wholesaler varies greatly. Some of them welcome small quantity buying, even one skin at a time; others insist upon only large volume purchases. You'll have to test out the particular supplier for yourself in his attitude toward the small craftsman. One way of getting onto the right track with the wholesaler is to bring him in a handbag you've made for his wife. The wholesaler can do a great deal for you; don't forget to do something for him. And don't overlook the local shoe repair shop as a possible source of leather supply, or for that matter, the local sandal shop. These two craftsmen are often willing to lump your small order in with their orders so that both of you can benefit from volume prices.

Garment Conversion Table: Fabric Yardage/Leather Footage

No two skins are uniform in their size, and no two tannage processes ever produce exact reproductions of the previous process in terms of duplicating color. If you're buying leather for a garment, buy it all at one time and out of one tannage lot. When buying garment leather, patterns usually call for material in designations of yards, while leather is sold by the square foot. There's a simple conversion formula for converting fabric yardage to leather footage. If the pattern calls for 36″ width material, the conversion factor is 9; if the patterns calls for 54″ width material, the conversion factor is 13. And then, when you convert yardage to leather footage, you should allow an additional 15% for loss in cutting. The following examples illustrate two conversions; one for 36″ width material, the other for 54″ width material.

Your pattern calls for 3 yards of material which comes in a width of 36″. The conversion factor for 36″ is 9.

First, multiply the yardage by the conversion factor. $3 \times 9 = 27$

Second, multiply the result by the 15% that you'll lose in cutting. $27 \times 15\% = 4.05$

Third, add 27 to your result.

The number of square feet of leather required is 31.05.

Your pattern calls for 3 yards of material which comes in a width of 54″. The conversion factor for 54″ is 13.

First, multiply the yardage by the conversion factor. $3 \times 13 = 39$

Second, multiply the result by the 15% that you'll lose in cutting. $39 \times 15\% = 4.85$

Third, add 39 to your result.

The number of square feet of leather required is 43.85.

Note: It's perhaps safest to round conversion square feet to the next highest number; in the two examples, the next highest rounded numbers would be 32 and 44 square feet, respectively. If the hide is very small, it's better to allow for a 20% loss in cutting.

On garments, the patterns will always call for the number of yards. A general guide for leather footage for a few garments is: 30 square feet for a short jacket, 55 to 60 square feet for a three quarter length coat, and 72 square feet for a full length coat. The safest method is to convert the yardage to footage for yourself and then apply it against the actual purchase of leather. (The author would like to thank Margaret B. Krohn and Phyllis W. Schwebke for their help in the above conversion charts. Their book, *How To Sew Leather, Suede, Fur* is published by The Bruce Publishing Company, of Milwaukee, Wisconsin.)

Some Additional Suggestions on Leather Buying

In garment leather buying, if it's at all possible, I suggest that you personally go down to the supplier with your pattern, select the leather, and then match the pattern against the given skins. This procedure will minimize waste, insure that duplicate skins come from the same tannage lot, and let you inspect the skins for the location of any and all imperfections. This of course is an ideal procedure. Personal selec-

tion of the leather guarantees uniform weight, thickness, color, and footage.

If you cannot buy your leather in person, but must rely on mail order, there are still a number of things you can do to insure uniformity and footage. You can, for example, send for sample swatches of colors. You might have to pay for these, but the small investment is well worth the assurance of uniformity in selection. These swatches will not only give you the color, but you can then see for yourself what the thickness and texture are like. When you do finally order by mail, I suggest you send your pattern along with the order, and ask that the supplier select matching skins, and skins small enough to eliminate as much waste as possible. He can then test the parts of your pattern by placing them directly on the skins to make certain that you get enough leather. It's also a good idea to remind him that you don't want imperfections, or thin spots appearing on the garment. I'd also suggest you specify that he roll the leather around a mailing tube when he returns it to you, and that he include your pattern in the package. The mailing tube idea reduces the possibility of heavy creasing in shipment. As an added insurance against the loss of your pattern, you can enclose a self-addressed, stamped, return envelope with your order. Don't be afraid to give the supplier as many instructions as possible. This will help both of you complete a satisfactory order.

If you're buying something other than garment leather, be sure to tell the supplier how you intend to put the leather to use, and what you want the leather to do. He can often make suggestions and improvements upon your own buying skills if he knows what you are about.

At some point in your development as a leather craftsman—and the sooner the better—I strongly recommend taking the time to visit a supplier in person. It's almost impossible for him to describe and catalog everything he sells. A couple of hours spent looking around and talking with him is certain to be an enlightening experience.

Leather Thickness Chart

The following chart is presented for general guidance in selecting leather thicknesses for a variety of projects as indicated. This chart is not meant as an exclusive guideline; you may want to deviate from these thicknesses, either more or less. The chart is general, and based on the average buying habits of small leather craftsmen at one given supplier. The specific brand name and type of leather is not mentioned because of the variety of species involved and the variance in the specific descriptive trade names used by tanners for given leather.

Handbags: 5-6 ounce leather for the body of the bag. Straps can be made from the same leather as the bag, or can be made from round industrial belting, such as ⅜″ and up United Round Leather Belting sold by The United Shoe Machine Company.

Belts, regular waist: 7-8 ounce leather. One very fine variety is English bridal backs, another is an A and B grade 8 ounce Russet Bridal Butt End, sold by A. C.

Products Company. Many craftsmen also use the belly section of horse for waist belts.

Belts, hunting, shell, and tool: 8-9 ounce leather

Billfolds: 2-3 ounce leather

Garment leather: 2-3 ounce leather; grains, splits, and suedes.

Lining leather: 2-5 ounce leather, depending upon weight and durability required. Lighter weight leather for informal wear, and heavier leather for work and cold weather. Cowhide purchased from commerical tanneries should present no problem with stretching, but leather such as buckskin and elk (often used in making leather trousers) may tend to stretch at the knee. If you use buckskin or elk, test the fabric first for stretch. If it stretches, you can minimize this stretch before you make the trousers by soaking the hide in water, and then tacking it onto a vertical board, or series of boards, to dry. As you tack the hide, you should stretch it tightly. This simple tip should help you to eliminate stretching at the knee when you use buckskin and elk.

Sandals: (*Bottom sole*) 11-12 ounce oil base leather, preferably a cod or fish oil tannage. (*Top sole*) 7-8 ounce oil base leather, preferably a cod or fish oil tannage. (*Straps*) 6-7 ounce curried and stretched industrial belting leather makes the best sandal strap material because it is both flexible and pre-stretched to eliminate stretching on the foot. Curried refers to pre-stretched leather.

Slippers and moccasins: 4-5 ounce leather.

Moc and Apache boots: 10-14 ounce oil tanned leather.

Necklace pendants: 8-10 ounce leather.

Hair barrettes: 8-10 ounce leather, preferably a dry leather.

Hats: 2-4 ounce leather.

Animal equipment (collars and halters): 8-10 ounce leather.

Upholstery and slip covers: 1-3 ounce leather; grain and splits.

Furniture, sling, strap, and suspended: 8-14 ounce curried and stretched leather (where weight is at a maximum as far as abuse, try to buy leather that has the barest minimum in stretch).

Watchbands: 4-5 ounce leather, also patent leather for laminated veneers.

Bracelets: 4-5 ounce leather, also patent leather for laminated veneers.

Leather cases: 4-6 ounce leather.

Leather sculpture: Skin coverings 2-3 ounce leather. *Wet, bent, and molded forms* 10 ounce and up, preferably oak and dry. *Laminated and carved* 10 ounce and up, preferably oak and dry. *Geometric solid forms* 10 ounce and up, preferably oak and dry.

Note: One can often pick up free or very inexpensive leather remnants, clicker negatives, and scrap for collage and other smaller projects from manufacturers of leather goods such as shoes.

How to Store Leather

If you're buying only one or two skins at a time, you'll have no storage problems because you'll be using up the leather. If, on the other hand, you buy in quantity, here are a few simple suggestions offered in the hope of preventing problems.

Unused leather should either be carefully rolled to avoid creasing, or else draped over a round bar and allowed to hang freely. Leather shouldn't be folded for storage. Folding causes deep creases, especially if several skins are folded and placed one on top of the other. Very stiff leather, such as oak bends, and sole leather, should be stored flat, and in layers, making certain there are no foreign objects between the layers which might dent the grain surface.

If you're using fatliquored leathers, keep them away from direct heat, especially furnace heat. A continuous blowing or hot air may cause the fatliquoring to dry out. Keep all unused leather out of direct sunlight. Sunlight may cause the color to fade. If possible, wrap the unused skins in brown paper, or at least cover the over–all pile. Do not store unused leather in an exceptionally moist place; moisture may cause mold. If mold should appear, it can usually be brushed off without damage to the leather. Also, beware of house cats around leather. Several friends of mine have had trouble with cats chewing on leather; they sense the animal skin, and are attracted to it.

CHAPTER FOUR

The workshop

Before unrolling that first purchase of leather, you should prepare a place to work. The ease with which you execute any design idea will, in large part, depend upon the convenience of your work space. You can eliminate the maximum number of bad starts by developing a creative atmosphere in which to work. Inadequate, or poorly planned work space produces a constant physical and emotional hassle for any craftsman. As a doctor operates in an operating room, so should a leather craftsman work at a bench in well planned studio space.

Ideally, if your house, offspring, and spouse can afford it, your work area should be at least a semi-private refuge from the normal business of family living. I'm one of the first to applaud the educational, not to mention the character value, of involving the wee ones in a family activity or craft, but after your Tiny Tim (if you have one) spills that first bag of rivets onto the floor and into the cold air duct, you'll well understand the need for your own refuge to work in.

Privacy, a large work table, a place to keep tools, storage for unused and scrap leather, and adequate lighting are the necessary ingredients for a creative work space.

Work Table

The work table should be large; the bigger the better. It should be flat and sturdy. Rolls of leather are often 3' to 4' wide, and when unrolled, they sometimes extend from 6' to 7' in length. Somewhere between hip and chest height is an ideal height for the table surface. With this height, you save wear on the back as well as on the knees of your bluejeans.

One of the quickest, and least expensive ways to construct a work table is to buy a 4' × 8' sheet of heavy, five-ply plywood and mount it over 2" × 4" legs, or even over three raised sawhorses; one at each end, and one in the center for added stability. A 4' × 8' plywood work surface will give you plenty of room and will make an excellent surface for cutting. You might also buy a smaller and thinner scrap of plywood to place on the table for a cutting backboard if you prefer not to scar the larger table surface with knife marks. I'd suggest that you also consider the purchase of a high stool to go along with your work table, as much of leatherwork can be done while sitting down.

Tool Storage

Tools should be stored within easy reach of your work table: a corner of the table reserved for tools, a rack above the table, or even a drawer under the table. As one of your introductory projects in leather, I suggest you construct a leather tool-storage rack for yourself. First, cut a long strip of leather about ½" wide and 24" to 36" long. It doesn't make much difference about the thickness of the leather; simply utilize a piece of scrap. Tack this strip of leather in loops to the wall, the front edge of a wall shelf, or onto the table surface (see Figure 2). The raised loops should be large enough to slide the given tool into. You can vary the loop sizes according to the diameter of the handles of the tools you have on hand. This looped strip of leather makes a fine rack for storing tools, because each tool will have its own snug leather loop to rest under.

A muffin tin, or better yet, an iron popover skillet, provides an ideal storage container for rivets, eyelets, nails, etc.; one separate cup for each item stored. With this type of cup arrangement, your rivets, etc., are open for quick and easy access, and you don't have to keep hunting around in drawers, bags, and cardboard boxes.

Leather dyes should always be stored away from the work table in order to avoid accidents. If a dye container left on the work table should accidently tip, and spill onto a piece of fresh leather, you'll spend a lot of time scolding yourself for not having read this paragraph.

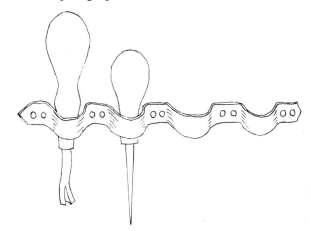

Figure 2. *A tool rack made from a strip of leather tacked in loops to the wall.*

Leather Scraps

As you accumulate leather scraps (and you will), I suggest that you plan to keep a box, or series of boxes available for scrap storage. The simplest procedure is to keep a series of labeled boxes for each type of scrap stored by color and thickness. Be sure to save all your scraps. Further on in the text you'll discover some profitable uses for what might appear to be a waste product.

Lighting

Adequate lighting is essential when working in leather. Pattern and tracing lines on leather are often difficult to see. If you don't provide for adequate lighting, especially when cutting, you may find yourself straying off the tracing marks, spoiling the leather, or even spoiling the project at hand. An overhead light mounted above the center of the work table is an excellent source of light. And in addition, a high-intensity swivel lamp is helpful for close work. As far as I'm concerned, you can never have too much light when working on leather.

Mess

Whoever heard of a paragraph entitled *mess?* Perhaps this is a literary first, but mess should be mentioned when speaking of leather because leather is such a clean material, except for dye stains, punch dots, and a few slivers of scrap. If you're careful about the surface on which you do your dyeing, the mess left over from working in leather can quickly be vacuumed or swept away with a broom. Unlike many other crafts, leather produces almost no mess. There's no sawdust, and no general glop to contend with afterwards.

Display Space

After you've completed work on a given design—be it a vest, a belt, or a piece of leather sculpture—it's a good idea to set aside an area of your work space as a visual gallery in which you can both display your work and at the same time protect it from abuse. This procedure might not only lead to sales, but it's an excellent visual stimulant toward keeping you enthusiastic, and toward generating further new design ideas. There's certainly no reward in packing away the fruits of your labors in boxes and trunks. Keep finished work out where you, and others, can see it. The final chapter in the book will give you some specific suggestions about setting up a sales area. Leather is complimented when displayed against brick, weathered wood, burned cork, burlap, white walls, and most metallic surfaces, especially copper and brass.

CHAPTER FIVE

Selecting your tools

Leather design requires only a minimum investment in tools, and most of the required tools are inexpensive. This isn't true with many other crafts, pottery, for example, where there is an immediate need for an expensive wheel, and eventually a kiln. Leathercraft, on the other hand, is a breath of fresh air as far as the pocketbook is concerned. There is absolutely no justification for economic shyness when considering involvement in leathercraft.

For example, if you decided to earn a living as a leather craftsman, you could set yourself up in business with an initial investment in tools of about $150.00, exclusive of any electrical machinery. With this initial $150.00 investment in tools and supplies, you would be fully equipped to make every item covered in this book. Remember now, I said $150.00 to earn a living, not just to discover a creative avocation. In what other craft or business can you earn a livelihood having invested only $150.00? Many professional craftsmen have actually done it on less. This isn't conjecture; I've met several craftsmen who've actually done it. And of course, the average reader has no intention of going into the full–time leather business, so his own initial investment in tools and supplies will be even less. My point here is that leathercraft is available to everyone.

This chapter is presented as a source of reference for professional tools available to the leather craftsman; nearly all of the tools available to the leather trade are described. Since there's no other published source on leather tools (other than supply catalogs), this chapter is long and detailed in order to acquaint you with the full range of tools available to the trade. You may never have occasion to use all of the tools described, but you should have a reference source for the day you do decide to expand your explorations beyond the basic tools. If you know what the tools are, and if the need arises, you'll be able to make intelligent selections by using this chapter.

After reading this chapter, I suggest you begin your tool explorations by sending for several of the supplier's catalogues listed in the back of the book. Or better yet, make a personal visit to a supplier, pick up a few tools, ask questions, and try them out on scrap. In this chapter I've tried to group tools together according to similarities and function. When you get further into the book, and begin reading about specific leather projects, you'll find many of the tools mentioned again—which tools to use on specific projects. If you read this chapter carefully, you'll know what I'm talking about when an eyelet is mentioned.

Tools should be purchased like hats, with discretion. You can wear only one hat at a time, and likewise you can use only one tool at a time; the time you specifically need it. Be fussy! Don't buy a tool until you do need it. Master the use of the tools you already have before you invest in others. It's your responsibility to boss that tool; don't let it boss you. If you start buying additional tools before you've mastered the use of the ones in hand, you may well become their victim. Every tool is only a dull club if you don't take the time to learn how to use it properly.

Practice with each new tool before you begin using it on a project. Some tools are easy to master; others are a bit harder to master than they might appear. Practice on scrap leather. Get the feel of the tool in your hand. Experiment with it. Find out for yourself what it will do; what it won't do. Work it fast, and then slow. This is the way to gain confidence, to transform that tool into an ally before you begin using it on a project.

Quality in Tools

Since the investment in leather tools is minimal, selection is of the utmost importance. How does one get the best value for one's dollar?

There's no substitute for quality in tools. As with all craft tools, the price of a given tool will range from inexpensive, to moderate, to expensive. This price variance results because there are many tools manufacturers, and many variations in quality. Each tool is an investment which depends upon your ability to perform with it. Don't be afraid of comparison shopping, or even of paying the higher price. Usually a higher price means higher quality.

I've made many deliberate mistakes buying leather tools while researching this book. I hope I've made the mistakes for you; to save you from making them yourself. This was my intention. I've purchased the same tool in a variety of prices and quality in order to test its performance. Without exception, a low quality tool will eventually break down.

I'll give you a specific example. I've tested several revolving punches ranging in price from just over $1.00, to upwards of $10.00. I've purchased revolving punches in hardware stores, chain stores, auto accessory stores, and through mail-order catalogues. I've also purchased them from tools manufacturers that serve the shoe and leather trade. For the most part, these revolving punches all look pretty much alike, and theoretically they were designed to perform identical functions. Inexpensive revolving punches don't have replaceable threaded punch tubes. These inexpensive punches are great for punching holes in paper, but are ineffectual for prolonged use on leather. Either the slot that holds the revolving punch wheel at a given stop shears off, or the punch tube ends up cutting through leather at an angle, leaving a ragged, or only partially cut hole. None of these inexpensive revolving punches will cut through 10 ounce leather with any degree of ease. On the other hand, the same punch manufactured in heavy–duty steel for the trade will cut through 10 ounce leather as though it were butter. There's a difference, and what a difference it is! Be prepared to pay a little more for your tools, and buy a tool that will do the job it was designed for. Or, better yet, if you can select your tools personally in the store, then test it for performance first on scrap.

A number of tools manufacturers are in the business to serve the leather and shoe trade. These firms make excellent tools; they charge more because they provide more. These are professional tools. You'd do well to stick with tools manufactured for the professional; tools advertised for heavy–duty use. The list at the back of the book provides information on tools suppliers. The rule is: Quality first, price second.

Using the Proper Tool

Under each tool discussed in this book, you'll find a brief description of how to use it, and when to use it. Again, don't try a tool out on a project until you've mastered its use on scrap leather. And don't assume that because you've read how to use it, and looked at its picture, you're automatically its master. Practice comes only from doing; not from words and pictures on white paper.

Another word of caution: very often, through your own ingenuity, you can make a given tool perform several functions. Before you do this however, especially if your justification is to save the few dollars it takes to buy the proper tool, ask yourself if that ingenious secondary use you've discovered really results in a professional looking job. This applies equally to making your own tools. I'll give you two examples.

A nail, backed by a piece of wood, will make a hole in leather, but a nail is *not* a punch. A nail slits, or tears a hole. It doesn't punch out a clean, smoothly edged negative leather dot as a revolving punch does.

A leather negative is that part which is left after cutting, punching, or clicking the positive pattern pieces from the hide. In other words, if you were to take a section of the hide, use an arch punch, and punch out 2″ buttons from that entire section, the piece of leather left after the buttons are punched is called the negative. On the one hand, you have your buttons—they're the positive pieces, and on the other hand you have the leftover piece of leather—which is called the negative. Positive pattern pieces can be ar-

ranged on the hide in order to produce a usable negative, even if that negative is nothing more than an abstract wall relief (see opposite page).

A nail punches nothing. It simply tears a hole in leather and doesn't remove negative material. Yes, you can make a hole in leather with a nail, but you can't make a punched hole. The visual difference stands out prominently to the discriminating eye.

As a second example, it's possible to set a rivet by padding the exposed rivet cap with leather, and then pounding the cap onto the rivet stud with a hammer. It does work, and the results aren't too bad, but nine chances out of ten you'll dent the rivet cap. On the other hand, an inexpensive concave rivet cap setter will prevent cap dents. The visual difference, again, is very evident. Why not undertake a professional job from the beginning? It's possible to rationalize by saying: "Oh, what's the difference?" But then you're beginning to compromise with craftsmanship even before you get your feet wet. Tools are designed for specific uses. It's always better to use the proper tool. I think you'll be much more satisfied with the end result if you do.

Beginning List of Tools and Supplies

The following list of tools and supplies will give you a basis on which to begin explorations in leather. I debated long and hard on whether or not to include a list of this type in the book. I do so with reservations.

As you've already seen so far, leather is a vast subject. There are literally hundreds of tools, supplies and findings which can be used in connection with leather. To set up a list of this type is to generalize on a reader's interest. I have no way of knowing what it is you plan to make from leather. The only guideline I can follow in this list is of a very general nature; to select tools of general use, findings with broad application, and supplies that everyone needs. The list therefore is far from exclusive. If you're a beginner, please read the list bearing in mind that these are only suggestions. You don't need all of these items to begin work in leather. You'll have to interpret the list by your own demands. If you were planning to go into the business, you'd eventually end up with many more items than those included here.

With the tools, findings, and supplies listed below, you can make vests, jerkins, sandals, handbags, billfolds, bracelets, hair barrettes, watchbands, pendants, belts, earrings, mobiles, sculptural figures, and many other items covered in the book.

1 Heavy–duty revolving punch
1 Single-prong thonging chisel
1 4-prong 3/32″ thonging chisel
1 Composition pounding board
1 Medium–weight mallet
1 7/16″ tack hammer
1 Fid
1 Automatic sewing awl
1 2-prong split needle for lacing
1 Straight Life–Eye needle
1 Assorted package of sewing needles

1 Spool of heavy-duty carpet thread
1 Spool of 5-cord linen thread
1 Spool of tan 3/32″ leather calf lacing
1 Cake of beeswax
1 Pair of heavy-duty leather shears
1 Steel straight-edge
1 Square point knife
1 Bevel point skiving knife
1 #75 X-Acto carving chest
1 Safety beveler
1 Adjustable gouge
1 Edge cutter, or #3 edge beveler
1 Bone folder and edge creaser
1 Circle edge slicker
1 Draw gauge or plough gauge for stripping
1 Packet of small, medium, and large brass rivets
  and a rivet setter
Grommets, eyelets, and setters as needed
Snaps and snap setters as needed
Buckles, loops, rings, and dees as needed
Soling nails as needed
1 Quart of leather cement
1 Small tube of Duco Household Cement
1 Roll of masking tape
1 Pair of rubber or plastic gloves
Pattern paper as needed
Dyes, finishes, and applicators as needed
Leather as needed

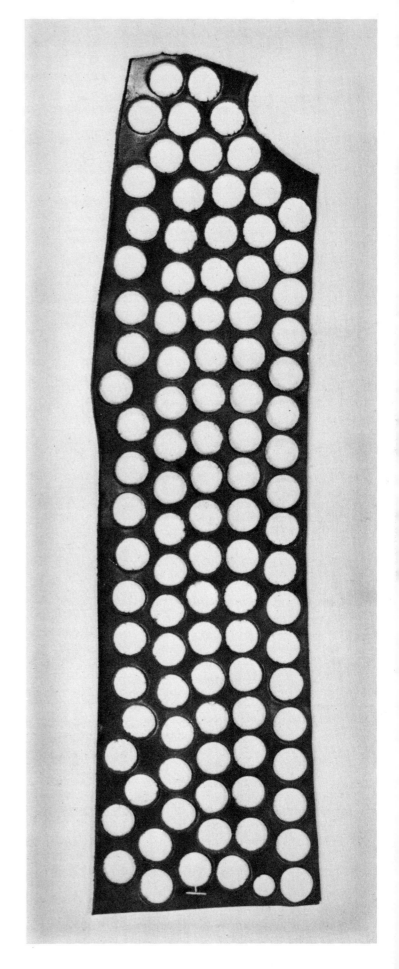

Abstract leather negative, left over after punching out leather buttons with an arch punch. (I've seen planned sandal sole negatives sold as whole hide abstract wall hangings, and bringing in more than the original cost of the skin.) Photo, Larry Hyman.

CHAPTER SIX

Punching tools

There are several types of punches for use on leather. Each punch has a specific use or advantage. Leather punches include the revolving punch, the round drive punch, the arch punch, the strap end punch, the bag, or oblong, punch, the oval drive punch, and the thonging chisel.

The Revolving Punch

The best revolving punch on the market is designated for professional and industrial use. It's equipped with six revolving punch tubes. This is a heavy–duty punch and the punch tubes are threaded for easy replacement. An even more elaborate version of the same punch comes equipped with additional tube sizes beyond the six; these are interchangeable. Figure 3 illustrates a revolving punch, and Figure 4 illustrates the actual size of the tubes available for the interchangeable variety. On the standard revolving punch without interchangeable tube threads, the tube sizes usually run in numbers from 1 through 6 (see Figure 4). The C. S. Osborne Company of Harrison, New Jersey, manufactures some of the best revolving punches in the industry.

The revolving punch produces a round hole and leaves a waste negative. It doesn't slit leather. It actually punches a round dot of negative waste leather to the size of the given drive tube. This hole is tapered; smaller at the tube tip, and larger at the top. The six tube sizes can be rotated into cutting position by twisting the wheel in the punch frame until it clicks into the next locked position.

The revolving punch can be used successfully on leather up to 10 ounces, or about ¼″ thick. On 8 to 10 ounce leather, use of the revolving punch does require a bit more oomph; a steady, even squeeze with both hands. Otherwise, on lighter-weight leathers, squeezing the handles together can be managed with one hand, while the other hand holds the leather firmly in place. The revolving punch has many uses. It's used whenever a hole the size of one of the punch tubes is required. For example, it can be used on rivet holes, eyelet holes, snap holes, belt buckle tongue holes, and holes for rawhide lacing.

It's operated by squeezing the handles together until the drive tube punches through the leather and stops flush against the anvil. Since the hole produced by the revolving punch is tapered, the tube should enter the leather from the finished, or exposed, grain side. Mark the location of your hole first, with either a nail, a pencil, or a scratch awl. Then select the tube size required to equal the diameter of whatever goes into the hole, be it a rivet, an eyelet, or a buckle tongue. Test the hole size on a piece of scrap for proper diameter first. Next, center the appropriate drive tube over your pencil mark and squeeze the two handles together. Be careful to go through the leather straight, and not at an angle. After the drive tube has punched the leather and is flush against the anvil, it's a good idea to squeeze the handles together once more, very hard, and then to rotate the leather. This insures that the punch negative, the small dot of leather, has been cut clean without ragged edges. When you release the handles, the hole should be perfect with the negative popping up inside the punch tube. Rotating the leather before releasing the handles also tends to burnish the edges of the hole.

If the hole goes at an angle through the leather, then chances are you're not giving the handles a firm, steady pressure. A good revolving punch will punch out a straight hole. An inexpensive punch, as we have seen, may angle; not because of anything you fail to do, but because the tool simply can't perform its intended function. If this happens, you may have to buy a better punch.

If you use this punch only on leather, the cutting tubes will remain sharp indefinitely. If a punch does get dull, it can be replaced by ordering a new tube as indicated by the number on the side of the tube wheel, or by matching its size against Figure 4. Once in a while, as with other steel tools, you might give the punch a light coat of machine oil, but be sure to wipe the excess off. You don't want oil on your leather.

The Round Drive Punch

The round drive punch, Figure 5, is a single hole, hand punch that produces a hole from 1/16″ up to 1″ in diameter. This punch is also tapered; smaller at the tube tip, larger at the top. The taper allows the negative to slip up easily into the tube. This punch is used for the same purpose as the revolving punch, in addition to being sold in larger hole diameters, and for use in producing deliberate usable negatives, as for example, small round buttons or leather beads.

The trick to working this tool is to hold it with one hand, straight up and down on the finished, or grain side, of the leather, and then, with the other hand holding a soft face mallet, to strike the head of the punch squarely in the center. The degree of straightness up and down, the strength of your holding grip, and the squareness of the mallet blow on the punch head will insure a clean, straight hole through the leather.

As you can see from the illustration, the shaft head on the round drive punch is all on one side. On thick leather, it's therefore very important to keep the balance of the tool straight up and down as it cuts through the leather. When practicing, you may have to lean on it a bit, pushing slightly toward the center to keep the direction straight.

As with all hand punches, it's important that the leather to be punched is placed on a solid corner of the work table, preferably directly over one of the table legs. It's also important that the leather be backed by a cutting pad, a piece of wood, or another piece of thick scrap leather, so that when the cutting edge of the punch pierces the leather it will have a soft surface to dig into so as not to dull the blade.

The Arch Punch

The arch punch, Figure 6, is also a single hole, hand punch. It's available in sizes of hole diameter from 3/16″ up to 2″. Because of the steel arch over the punch barrel, the shaft of the punch is centered over the barrel. This punch is designed for an even, downward cut without additional side pressure to keep it vertical. It's a stronger punch than the round drive punch, it produces larger holes, and can be successfully used on heavy leather to punch buttons and larger bead discs. It's used in the same manner as the round drive punch; one hand holding the shaft perpendicular to the finished side of the leather, and the other hand on the mallet to strike the punch head in the direct center. I suggest you save all but the very small punch negatives. As mentioned earlier, punch negatives make leather necklace beads, earrings, pendant trim and collage material. Later on in the text, I'll describe some specific uses for these negatives.

The larger diameter arch punches require several square hits on the punch head to pierce thick leather. Unless the work surface is rigid, the punch has a tendency to bounce. If this happens, move your punching to a solid place, or even onto the floor above an upright beam. It takes a good deal of heft to get a 2″ arch punch through a 10 ounce piece of leather. Remember to strike the punch head in direct center.

The Strap End Punch

The strap end punch, Figures 7 and 8, is designed to cut either a *V* or a *C* end on a belt, handbag or garment strap. Figures 7 and 8 illustrate the cut made by the half round *C* punch and the English Point *V* punch. Both of these punch styles are available in sizes from ¼″ up to 2″ in diameter. These punches are used in the same manner as the round drive

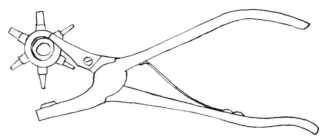

Figure 3. *A revolving leather punch.*

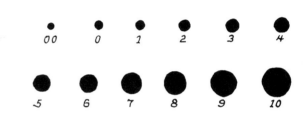

Figure 4. *A template showing actual punch tube sizes and size nomenclature.*

Figure 5. *A round drive punch, which is used for punching small round holes.*

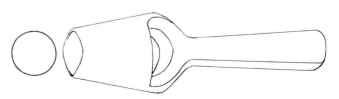

Figure 6. *An arch punch, for punching large round holes.*

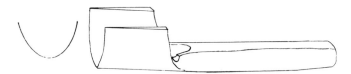

Figure 7. *A strap end punch (curved), for cutting rounded belt tips.*

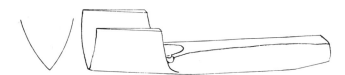

Figure 8. *An English point strap end V punch, for cutting pointed belt tips.*

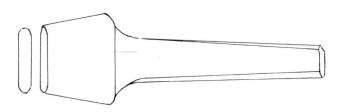

Figure 9. *An oblong, or bag, punch, for punching sandal and handbag strap holes.*

Figure 10. *An oval drive punch, for punching the dowel hole in hair barrettes.*

punch. The trick here is to again keep the punch blade headed straight up and down into the leather, and to make certain the cut is made all the way through the leather leaving a clean, smooth edge. As with the round drive punch, you may have to offset the side shaft with some additional center pressure.

The Bag, or Oblong, Punch

The bag, or oblong, punch, Figure 9, is a single hole, hand punch designed specifically to punch an oblong, slot–shaped hole for installing clasps, buckles, and straps on handbags and sandals. This punch is available in lengths from ¼″ up to 1½″.

Whenever you need a slot to accommodate a finding, or a strap, you'll find this an indispensable punch. This punch is used in the same manner as the other hand punches previously described. One word of caution: if the punch is used for a strap hole, and the strap is meant to slide in and out of the slot, you'll find that you'll have to use a punch at least one size larger than the actual width of the strap. In other words, the hole must be larger than the strap, if the strap is to slide easily in and out of the slot.

This punch produces a unique leather negative. Plan to save these negatives.

The Oval Drive Punch

The oval drive punch, Figure 10, is still another, single hole, hand punch. Occasionally, you'll run across a finding that will require an oval hole. Also, it's an excellent punch to keep in mind when you need a hole a bit larger than the next size round punch, but still not a full size up. The oval hole graduates in size like an egg and will allow roomy end space when a loose fit is required of an otherwise round hole. It's used in the same manner as the other hand punches previously described. Again, save these oval negatives. One common use of the oval punch is to punch out the holes on hair barrettes which accommodate the barrette dowels.

The Thonging Chisel

The thonging chisel is a slit punch that is available with prongs extending from a single shaft, in sizes ranging from 1, 2, 3, 4, 5, 6, and 8. Figure 11 illustrates the variety of chisel prongs available on a single shaft.

This tool is used to produce slit holes for lacing. Since most lacing is sold in widths of 3/32″ and ⅛″, the thonging chisel is available in both of these sizes in the various prong styles. A 3/32″ pronging chisel means that the width of each prong slit produced is 3/32″ wide; a ⅛″ pronging chisel means that the width of the prong slit produced is ⅛″ wide.

The reason for the variety in the number of prongs on a single shaft is to facilitate speed and access when lacing. For example, if you were hand lacing a hand-bag with long side seams (straight edges), an 8-prong chisel would cover the distance much more rapidly than a 2-, 3-, or 6-prong chisel. On the other hand, if the edge had a continual curve, as on a circle, you might select a 3-prong chisel. (In the last example, an 8-prong chisel would not allow you to bend with the edge curve.) And then, supposing you had a 90 degree corner to turn, and you wanted a single stitch to hold down the curve of the corner. In this example, a single prong chisel would follow that sharp curve; it would allow you to place one slit at an angle to the two perpendicular edges (a 3- or an 8-prong chisel could not do this).

The thonging chisel is available in two styles of prongs, straight and diagonal. The chisels on the top of Figure 11 illustrate the straight pronging chisel, where the prong points are all evenly spaced to produce a straight line of slits parallel to an edge. The last drawing (bottom) illustrates the diagonal prong where the prong blades are on an angle, parallel to each other. The straight prong chisel is perhaps the more widely used of the two styles. The diagonal pronging chisel produces slits that run at an angle (approximately 45 degrees) to the outer edge of the material being laced. Many craftsmen prefer the diagonal pronging chisel, feeling that since the total length of the slit doesn't run as close to the edge as with a straight prong, the lacing will therefore be tighter and less likely to stretch the leather. They also feel the diagonal prong produces a neater finished appearance to lacing.

The thonging chisel, as we have seen, slits leather; it doesn't produce a negative punch-out. It's designed to be used with standard, flat lacing. The Tandy Leather Company also sells a 4-in-1 round hole punch illustrated in Figure 12 that operates on the same principle as the thonging chisel, but is used for round, rather than flat lacing on leather up to 5 ounces thick.

All of these thonging chisels are used much in the same manner as the drive, arch and end punches previously described; one hand firmly holds the chisel perpendicular to the finished side of the leather, while the other hand produces the mallet blow that forces the chisel through the leather. When using the thonging chisel, the path of the lacing slits should be marked ahead of time on the leather with a pencil. This is the only way you'll keep all the slits at an even distance from the edge. With all of the thonging chisels larger than 1-prong, most craftsmen prefer to use the first slit on the previous hit as the guide slit on the current hit.

For example, if I were using a 3-prong chisel, I would first mark, at an even distance from the edge, a penciled guideline for my slits. I would then make my first punch of three slits along that line, as close to the edge as I'd want to lace. To make my second punch, I would place the last prong of the chisel in the first split of the first triple punch. My second punch would produce only two new holes because I would use the first slit of the previous punch as the last slit on the current punch. The reason for doing this is to insure keeping all the slits an even distance apart. After the first punch, each successive punch would produce only two new slits with the third prong always acting as a space guide. (Figure 13 illustrates this procedure with a 4-prong chisel.)

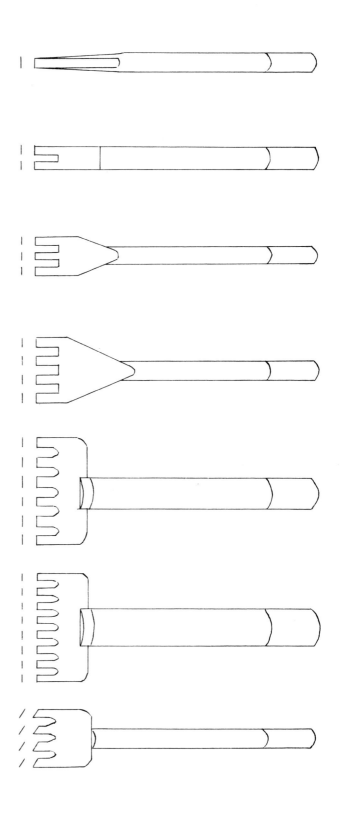

Figure 11. *Regular thonging chisels (1-, 2-, 3-, 4-, 6-, and 8-prong), and a diagonal thonging chisel, used to punch lacing holes.*

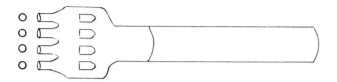

Figure 12. *A 4-in-1 round hole punch, for punching lacing holes when using round lace.*

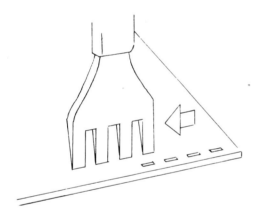

Figure 13. *A 4-prong thonging chisel in use (arrow shows direction of movement), with last prong using last hole on previous punch as a spacing guide.*

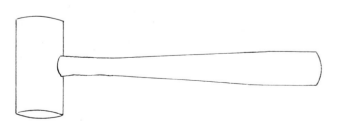

Figure 14. *A rawhide mallet, for light work such as securing cemented seams.*

Miscellaneous Punches

There are a number of additional leather punches available for special problems. One of these is the lacing hole nipper. This tool operates like a revolving punch in that you squeeze it together, but this tool develops a single slit instead of a hole. Another tool is the single tube spring punch which operates in exactly the same way as the revolving punch, but has just one punch tube instead of six. This is designed for punching very thick leather. And then, there are combination spring punches that have interchangeable punch tubes to develop either round or slit holes. The combination punch, for the most part, isn't as durable as the punch designed for a single purpose. Combination punches are designed to save you from buying one of each single type of punch. They're designed as money-savers so that you can adapt one tool to serve several purposes by means of attachments and alterations.

Pounding Board

As mentioned earlier, it's essential to use some type of pounding board as a backing for hand punches. A pounding board not only provides a flat surface on which to pound, but also minimizes wear on the punch cutting edge. Without an absorbent backing, a punch blade will quickly lose its sharpness. Never punch leather directly upon a metal surface.

Several types of manufactured pounding boards are available. Probably the most common pounding board is a large rectangle of smooth hardwood, for example, solid rock maple or white birch, of about the same dimensions as a kitchen breadboard. Many craftsmen use one side for pounding and the other side as a backboard for cutting.

Another type of pounding board is one made out of composition material designed to absorb sound, and to minimize wear by cushioning the punch blade. Continual punching does become a bit ear splitting. Any material that will absorb sound is an added bonus for the nerves. Whichever you use, even if it's the wooden table surface itself, make certain that it's solid in order to eliminate any bounce. A bouncing punch can't cut a straight hole and it requires double or triple the number of strikes to get it through leather.

The Mallet

A mallet is used in leatherwork to press two cemented surfaces firmly in place, as a drive force on hand punches, for stamping, and for setting snaps, rivets, etc. Because of its rawhide or wooden head, a mallet produces much more of a cushioned blow than a steel-headed hammer. Mallets are sold by the weight of the mallet head. A lightweight head (2 to 6 ounces) is used for light strokes, for example on thin leather, or for light stamping. A medium–weight head (8 to 12 ounces) is used in general leatherwork, and a heavy head (14 to 20 ounces) is used where a hard blow is needed on thick leather, for example when using an arch punch on leather over 8 ounces.

The Tandy Leather Company also sells a 5-in-1 Select-a-Stroke mallet where weights can be manually added to create a variety of head weights from 8 to 12 ounces. Several mallets are sold so that heads can be purchased separately to replace worn ones. A rawhide head, for most craftsmen, seems to offer more control than a hardwood head. It's certainly less likely to slip.

When you use a mallet to flatten seams and creases, or to pound cemented surfaces together, the mallet is struck so that the flat surface of the head hits the leather squarely. When the mallet is used for punching and stamping, the center of the mallet head should strike the punch in a vertical blow. A glancing, or angled, blow off center usually causes problems; either the punch cuts the leather at an angle, or the mallet head slips off the punch. Figure 14 illustrates a rawhide mallet.

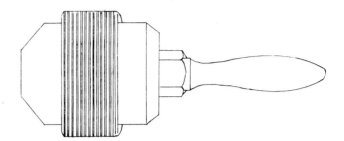

Figure 15. *A rawhide maul, for heavy work such as punching and die cutting.*

The Maul

A rawhide maul (Figure 15) is extensively used with cutting dies, hand punches, and for grommet (metal eyelet, or ring) settings. It's a tool that's reserved for heavier work. The striking face on the maul is made from compressed rawhide. A maul is likely to last longer than a mallet because the face of the maul head is round. This roundness provides a larger surface area; the maul can be rotated for even wear.

A maul is struck on the side; the rawhide on the side strikes the punch head. Because it doesn't have a flat surface, use of the maul requires a bit more practice than a mallet. The maul is sold in head weights from 2¼ pounds to 7½ pounds. Selection of the proper head weight depends upon how much of a blow you need for a given pounding project. Most hand punch manufacturers recommend the use of either a mallet or a maul with their tools, and specifically warn *not to use these punches with a steel headed hammer.*

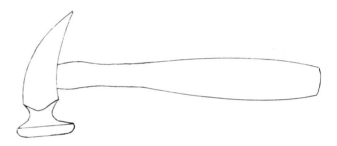

Figure 16. *A shoe hammer, for use on thick leather.*

The Hammer

The two hammers illustrated in Figures 16 and 17 are made with forged steel heads. Figure 16 is a shoe hammer. It has a rounded head face to prevent marring the leather. This hammer is used to form thick leather into a given shape, to flatten creases and seams, and to pound thick, laminated leather surfaces together, as for example, sandal soles. Its use is actually about the same as that of a mallet except that it has a forged steel head rather than a cushioned head. It should not be used on hand punches.

The heel, or tack, hammer illustrated in Figure 17 is used to drive cobbling or soling nails into sandal and shoe soles. The face head on the hammer has a very narrow diameter (from 5/16″ to 7/16″) to allow you to hold the nail in place while you pound. Using this hammer requires practice. Since the face is narrow, the hammer requires expert aim. Don't try to use a carpenter's hammer with cobbling or soling nails. The head is too big. An inexpensive heel, or tack, hammer makes the task much easier and much less subject to error.

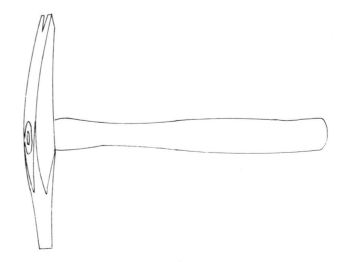

Figure 17. *A heel hammer, for cobbling sandal soles.*

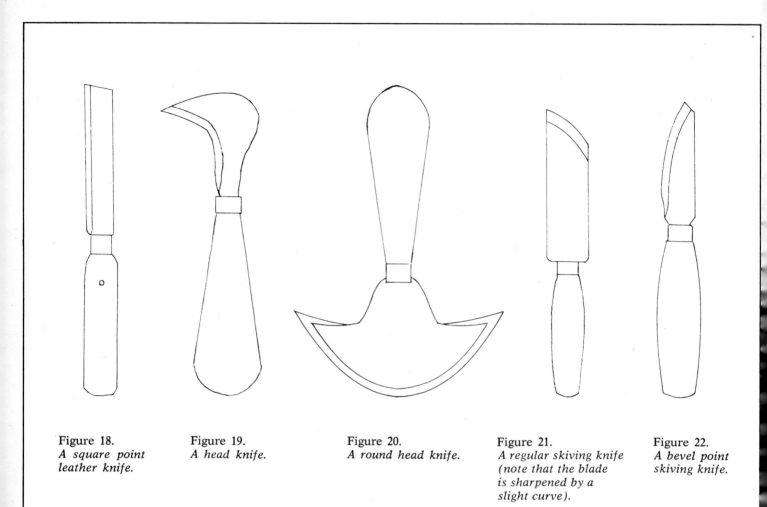

Figure 18.
A square point leather knife.

Figure 19.
A head knife.

Figure 20.
A round head knife.

Figure 21.
A regular skiving knife (note that the blade is sharpened by a slight curve).

Figure 22.
A bevel point skiving knife.

CHAPTER SEVEN

Knives and gouges

There are a variety of knives designed for use on leather. This chapter will introduce you to the square point knife, the head knife, the round knife, two styles of skiving knives (the regular skiving knife and the bevel point skiving knife), and an assortment of interchangeable blade knives (X-Acto knives). The chapter will also include instructions on skiving leather, and a step-by-step description on how to sharpen knives.

Many leather knives overlap in their functions; one knife can be used to perform several cutting tasks. For example, both the head and round knives can be used to skive leather as well as to cut leather. Once you understand your cutting problem, and what the various knives will do, you'll be able to tell which knife to select.

As a general rule, knives are used to cut thick leather over 6 to 7 ounces, and they are used when skiving, and for cutting strips with a steel straight–edge. For cutting thin leather, most craftsmen prefer using a leather shears. When buying knives, I suggest you stick with knives manufactured specifically for the leather trade; this way, you can't miss on quality no matter what job you're working on.

The Square Point Knife

Figure 18 illustrates the square point knife. There's hardly a leather craftsman in business who doesn't own a square point knife. This knife is used either to cut leather flat against a work surface, or for trimming leather that can be held in the hand. It can be used for cutting strips with a steel straight–edge, for cutting out footwear patterns in thick leather, for cutting sculpture patterns, for edge beveling by hand, for skiving belt ends and for many other leather–cutting problems. The handle of the knife is gripped in the palm, the same way in which you would hold an ice cream cone, with the blade extending either up or down, depending upon the particular cutting problem. The cutting edge can be either pushed or pulled. When a perpendicular leather edge is desired, the cutting blade should be held at a 90 degree angle to the leather. When a beveled edge is desired, the blade can be tipped to the angle of the bevel, and both the bevel and the cut can be made in one stroke. I've watched many bootmakers who can not only draw this knife through 14 ounce leather in one smooth stroke, but who can also cut the leather at nearly to

a perfect 45 degree bevel in the same motion. When using this knife, or any other knife on a work surface, the surface should be free of debris before the leather is placed on it, and the surface should always be made of wood. As I've mentioned before, never cut leather against a metal surface.

The Head Knife

Figure 19 illustrates the head knife. This is also a very popular knife among leather craftsmen. It resembles a linoleum knife; the hook on the knife blade acts as a safety guide when drawing the knife through leather. This hooked tip travels ahead of the actual cut, and prevents the knife from slipping out of the cut. The hook also indirectly serves as a visual guideline for the cutting direction. This knife can be used in either a pulling or a pushing motion; it's held in the hand in exactly the same manner as the square point knife. You're more likely to use this knife for trimming, or when cutting leather away from the work surface. It's designed to be used so that the hand travels under the leather. The round end of this knife can also be used for skiving.

The Round Head Knife

Figure 20 illustrates the round knife. The round knife is sort of a double-sided head knife; it has the head knife blade hook on both sides of the handle. It can be used as a head knife, or it can be used in a chopping position, with the leather flat against a wooden work surface. This knife is unexcelled for cutting out round corners when it's held in a chopping position. To cut a round corner, the hand grips the handle with the blade extending below the fist. With the leather flat against the work surface, a round corner is cut by rolling the knife blade forward on the line of the cut. What you try to do is to produce somewhat of a rocking motion; you press down hard on the blade, rock it forward along the line of the cut, and turn the leather as the blade cuts. This simultaneous cutting and turning produces a smooth corner.

The round end of this blade can also be used to skive leather. When skiving, the knife is held like a windshield frost scraper and pushed toward the outside edge of the leather.

Skiving Knives

Figures 21 and 22 illustrate two styles of knives designed specifically to skive leather; the regular skiving knife and the bevel point skiving knife. The only difference between these two knives is the angle and length of cutting edge. Figure 21 is used more as a pushing tool, whereas Figure 22 is used more as a slicing tool. Figure 22, as you can see, has the longer cutting edge and blade angle. The regular skiving knife is the most widely used of the two knives.

What is Skiving?

Skiving is the process of reducing the thickness of leather, of actually slicing away negative leather from the original thickness. Skiving is a functional procedure rather than a decorative embellishment. In order to give you some idea of why skiving leather is necessary, let's look at three common problems presented by thickness.

In this first example, let's suppose you were making an ordinary waist belt out of 8 ounce cowhide. You've finished the whole belt; the buckle is attached, the belt is dyed and edged, and you're ready to give it a trial run through the loops on a pair of trousers. As you bring the belt end up through the buckle, poke the belt hole over the buckle tongue, and are about to tuck the belt end back down over the other side of the center bar, you discover that the belt end is too thick to slide comfortably under the opposite side of the buckle. Your problem is that the space provided between the buckle center bar and the outside frame of the buckle is too narrow for the thickness of the belt end. For convenience and ease of wear, the belt end should slide effortlessly under the outside buckle frame; but it doesn't. You discover that you must force it, almost stuff it under the frame, and you're afraid that this much stress may crack and scuff the leather. What do you do?

The whole problem can be solved by skiving the belt end, making it thinner from the point of the first hole to the tip. If you neatly skive the belt end on the flesh side, you've thinned the leather and made it much more flexible. You've shaved off some of the thickness by skiving, and you've solved the problem.

Another example might be the strap of a handbag. (This example could apply equally to other parts of the bag, as well as to garments where the same problem arises.)

Let's suppose that on this handbag, you want a finished shoulder strap 1½" wide. You've decided that you don't want to leave raw edges on the strap. You prefer turning these raw edges under and cementing them down. You've decided to turn ¾" of leather under on each side of the strap. This means that for a finished strap 1½" wide, you must cut a 3" strip of leather to allow for a ¾" turned edge on each side. After you've cut the 3 inch piece of leather, you lay it flat on the work surface, grain side down, and then try with your fingers to turn this ¾" edge. In trying it out, you discover that this particular thickness of leather doesn't want to turn; it's too springy and wants to flop back, or else it leaves too much bulk at the fold. You're afraid this thickness may pull the cement or crack the leather. What do you do?

Again, you can solve your problem by skiving. You can skive that ¾" outer edge on each side making it thinner; you can remove some of the flesh side thickness. You can either skive the whole ¾" all along both sides of the strap, or you can run a shallow groove on the flesh side at the bend line. You've once again solved the problem by skiving. If leather is too thick, you might also encounter this problem on the turned edges of garments.

Still a third example of solving a thickness problem with skiving is in turning and cementing leather edges when bookbinding. Your problem here is that you want to turn your outside leather edges, you want to flop them over the cover board, turn them inside and cover them with cemented endpapers. You discover that your leather is just too thick to be neatly covered by the endpapers. Here again, if you skive the outside edges to the point where they make the bend, you'll have reduced the thickness of the leather so that the endpapers will cement down over the turned leather edges. You've again solved the problem with skiving.

We could look at many more examples of when skiving leather is necessary, but I hope that by now you've gotten the point. While reducing thickness, the process of skiving also makes leather more flexible. Skiving is therefore used whenever you run up against any thickness problem in folding, creasing, flexing, or edge turning.

How to Skive Leather

Skiving is normally done on the flesh side of leather, unless you have a particular reason to do it on the grain side. The process is not difficult on thick leather 5 ounces and up. Skiving leather under 5 ounces, especially under 3 ounces, is much more difficult. The process for all thicknesses is the same, but with thin leather, there's a much greater chance of cutting through to the grain side. A professional bookbinder can skive leather to the thinness of onion skin without cutting through to the grain side.

The primary ingredients for skiving are an extremely sharp knife, a steady pressure, control, a watchful eye, a hard surface against which to place the leather and a lot of practice. Skiving control comes from the muscles in the forearm, between the wrist and the elbow. The hand operates only as a guide and as an instrument with which to hold the tool; it's the knife blade and the forearm that perfect the slice.

Sometimes it's possible to avoid the necessity of skiving by planning ahead and using the proper thickness of leather to begin with. In other words, if you know ahead of time that on a given project you intend to turn edges, you can very often eliminate the need for skiving by selecting a thin, flexible leather. If, on the other hand, you prefer using a thicker leather, then you must plan to skive in order to obtain a professional finish.

As mentioned earlier, skiving can be done with a number of tools in addition to knives. The Tandy

Leather Company sells a safety beveler that can be used for controlled depth skiving. The C. S. Osborne Tool Company sells a tool they call a "skife," which is identical to the safety beveler, and is also used for controlled depth skiving. And then there are gouges and adjustable *V* gouges for skiving grooves at controlled depths and widths. These tools are described at the end of this chapter.

At this point I'll describe the procedure for skiving with a regular skiving knife (Figure 21). The process is virtually the same for all knives. Once again, you'll need a sharp knife, and a hard flat surface against which to place the leather. The sharpness of the blade is in direct proportion to how successful you are. The blade edge should be razor sharp (sharp enough to cut the hairs on your forearm). Many people prefer using a lithographer's stone against which to place the leather while skiving. A piece of granite, or a slab of marble works equally well. Something perfectly flat and very hard is the surface requirement.

The important points to remember in skiving are to maintain an even depth to the slice, and to keep the knife blade under maximum control at all times. Begin by placing the leather flat on the hard surface, flesh side up. Make sure the edge to be skived is on the hard surface. In skiving, you always work the blade in a slicing motion toward the outside edge of the leather.

The regular skiving knife is a pushing tool; one side of the blade is flat, and the other side is beveled into a fine cutting edge. Your knife may come with a perfectly straight cutting edge. If this happens with your knife, skiving works much better if you can develop a bit of roundness to the blade edge; higher in the center than on the ends. The knife handle is cupped against the heel of the palm. The blade should extend straight out beyond the index finger. The index and third fingers should be on top of the blade, and the thumb under the blade. The blade edge should face the outside edge of the leather, with the beveled cutting edge facing up. The knife should be held so that the fingers, hand, and wrist are all in a straight line with the forearm. The position here is very similar to holding a putty knife when using is as a forward scraper.

To skive, place the blade flat on the leather. Then lift the knife handle just enough to get a slight angle. Now stroke the blade into the leather, a shallow cut, moving the blade in either a forward or a slightly clockwise circular motion toward the outside edge of the leather. The knife blade should be almost horizontal to the leather. What you're trying to do is to cut either short circular slices, or one long slice into the leather thickness, maintaining the same depth of slice all the way along the length of the skive. Figure 23 illustrates the procedure visually. This is the procedure I use. It isn't necessarily the only procedure. If you can find a more comfortable procedure, you're welcome to do so. Control over depth is maintained by using the forearm as though it were a carpenter's plane; the wrist should be kept straight.

It's also a good idea to mark the path of your skive beforehand, and to keep the leather flat to the hard

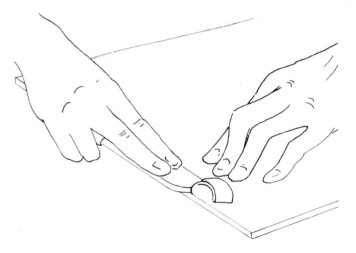

Figure 23. *Position of the arm and hand while skiving.*

surface at all times. If you don't hold the leather flat, it has a tendency to bunch up, or ripple, especially thin leather. The more points of pressure you can apply against the leather to hold it flat, the less likely it will be to bunch up.

Interchangeable Blade Knives

An interchangeable blade knife is a two-part tool comprised of a handle and a variety of interchangeable blades. The blades are disposable. When blades get dull, they can be replaced with new ones. The blades to these knives are surgically sharp. Figure 24 illustrates a selection of X-Acto brand knives and blades, including knife blades, curved blades, chisel blades, gouges and routers.

I've experimented with a number of these knife blades on leather. Quite a number of them work beautifully for a variety of purposes. Blade #28, the curbed blade, is excellent for cutting from 7 to 10 ounce cowhide; it works just as well, if not better, than a leather head knife. The X-Acto blade is much thinner than a regular head knife, and there's therefore less resistance when pulling the blade through leather. Blades #'s 19 and 24 work well for cutting thin leathers (under 6 ounces) with a straight edge. And the gouge and router blades work well for skiving, for cutting folds, stitching grooves, and for edge beveling. The only drawback I've found to the tool is that the aluminum collar threads on the knife handle wear out. It's difficult to understand why, with such an otherwise fine tool, there's this element of built-in obsolescence. Even with its threading drawbacks, it's a difficult tool to be without. These disposable blades save endless time in sharpening.

How to Sharpen a Knife

Knives can be sharpened by hand, on a grinding wheel, or even, in some cases, on an electric knife sharpener if the knife has a thin, straight blade. For a very fine cutting edge, most craftsmen prefer sharpening entirely by hand.

With most leather knives, the cutting edge of the blade should have one beveled side and one flat side. The cutting edge is shaped into a thin wedge. Tools needed for sharpening are a flat oilstone, a small can of household oil, and a strip of 12" to 16" scrap leather, 2" to 3" wide, to act as a strop. Oilstones are sold according to grade, from coarse, to medium, to fine, to extra fine and should be used in that order depending upon how dull the blade is to begin with. Unless the blade is really in bad shape, you should be able to get along with a fine or extra fine grade stone. A drop or two of light household oil on the stone will lubricate the pores in the stone. Don't, however, use oil on the strop.

There are a number of craftsmen who feel there's only one correct procedure for sharpening a leather knife on a stone. I've found, however, that several ways work. This is the procedure I use:

I begin by placing the wedged side (not the flat side) of the cutting edge on the blade flat against the

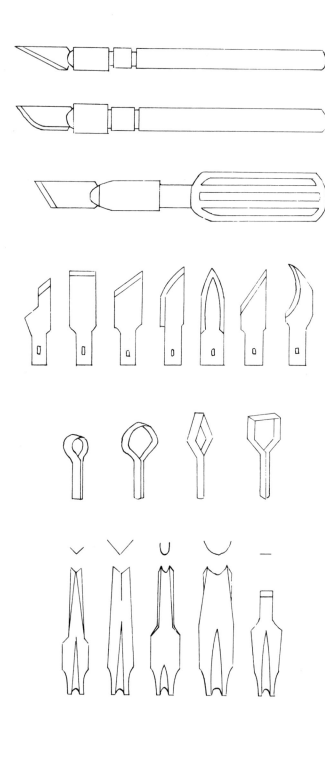

Figure 24. *A selection of X-Acto knives, blades, routers, and gouges.*

stone, and then moving the cutting edge along the flat surface of the stone in a clockwise, circular motion. What I'm after is to create an even, gradual taper to the beveled side of the cutting edge until I begin to see a fine, wire edge appear. I then repeat this same motion on the leather strop until the edge disappears. The other side of the cutting edge should be left flat. In the event that it too has developed a taper, you'd be better off to flatten it back out on the same stone.

Some people prefer holding the stone in their hand and moving it across the beveled cutting edge. Still others prefer stroping the blade back and forth across the stone. It makes little difference which method you use as long as you develop a fine edge. The principle is to keep one flat side and one beveled side to the cutting edge; the thinner the taper, the sharper the edge.

For the curved areas on head and round knives, it's best to run the stone along the bevel of the blade; that's about the only convenient way you can get at those inside curves. As mentioned earlier, it's well to remember that for skiving, a slightly curved blade works better than a perfectly straight one.

Take care of your knives, and protect the blades from abuse. When not using a knife, you can run a strip of masking tape along the blade as an inexpensive, temporary sheath. Leather doesn't dull a knife as other materials do. If you use the knife only on leather, about all you'll ever have to do is to temper the fine edge.

The Safety Beveler and the Skife

A brief mention of the safety beveler and the skife were made under the section, "How to Skive Leather." Figure 25 illustrates the safety beveler in use. The C. S. Osborne Company's skife is a similar tool. A description of one is literally a description of both.

The safety beveler is a leather skiving tool that uses a disposable Schick razor blade as a cutting edge. The cutting surface of the tool is curved; the blade is forced into a curved frame. This curve controls the depth of cut. The tool is designed to be used in the right hand. It's pulled toward the body and works on the same principle as a vegetable pealer. The curve of the blade and the rear blade guard limit the depth of cut; the tool peals off thin slices of leather. The tool cuts a concave slice; the completed area of skiving will look more like a series of shallow dents than a completely flat surface.

The tool is operated by first grasping the handle in the right hand and extending the thumb for a brace against which to hold the leather and pull the tool. Tilt the back of the tool slightly forward so that the blade is tipped down toward the leather. Then pull the tool toward the body, pulling the blade into the leather and using the extended thumb as a holding device and guard stop ahead of the tool.

The Adjustable Gouge

Figure 26 illustrates the adjustable gouge. This tool is used for cutting 3/32" width grooves in leather. The

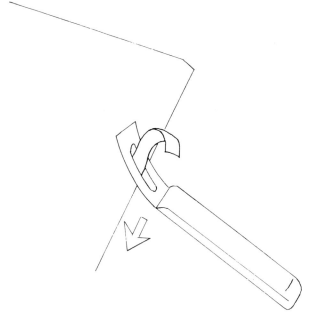

Figure 25. *A safety beveler, or skife, in use.*

grooves can be used to recess thread, and as an aid in folding or creasing leather. The adjustable gouge has a wooden handle and a *U* shaped gouge blade that can be adjusted for groove depth by a thread screw under the handle. The blade extends up and down between two metal guide posts. These two guide posts slide along on the leather surface while the gouge blade dips into the leather from in between.

The adjustable gouge is a pushing tool. Before you use this tool you should mark your line of direction on the leather surface as a guide to follow. First, adjust the blade to the desired depth of cut by turning the thread screw. Next, hold the tool at about a 45 degree angle to the leather so that the guide posts run flat on the leather. As you push the tool along, make sure you hold it at the same angle during the entire length of the cut. It's also important to make one continuous cut without stopping. This insures a smooth, clean cut. If the first groove isn't deep enough, simply adjust the blade for a deeper cut and then go over the groove a second time. If you want a wider groove than the one cut by the tool you can tilt it to one side or the other and then run it along the same groove at an angle. This action broadens the width of the existing groove.

When the tool isn't being used, the blade should be screwed up inside the guide posts to protect it from nicks. The screw is turned clockwise to extend the blade and counter-clockwise to recess it. One final word of caution; don't press down on this tool too hard. The guide posts that slide along on the leather may leave dents if you do.

The Adjustable V Gouge

Figure 27 illustrates the adjustable *V* gouge. This tool cuts a *V* groove whereas the adjustable gouge just described cuts a *U* shaped groove. The *V* gouge operates on the same principle as a carpenter's plane. It offers controlled depth and direction on the groove. The tool has a flat base like a carpenter's plane where the blade dips down below the base. The tool is shaped to push with the heel of the palm. First, you mark your line on the leather, then adjust the blade depth by turning the set screw, and then push the tool in one even stroke from the beginning to the end of the groove.

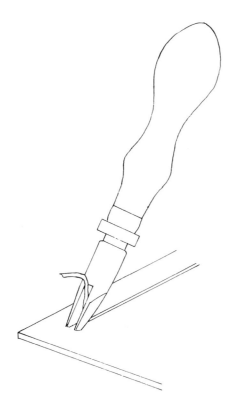

Figure 26. *An adjustable gouge in use.*

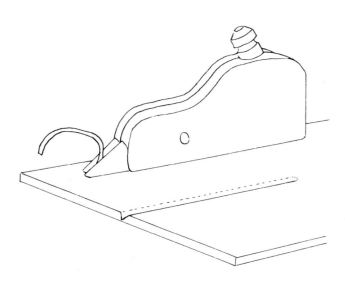

Figure 27. *An adjustable* V *gouge in use.*

CHAPTER EIGHT

Edging, folding, and creasing

There are a number of tools available for cutting and beveling edges. These are pushing tools. They vary in depth of cut and in shape of blade. One style may have a bent-tip blade while the next style has a straight or curved blade. Because there are just too many styles to describe here, I'll limit our discussion to four, all for general use: the common edge beveler, the edge cutter, the bone folder and edge creaser, and the circle edge slicker. All of these are inexpensive tools. For most leather projects, any combination of the four will work.

An edge is put on leather to dress it up, to give it a professional finished look. These tools are used on leather thicknesses from about 6 ounces and up. Leather thinner than 6 ounces is too flimsy to dress on the edges; usually the edges of thin leather are turned under as a means of dressing. A finished edge is used on such projects as belts, straps, handbag flaps, sandals, and leather sculpture. Unfinished edges often look uneven, tattered, or even feathery, an unattractive touch which hurts the over-all effect.

The Common Edge Beveler

Figure 28 illustrates the common edge beveler. This tool is sold by number; the lower the number, the shallower the cut. Numbers 2, 3 and 4 are suitable for general use. The tool rounds off a sharp edge by cutting off a sharp sliver of corner leather. Leather is placed flat on the work surface, grain side up. One hand pushes the tool while the other hand holds the leather flat against the work surface to prevent it from slipping. The tool works best if you try for one continuous stroke over the entire length of the edge. As you move forward with the tool, you can creep your holding hand along ahead of it. Figure 28 shows the tool in use. The tool can also be used to countersink rivet heads below the grain surface of leather.

The Edge Cutter

The edge cutter is illustrated in use in Figure 29. It's sold by the Tandy Leather Company and offers a little more control than the edge beveler. This tool has a guard-like flange that rests against the outside edge to eliminate over and under cutting, and keeps the blade from slipping off the edge. This again, is a pushing tool.

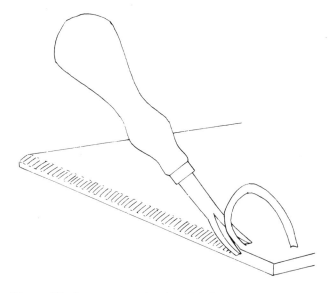

Figure 28. *A common edge beveler in use.*

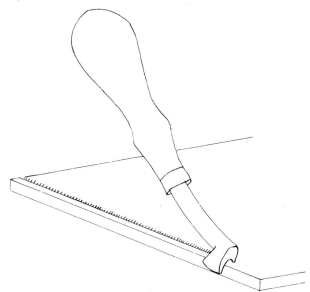

Figure 29. *An edge cutter in use.*

The Bone Folder and Edge Creaser

Figure 30 illustrates the versatile and very inexpensive multi-purpose bone folder and edge creaser. One end of the tool has a hard plastic half-circle made with two grooves 3/32″ and ⅛″ wide cut into it. The blade end resembles a letter opener and is used for folding, creasing, and slicking.

The grooves in the plastic half circle are used to burnish leather edges. Simply select the right groove for the given leather thickness, and then run the groove along the length of the edge, back and forth, until the leather begins to shine.

The other end of the tool is used to "press" a crease or fold in leather. It's used in exactly the same manner as using the blade of a letter opener to fold a letter.

Figure 30. *A bone folder and edge creaser.*

The Circle Edge Slicker

Figure 31 illustrates a circle edge slicker. This tool is made of wood, usually *lignum vitae*. It's an edge burnishing tool that can either be used by hand, mounted from the arbor on an electric motor, or mounted from the chuck on an electric drill. It consists of a round, hardwood circle with a *U* groove cut into the outside circumference. When using it by hand, the groove of the slicker is run back and forth along the leather edge. If mounted on a machine, the leather edge is run back and forth along the groove of the revolving slicker.

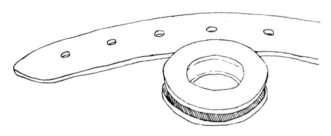

Figure 31. *A circle edge slicker in use along a belt edge.*

Putting an Edge on Leather, Step–by–Step

Our step–by–step example here is an ordinary leather belt. Even though a belt isn't very thick, it's still a rectangle with four edge corners; two on the grain side and two on the flesh side. Before you begin you must make a choice. Do you want 90 degree edge corners, or do you want rounded edge corners? And if you want rounded edge corners, do you want them on just the grain side, or on the flesh side as well? What you do with the corners of a belt is a matter of personal taste.

Using the example of edging a belt, let's say that you plan to round only the two grain surface corners and then dye and burnish the edges. You've elected to dye the edges a darker shade than the belt's grain surface in order to highlight it and at the same time minimize any imperfections along that edge.

Begin by laying the belt flat on the work surface, grain side up. To slightly round the two grain surface corners, you've chosen the common edge beveler as the tool. With the tool in one hand, and the other hand holding one end of the belt firmly against the work surface, run the edge beveler along the first grain side corner; the corner on the edge facing you. You're working from right to left, one end to the other, in a smooth, even stroke along the belt. As you progress along the edge, your free hand should creep along just ahead of the tool in order to hold the belt flat. After you've gone the entire length of the belt, turn it around and repeat the process on the opposite grain side corner. You should now be ready to dye and burnish the edges. Up to this point you've removed a light sliver of leather from the square corner in order to make it slightly rounded.

With either the edge creaser, the circle edge slicker, or a piece of coarse canvas held flat in the palm, you can now burnish the belt edges. Strop them back and forth continually until they begin to shine, or until the edge appears as one uninterrupted flow of leather and all the fuzzy edge fibers disappear. Next take a clean dye dauber, dip it into the dark dye or edge dressing, and blot the excess dye off onto a piece of scrap fabric. Now run the side of the dauber from left to right along the belt edges, being careful not to slop dye onto the belt's grain surface. If you want a deeper edge tone, you can give the edge another coat of dye. My own preference is to dye the grain surface first, and then dye the belt edges. At this point the belt is now ready for a finish coat, including the edges. After the finish coat is dry, you can again burnish the belt edges a few more strokes and finally polish the belt with a soft cloth. Your belt edges are now finished; they've been rounded, burnished, dyed, finished and reburnished, and they should now slide easily into belt loops.

If you use coarse canvas to burnish belt edges with, lay the canvas in the palm of the hand, place the belt on the canvas, and then squeeze your hand around the canvas and the belt. If you pull the belt back and forth through this canvas with your free hand, you'll be able to develop an excellent edge.

How to Fold and Crease Leather

The procedure for a fold and a crease are the same. Technically, a fold is a bend in leather of more than 90 degrees, but less than 180 degrees. On the other hand, a crease is a fold that completes a full 180 degree bend; it's bent back upon itself.

Folds and creases are common on leather projects. They occur on handbag flaps, briefcases, leather envelopes, billfolds, garment hems, garment seams, garment edges, and even on book spines when the book is bound in leather. Leather 3 ounces and under is so thin that it will usually fold and crease by just flopping it over. Thicker leather, especially leather over 6 ounces, doesn't flop over. A tanned hide is a flat plane. This is the natural plane of leather. A fold or a crease in leather changes this flat plane; the leather is being asked to assume a new position which is alien to its original shape. If you try bending thick leather, it has a natural tendency to revert back to its original flat plane. To make a fold or crease permanent on thick leather, the bend will require special treatment.

Here are some tips to remember when attempting to fold or crease leather.

1. The area of leather that actually does the bending consumes length. The thicker the leather, the more length it will consume at the bend line. Before you cut a piece of leather out, be sure to account for the length which will be consumed in the bend. In other words, if you wanted to fold a piece of leather in half so that each finished half was exactly 3″ long, you'd have to begin with a piece of leather longer than 6″ in order to account for the length consumed in the bend. This bend length can be tested ahead of time by simply bending a leather sample and measuring the amount of extra length consumed by the bend. You'll run across this in billfolds, briefcases, book covers, and any other fold where the finished length is specific.

2. If a fold on thick leather is too bulky, you may have to skive the folded section as described in the previous chapter under the heading, *How to Skive Leather.*

3. Leather will always bend easier when dampened with water at the bend line.

4. A *U* or *V* groove skived into the flesh side of leather at the bend line will not only reduce the surface length of the bend, but will fix the fold permanently, and remove some of the leather that naturally inhibits the bend.

5. On creases that are cemented, the springiness of the leather should be reduced to a minimum before the cement is applied.

6. When creasing leather over 6 ounces thick (bending it back upon itself), I suggest that you lubricate both sides of the bend line with Vaseline Petroleum Jelly to prevent the leather from cracking.

7. Once leather is bent, it can be creased with a bone folder, creased in a padded woodworking vise, creased in a book press, pounded with a mallet or simply creased by piling weight on the bend line. The method you choose will depend upon the thickness of the leather.

The uses of bends, folds, and creases vary so much between projects, leather thicknesses, and desired results that it's impossible to set down step-by-step procedures. If I did this I would have to describe in detail every possible step-by-step fold on every project where it might occur. You'll have to proceed by instinct with much of the folding and bending. The tips just listed should be a big help. You'll just have to experiment for yourself. Wetting the bend line with water is generally applicable when working with thick leather, especially on sculpture. Skiving a *U* or *V* groove into the flesh side is generally applicable on right angle folds, thick leather folds, and on projects such as briefcases, book covers, and when covering over any other material with leather. Lubricating the bend line generally applies to thick leather over 6 ounces. Creasing with a bone folder is generally reserved for thin leather, while creasing with weights, vises, and presses is generally restricted to thick leather.

Stripping Tools

There are three tools available for stripping leather belts and straps; the Strip Ease, the draw gauge and the plough gauge.

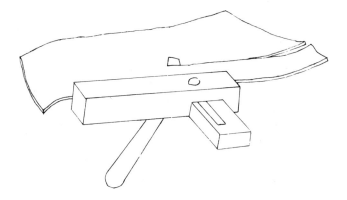

Figure 32. *A Stript Ease in use.*

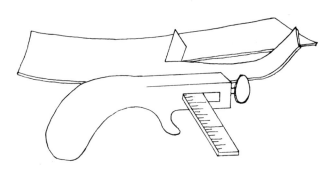

Figure 33. *A draw gauge in use.*

The Stript Ease

By rights, I should have a pun for a tool with a name like Stript Ease. Perhaps it's enough to say that a Stript Ease barely pulls it off (leather, that is). The Stript Ease is a very inexpensive pull tool; it's illustrated in use in Figure 32. The tool has a wooden frame and is equipped with replaceable razor blades that, according to the advertisement, are supposed to be designed to strip leather of any thickness up to 2½″.

My pun was that it "barely pulls it off," and this is an accurate description of the tool's performance. It might well be a handy gadget to have around in case of an emergency, but it's not a tool for accuracy in cutting belts and straps. Even though the tool is widely advertised, it's inefficient for use by a craftsman who takes pride in accuracy. The razor knife on the tool is so thin that it bends, or will even break off under the stress of recommended 8 ounce belt leather. And the blade is so short that the leather almost always rises up over the blade and pops out of place. I'll say no more except the *coup de grâce:* forget it!

The Draw Gauge

Figure 33 illustrates the draw gauge. Now here you have a *real* stripping tool. This tool is what the Stript Ease tries to be, but isn't. The draw gauge is also a pulling tool. This tool strips leather accurately in widths from ¼″ up to 4″ wide. It has a pistol grip handle, a long quality blade and an accurate measuring rule. The tool is all metal. The C. S. Osborne Company manufactures an excellent draw gauge.

The draw gauge is simple to operate. You merely select the belt width, turn the thumb screw, adjust the blade width, tighten the thumb screw and pull the leather through the tool. The only word of caution needed on any of these stripping tools is that you do need an accurate straight leather edge before you begin stripping. If the edge is curved, the tool will follow the curve. It cannot straighten a poor start.

The Plough Gauge

Of all the stripping tools, the plough gauge is undeniably the best. The Joseph Dixon Tool Company manufactures a heavy-duty variety. This is a pushing tool rather than a pulling tool. The pushing motion provides full visual access to where you're headed instead of where you've just been. When stripping belts and straps, it's much more interesting to see where you're going than where you've come from. This tool is the most expensive of the three stripping tools, but if you plan to make belts in quantity, I highly recommend it.

It operates on the same principle as the draw gauge, except that you push rather than pull. In addition to the push feature, the tool also has a clamp–like device that holds the leather firmly against the tool; the belt therefore can't pull away from the straight edge of the tool.

CHAPTER NINE

Sewing and lacing

Sewing and lacing (exclusive of machine sewing), are entirely handwork skills. In addition to thread or lace, there are a number of other tools available to simplify and perfect your sewing skills. These tools will be introduced in this section. Most of them are inexpensive, and many of them are as helpful to the leather craftsman as a hammer is helpful to the carpenter. Hand lacing and sewing is very often a slow and meticulous process. Many of the tools described in this section will not only speed up your skill, but will provide the bonus of giving you additional self-confidence in the fussy spots, or what otherwise might have appeared to be complicated sewing situations. Even though every leather tool isn't included in the beginner's tool list, don't be afraid to explore the unlisted tools. You may find one of the lacing and sewing tools to be just the tool you were looking for, even though it isn't included in the list.

The Scratch Awl

Figure 34 illustrates a scratch awl. This tool resembles a short ice pick and is used for tracing patterns onto leather, marking cutting lines, and for piercing holes in thin leather. The scratch awl can be held either like a pencil or an ice pick, depending upon how deep a mark is required. I use a scratch awl to scratch my pattern marks right into the leather grain surface, so that I can follow these lines easily with a knife or shears. Trying to follow a pencil mark on leather, especially on dark colored dyes, is next to impossible. The scratch awl eliminates guess work.

Haft and Awl Blades

In order to avoid language confusion, a haft is nothing more than a handle, and an awl blade is an interchangeable blade that fits into, and works with, a haft. In order to get one functioning tool, both a haft and an awl blade are required.

There are many styles of hafts. Figures 35 and 36 illustrate two of these styles. Figure 35 is called a sewing haft. This haft is shaped to hold in the palm of the hand, or to grip as one would grip a screwdriver.

Figure 36 is a peg awl haft. The only difference between this haft and the sewing haft is the shape. The peg awl haft, as you can see from the illustration, has a butt-type end made out of rawhide so that it can be struck with a mallet. This type of haft is used with

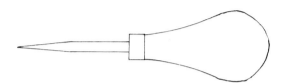

Figure 34. *A scratch awl, used for marking leather and indicating tracing patterns.*

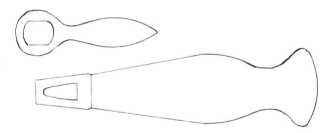

Figure 35. *A sewing haft (below) with a wrench (above), used with awl blades.*

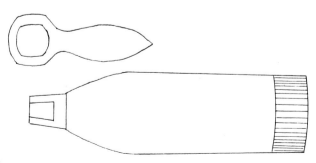

Figure 36. *A peg awl haft with a wrench (rawhide-tipped handle allows it to be used for hammering also).*

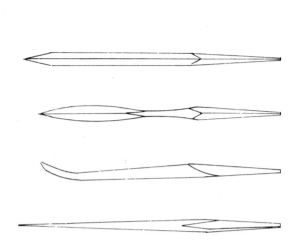

Figure 37. *A selection of awls (from top to bottom); a saddler's awl, a saddler's stitching awl, a curved sewing awl, and a round point stabbing awl.*

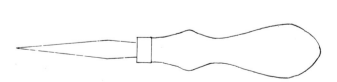

Figure 38. *An automatic awl with thread spool built into the shaft.*

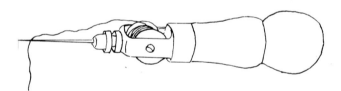

Figure 39. *A lacing fid, used to enlarge lacing holes and pull lace tight.*

awl blades for poking holes in leather, rather than for sewing. Both of the hafts illustrated are equipped with an adjustable chuck and a wrench for changing awl blades.

An awl blade is a separate metal shaft that is designed to fit into a haft. Several styles of awl blades are available including the harness awl, the stitching awl, the curved awl, and the stabbing awl illustrated in Figure 37. Awl blades are used with a haft for either sewing, poking holes in leather, or for enlarging existing holes. Awl blades are sold by their length, thickness and shape. The lengths range from about 1¾" to 3½".

When compared with the thrust and piercing ability of a needle and thimble, an awl blade and haft provide many times the control. An awl blade and haft are especially useful when hand sewing such items as belts, handbags, moccasins, or other projects using medium to heavy leather.

The curved, stabbing, or piercing awl blade is used when hand sewing such items as moccasins where a shoe last is required. The curve of the awl blade pierces the two thicknesses in such a way that the hole is angled, rather than straight, through the fabric.

Automatic Awl

Figure 38 illustrates an automatic awl. This awl is excellent for hand sewing because it both pierces and sews in one operation. To work this awl requires practice. The awl carries a spool of thread on the handle which feeds out as you stitch. The handle is hollow and holds a wrench and extra awl blades.

The Fid

Figure 39 illustrates a fid. A fid is designed to enlarge lacing holes; it's a time–saving tool. The fid has a wooden handle and a flared steel shaft about 2¼" long. The flared shaft is poked into the existing lace hole and pushed against the leather until the hole is enlarged to the required size. The fid is also a handy tool to loop under lacing in order to pull it tight while sewing. The tip of a fid can also be used as a stippling device to shade the background of relief tooling on leather. The fid is inexpensive, and a very handy tool to have around.

The Stitching Groover

Figure 40 illustrates a stitching groover. This tool is used to produce a shallow groove in the surface of leather into which the thread is recessed below the leather surface. The tool has a snub end with an adjustment screw recessed into the end. The groove cutter extends out from the tool on a metal shaft that can be adjusted in length by means of the recessed screw. The shaft adjusts from 1/16" to ¾" out and away from the tool. The Tandy Leather Company sells one version of this tool.

The cutting blade on the stitching groover is actually a tiny sharp cutting hole in the end of the extension shaft. The snub end of the tool is placed as a guide along the edge of the leather. The cutter shaft is adjusted to the desired width, and the tool is moved in an upright position along the edge of the leather. The snub end of the tool follows the edge of the leather and keeps the groove an even distance from the edge.

The cutting blade on the stitching groover is replaceable. This tool cuts a very fine groove. If you need a wider groove, you can cut it with an ordinary gouge, even a gouge blade on an X-Acto knife.

This groove cut is functional. It allows the thread to be recessed below the leather surface. If thread is left above the grain surface on certain items, it will break off from wear. For example, if you were to attach the sole of a moccasin leaving the thread above the surface, you'd end up walking on the thread and it would immediately wear out because it would be the first thing in contact with the floor. By recessing the thread into the leather by means of a groove, you've saved it from wear.

Needles

Essentially there are three types of needles: thread, lacing and machine needles. Each type of needle is available in several styles, varying in length, shape, and diameter.

Thread Needles

Thread needles are needles for hand sewing with thread. They're sold according to gauge and are available in a wide variety of shapes and sizes. The Singer Sewing Company and The Tandy Leather Company both sell an inexpensive assorted package that contains bent, curved, and straight needles. I suggest that you begin with one of these assorted packages and select the appropriate needle when the sewing problem is immediately at hand. These needle packs contain general suggestions as to which needle to use on which kind of project. Once you reach the point in your project when you're about to begin sewing, you'll be able to visually tell for yourself the shape and size needle required. The needle requirement depends greatly on the sewing problems and the type of stitch you select. With an assorted package of hand thread needles, you'll have a needle available for every sewing problem.

Lacing Needles

Lacing needles are hand needles designed to be used with leather and vinyl lacing. Figure 41 illustrates four styles of lacing needles: the top needle is a hook and eye flat lacing needle; the needle underneath it is a 2-prong split needle; the other two needles are a curved Life-Eye needle and a straight Life-Eye needle.

The two top needles differ only in that one has an eye and the other doesn't. Both of these needles have split ends. I've found that the needle with the eye is more apt to keep the lace from slipping out the side

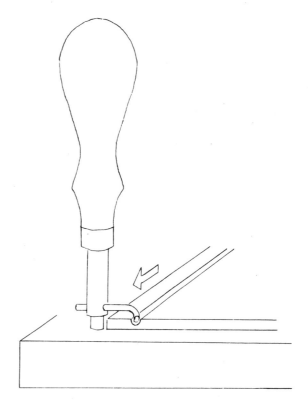

Figure 40. *A stitching groover in use.*

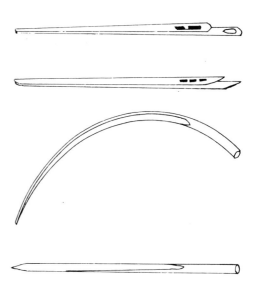

Figure 41. *A selection of lacing needles (from top to bottom); a hook and eye needle, a 2-prong needle, a curved Life-Eye needle, and a straight Life-Eye needle.*

of the split end. The hook and eye needle (top needle) is threaded by running the tip of the lace through the eye, spreading the split end and resting the tip of the lace above the prongs. Then with a mallet, lightly tap the split ends together forcing the needle prongs through the lace. The prongs hold the lace in place. The 2-prong needle (second from top) is threaded in the same way, except that there is no eye.

The curved Life-Eye needle is used in tight places and on corners where the curved tip provides something to grab onto in order to pull the needle through the fabric. This needle is used with both lacing and heavy thread. It's threaded by first cutting the lace to a sharp point, then inserting the point in the open end and twisting the needle clockwise several times until the lace is secured firmly within it. The open end of the needle threads the lace into a firm grip, similar to the way a woodscrew works. If the needle fails to thread properly, there may be dirt lodged in the open end. You can remove this with the tip of a common pin. If the lacing accidently breaks off while sewing, the threaded end can be dislodged by twisting the lace counter-clockwise with a pair of tweezers.

The straight Life-Eye needle (bottom needle) is threaded in exactly the same manner as the curved Life-Eye needle (second from bottom). If, in the process of lacing, the lace should accidently break, or you've misjudged the amount of lace needed, the lacing can be spliced by skiving the ends of both the old and new piece, and then cementing them together with transparent household cement.

The needle you use is, again, a matter dictated by the given sewing project. The Life-Eye needles are sold through Tandy Leather stores, and are perhaps the easiest to thread. The split end needles, on the other hand, seem to keep the lace intact longer, but are more apt to break if care is not exercised when spreading the prongs. These needles are so inexpensive that you can easily afford to try them all. When you've found one you like, keep an ample supply on hand. These needles are not something you can run down to the local drugstore to replace.

Machine needles

Most sewing machine manufacturers sell special needles for heavy–duty use on leather. Regular household sewing machines use a leather-point needle, size 14 to 15, which has a wedge point to make a clean cut through leather. Singer Sewing Machine stores throughout the country sell leather needles for household machines. If you're in doubt as to needle size for a given leather thickness, I suggest that you bring your leather and your pattern into one of these stores and ask the attendant for suggestions. As a general guide, lightweight leathers use a size 11 needle, medium-weight leathers use a size 14 needle, and heavier garment leather, or multiple layers use a size 16 needle. You can vary this general guide by testing the needle size on scrap leather. If the needle seems to be having a tough time piercing the leather, move up to the next needle size; if the hole is loose, drop back a size.

Thimble

A thimble, or a scrap of 4 to 5 ounce leather wrapped around thumb and index finger is an excellent aid to sewing. A needle requires a great deal of pushing to get it in and out of leather. Human skin just isn't durable enough to withstand this pushing; some type of thimble protection will solve this problem.

Thimbles are theoretically designed to be worn over the third finger of the right hand. When sewing on leather many people never use this finger. They're more apt to use the thumb and the inside heel of the index finger. Because of this, most craftsmen seem to prefer a scrap of leather to a commercial thimble. The leather idea gives you a larger protective surface, and isn't as bulky to wear as a thimble is. When sewing thick leather, a needle is also more apt to slip on a thimble than when pushed against a cushion of leather. What most craftsmen do is simply to sew or rivet a scrap of flexible leather into a ring to fit the particular finger or thumb.

Threads

The type of thread used on leather will depend upon the sewing problems of the given project, the thickness of the leather, and the amount of stress which the given seam is subjected to. Thread is either used functionally to join two pieces of leather together, or it's used ornamentally as an edge trim. If it's used functionally, it must be strong enough to withstand the maximum seam stress of the given project. If it's used ornamentally, then stress, or the inherent strength of the thread, is not an important consideration, and the thread selected can then be of a finer gauge. A few thread suggestions follow:

For buttons, belt keepers, handbag seams and thick hand–sewn garment seams; a heavy–duty button and carpet thread or a dacron thread.

For hand sewing thick leather on sandals, moccasins, slippers and sheepskin jackets; preferably a polyester dacron thread, as manufactured for the shoe trade. This thread is sold by cord count and is available on spools. Depending on the leather thickness, the cord count should run from 5 to 8 (the moc boots illustrated on page 88–90, made from 14 and 15 ounce cowhide were sewn with 8-cord, polyester dacron thread). 8 to 10 ounce leather can be hand sewn with lighter gauge thread 5- to 6-cord. The Tandy Leather Company also sells a linen thread for heavy sewing projects. Many craftsmen use this linen thread, but it is more apt to fray than polyester dacron thread.

There seems to be an "authorative" controversy over the use of thread when sewing garment seams by hand. One of the major pattern companies recommends using mercerized, 2- to 3-cord cotton thread (mercerized thread is thread which has been treated with caustic soda for strength and luster), and one of the major suppliers cautions craftsmen against using anything but silk thread, claiming that cotton has limited durability, and that nylon picks up lint. In actual practice, however, leather craftsmen are using all sorts of threads—silk, cotton, nylon, dacron—and none of their garments are falling apart. Silk is perhaps the better thread to use, but the most important thing to keep in mind is to use a strong thread and to perfect the stitch.

For machine sewing garments of lightweight to medium–weight leather, either a heavy–duty silk thread or a 2- to 3-cord heavy–duty mercerized cotton thread should be used.

For ornamental hand or machine sewing, a silk buttonhole twist thread should be used.

As a general rule, its better to risk a heavier thread on leather than to use a flimsy thread and have the seams tear apart.

When hand sewing, each stitch should be locked or knotted before proceeding to the next stitch. This prevents the whole seam from opening if one stitch should wear out. Locking or knotting can be done with a simple thread loop, running the thread back through the loop and then pulling it tight.

When machine or hand sewing leather, the thread should either be commercially beeswaxed or waxed by hand before it's sewn into the project. Nylon Monofilament fishline is also usable for special sewing problems, stringing leather beads for example.

If thread is visible to the eye, you should carefully consider its color as a complement to the finished piece. Undyed, or natural, thread can be dyed by pulling it through a saturated dye applicator. It should then be coated with beeswax.

Lacing

Lacing, as compared with thread, is thicker, wider, and stronger. Lacing is both ornamental and functional; if a decorative stitch is used, there's no objection to the lace remaining visible; in fact, the lacing on billfolds, cases, belts, and even garment seams and edges is normally left visible as a decorative touch. Whether you use lace or thread is a matter of personal preference on many items.

Lacing is available in both leather and vinyl. I don't recommend vinyl. The vinyl coating over the inner thread core is likely to peel off. Leather lacing, on the other hand, is consistently durable. Leather lacing is available in calf, goat, and latigo, all in a wide assortment of commercially dyed colors. Lacing is sold by width (usually from 3/32" to 3/16") and comes rolled on a cardboard spool in lengths of from 25 to 50 yards, depending on width. The Tandy Leather Company sells a wide selection of leather lacing with recommendations on which lacing should be used for specific projects.

Lacing is either flat or round. On flat lacing, the exposed side, or facing, is either flat or slightly rounded; the right side of the lacing is usually obvious by a siight degree of roundness or by a shinier finish. Make sure that this finished side always faces out on your project.

Latigo lacing is the strongest kind and is used on the thickest leathers; calf is a medium weight, and

goat is a fine lacing. Lacing is hand sewn with the lacing needles described on page 49. Light–colored lacing can be dyed darker in the manner described in Chapter Fourteen. On pages 54 and 55 there are detailed diagrams showing a number of lacing styles.

Rawhide lacing is designed for extra heavy–duty use on projects such as front and side closings on vests, for closing shoes, boots and mocassins, for bracelet ties, for hair ribbon and for stringing necklace pendants.

Beeswax Compound

As mentioned earlier, a small cake of beeswax compound is a must when hand sewing with thread and lacing. The Tandy Leather Company, as well as most neighborhood shoe repair shops, sell inexpensive beeswax cakes of about 1½ ounces. Thread and lacing should always be coated with beeswax before they're used in leather. A wax coating not only adds strength and durability, but reduces fraying and allows the thread or lace to glide smoothly into the lace holes.

To coat thread and lace with wax, you simply cut the required length and then pull it along the cake of wax enough times so that you cover all sides. If wax residue builds up on the thread or lace, this should be removed before sewing begins. If you don't wipe away the excess, it will come off in the first lace hole and glop on the leather.

The Lacing Pony

If you plan to do much hand lacing, you might be interested in eventually buying a lacing pony. Figure 42

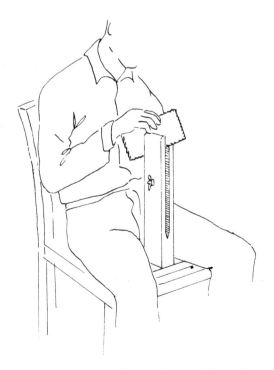

Figure .42. *A lacing pony in use (notice how the pony is held upright by the craftsman's legs).*

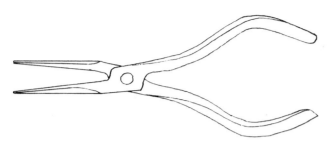

Figure 43. *A pair of lacing pliers, for pulling the lace through the punch holes.*

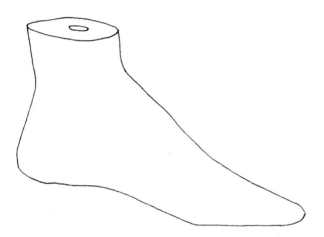

Figure 44. *A shoe last; the hole at the top fits down over the last jack.*

Figure 45. *A last jack made of a continuous leather belt; tension is gained by spreading the feet farther apart.*

illustrates a lacing pony in use. This clamping tool is shaped like an inverted *T*. The trunk of the *T* is split into a vise clamp to hold the project in place while it's being laced. The clamp jaws are made of wood and tightened by means of a wing nut. When lacing smaller items, such as small handbags and billfolds, the lacing pony holds the project in place and leaves both hands free to lace with.

One side of the *T* bar is placed under each leg to keep the pony vertical and solid. The lacing project is then placed between the clamp jaws at a comfortable angle, and the wing nut is finally tightened. It's a good idea when using a lacing pony to place a buffer of leather between the clamp jaws and the project. This leather buffer will keep the clamp jaws from scratching or denting it.

Lacing ponies are a very old leather craftman's tool. In Colonial America they used to be incorporated right into a cobbler's bench. Many of the old ones are still around and in use today. The Colonial leather-maker knew that he could work faster and exercise much more control if he had both hands free. A belt-type boot–lacing vise is described in this chapter under *Last jack.*

Lacing Pliers

A lacing pliers, or any tapered needle-nose pliers is a valuable aid to lacing. Figure 43 illustrates a pair of lacing pliers. The narrow tip on the pliers aids in pulling the lace through the lace hole, much in the same manner as a pair of tweezers is used for pulling out a sliver. A lacing pliers is primarily a time–saver.

The Last

Figure 44 illustrates a shoe last. A last is a form shaped like the human foot. The last is used in form-ing and hand sewing on moccasins, moc boots, and shoes. The moc boots illustrated in Chapter Sixteen were formed and hand sewn on a last. Lasts are sold in both men's and women's sizes, are available in wood and plastic and can be specially ordered to fit a particular shoe or moc style. The suppliers listed at the back of the book include last manufacturers. Very often used lasts can be purchased from shoe manu-facturers and then reshaped to a new style.

The last provides a rigid inside form around which the footwear is built; a specific last for both left and right foot for each style and size. The last is non-metal so that the piece of footwear can initially be tacked to form around the last before being sewn. Since the whole piece of footwear is built around the last, the outside shape and dimensions of the last will deter-mine the exact inside measurements of the footwear.

If you do nothing more then lace the kit-type foot-wear sold by the Tandy Leather Company, you won't need a last because these kits are already precut and partially formed. If, on the other hand, you plan to make footwear (moc boots, boots, Apache boots or shoes) from the ground up, a last is an absolute must. Without a last, a piece of footwear has no inside form.

Last Jack

A last requires some type of last jack, or holding device, to keep the last rigid while it's being used. The United Shoe Machinery Company (listed at the back of the book) sells both a regular last jack and an offset last jack. Both of these can be fastened to a bench. A last jack not only holds the last, but is constructed so that when sewing, the last can be turned to convenient sewing angles. The chapter, *Moccasins, Slippers, and Moc Boots*, goes into greater detail on the construction of moccasins and moc boots.

The early American moccasin maker used a continuous leather belt as his last jack. This continuous leather belt was 2″ to 3″ wide and long enough to go under his feet and over his knees when he was in a sitting position (see Figure 45). He would place the moc on his knee, loop the belt over the moc to hold it tight to his knee for sewing and then stretch the belt tight with his feet. Walter Dyer, one of New England's most successful makers of hand-sewn mocs, whose boots are illustrated on pages 88, 89, and 90, still sticks to this old custom of using a belt at his last jack.

Lasting Pincers

Figure 46 illustrates a pair of lasting pincers. Lasting pincers are used when tacking and sewing footwear on a last. This tool combines a pliers, a hammer head (for nailing tacks to form leather to the shape of a last), and a claw handle for removing tacks once the seams are sewn. This tool is used by almost all professional boot, shoe, and moccasin makers. The C. S. Osborne Company sells a professional version of this tool.

Still another supply item is tacks. If you expect to do any hand sewing of moccasins, moc boots, Apache boots, or shoes on a last you'll need a supply of tacks. Tacks are used to form the leather to the last until the seams are sewn; they're then removed.

Sewing and Lacing Styles

Whether you use flat lace, round lace, or even if you sew by hand with thread, there are two basic types of sewing styles; the *line* stitch, and the *edge* stitch. The line stitch is a purely functional stitch; it's used to seam two pieces of leather together, the stitch runs along a line, and is set in, back away from the leather edge. The edge stitch, on the other hand, is both decorative and functional. With an edge stitch, the thread or lacing loops over the leather edges, and can, with some styles, completely cover up the raw fabric edges. Normally, the line stitch is used when sewing garment seams; most craftsmen feel that the line stitch is entirely too bland to use along exposed edges. The edge stitch, on the other hand, is used on all types of leather projects, from billfolds, to belts, to handbag seams, and especially when sewing together the parts of small leather cases.

There are variations within each of the two sewing types. The most commonly used line stitch is the *run-*

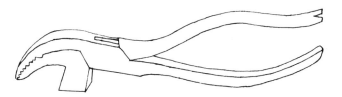

Figure 46. *A pair of lasting pincers, used when forming leather to a last.*

ning stitch illustrated in Figure 47. This stitch is applicable to both lacing and thread. It's similar to the straight stitch produced by the sewing machine. The edge stitch, on the other hand, has a much wider application of styles, from the simple *whip* stitch illustrated in Figure 48, to the more complicated *single loop* stitch illustrated in Figure 49. This section then, will illustrate one type of line stitch (the running stitch in Figure 47), and three types of edge stitching (the whip stitch in Figure 48, the single loop stitch in Figure 49, and the *cross loop*, or *baseball X* stitch in Figure 50. In addition to the styles illustrated in this section, there are still several other lacing styles not shown. If you want more information on the subject of sewing and lacing, I suggest you consult one of the Tandy Leather Company catalogs, or read their excellent pamphlet entitled "Braiding and Lacing for Fun."

The Running Stitch

This is a simple over and under stitch used to hold two pieces of leather together with the line of stitching set back away from the leather edge. The length of the stitch runs in a more or less straight line at a constant distance from the outside edge (never looping the edge). As mentioned earlier, it's used primarily when sewing garment seams, and it's generally a recessed stitch which is hidden from view. Figure 47 illustrates the whole process of stitching a running stitch with lace from beginning to end. In the top left illustration, a tiny slit about ⅛″ long, is cut in the center of the lace. If you follow the progression of drawings, you can see how this slit forms a tie loop to begin the lace. If you were using thread rather than lace, you'd have to tie a knot in the thread to take the place of this slip-loop beginning. The stitch then proceeds around the circumference of the project, over and under, at the same distance from the edge until it reaches the place of beginning. The bottom right drawing in the sequence illustrates how the running stitch is ended by simply running it back under the previous stitch on the non-exposed side of the project, and then cutting the lace end off. Care should be exercised with this stitch to keep equal tension on all separate stitches, and not to let one section of stitches bunch up, or pucker the fabric. The length requirement for the running stitch is approximately 3 times the distance covered.

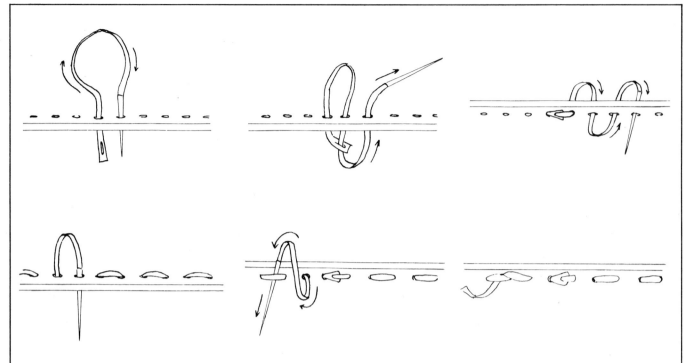

Figure 47. *The running stitch: this is a simple over/ under stitch. The top left drawing shows how the stitch is begun; a ⅛" slit is cut in the lace, and the first loop of lace is run through this slit in order to fasten the beginning of the stitch securely. The running stitch is then continued all the way around the circumference of the project, over and under, until it reaches the point at which it began. The lower right drawing illustrates how this stitch is ended; the lace is drawn back under the previous loop (on the non-exposed side of the project), and then cut off.*

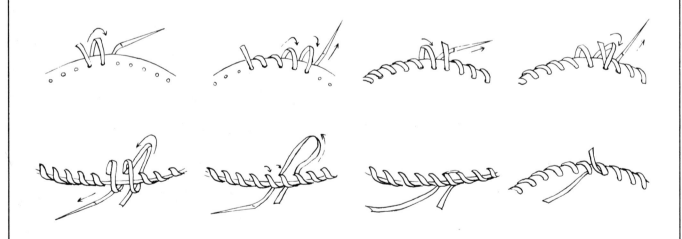

Figure 48. *The whip stitch: this stitch covers the edge of the project with one simple loop. If you follow the sequence of the drawings and pay attention to the arrows, you'll be able to see clearly how this stitch begins and ends. Make sure that all ending loops are pulled tight, and tap the end piece flat with a mallet.*

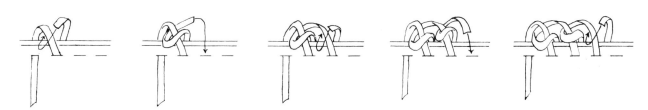

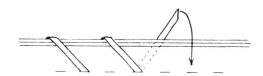

Figure 49. *The single loop stitch: this is an edge stitch like the whip stitch, but it's more decorative than the whip stitch. It's made in the same way a whip stitch is, except that an additional back loop is made on each stitch before proceding on to the next one. Corner holes should be laced through three times in order to cover the corner and spread the lace out evenly. Make sure to keep the lace from twisting. The single loop stitch begins and ends in the same way that the whip stitch does.*

Figure 50. *The cross loop, or baseball X stitch: this is a very popular stitch and is used on billfolds, belts, garment seams, and when attaching straps to handbags. Simply skip every other hole and then reverse direction, hitting every odd hole on the way back.*

The Whip Stitch

The whip stitch is a simple edge stitch; it covers the raw leather edges with a single loop. It's the easiest of the many edge stitching styles, and can be used on most small projects from cases to billfolds. Figure 48 illustrates the whip stitch being used with lacing. This same style can also be used with thread, but again, as with the running stitch, a knot takes the place of the beginning lace technique illustrated in the first of the sequence of drawings. If you closely follow the arrows along the sequence you can see the method of beginning and ending the stitch. Remember to keep all loops of the whip stitch tight and evenly spaced. After you've cut both end pieces, tap them flat against the project with a mallet. The length requirement for the whip stitch is approximately 3½ times the distance covered.

The Single Loop Stitch

The single loop stitch is another style of the edge stitch. This stitch is actually nothing more than an extension of the whip stitch. It's a bit more complicated, but it produces a much more decorative edge. With this stitch, you can completely cover raw edges on a project. The single loop stitch can be used on most

small projects including cases, belt edges, and billfolds. Figure 49 illustrates the technique of the single loop stitch. It differs from the whip stitch by an additional single back loop made through the previous stitch before proceeding ahead. Points to remember when using this stitch are to keep the lace from twisting, and when going around corners, it's suggested that you lace through the corner hole three times and then spread the three stitches evenly around the corner. Begin and end the stitch as was done with the whip stitch. The length requirement for the single loop stitch is approximately 5½ times the distance covered.

The Cross Loop, or Baseball X Stitch

The cross loop, or baseball X stitch is a third variation in the edge stitch. It is very decorative because of its unique design, especially on billfolds, small cases, and even when used as a single X in attaching handbag straps. Figure 50 illustrates this technique. It consists of simply skipping every other hole along the edge from beginning to end, then reversing direction, and catching the odd hole in the opposite direction on the way back. The length requirement for the cross loop or baseball X stitch, is approximately 6 times the distance covered.

CHAPTER TEN

Bonding and laminating

To laminate is to sandwich layers of leather together; one on top of another. The technique of lamination is primarily used to gain thickness or volume, as for example when laminating two layers of leather together to form a sandal sole. This double thickness of leather on a sandal sole not only creates a heavier sole, but also insures longer wear.

The technique of laminating layers of leather together is also used when making leather sculpture, leather jewelry such as pendants, pins, and bracelets, when constructing leather wall reliefs and when making leather beads. In all of these examples, the technique of lamination is used to produce volume. In these instances, lamination has nothing to do with producing longer wear, but is used for purely visual purposes.

Lamination can also create line, as with a wood grain effect, and it can create contrast when the layers of leather alternate in color and texture. For example, an embossed grain laminated over a smooth grain creates a contrast in texture; a tan leather laminated over a brown leather creates a contrast in color.

Lamination is normally accomplished with leather contact cement after first texturing or roughing–up both matching surfaces with a fine grade sandpaper. This roughing–up produces a deep penetration of the cement and creates a stronger bond. Don't use rubber cement when laminating; the bond isn't strong enough.

Leather Cements and Glues

A number of bonding agents will be covered in this section; both cements and glues. There are two types of bonding agents, one bonds wet and the other bonds dry. The wet bonding agents are applied evenly to both surfaces and the bond is made while the agent is still wet. The dry bonding agents are applied evenly to both surfaces, allowed to dry, and then bonded.

Wet bonding agents include Duco Household Cement, Testor's Glue, Elmer's Woodworking Glue, Franklin Glue, and other white glues. Wet glues generally aren't flexible, some of them stain, others are difficult to clean up, and all of them require pressure or weight on the bonded area while drying.

Dry bonding agents include Master's Quick-Drying All Purpose Cement, Barge's All Purpose Cement, The Tandy Leather Company's "Craftsman" All Purpose Cement, epoxy cement, Goodyear High Speed Neolite All Purpose Cement, and Elmer's Fast Dry Cement. Master's and Barge's Cements are manufactured for the leather trade. These two cements must be purchased through a local shoe repair, a jobber or directly from the manufacturer. Goodyear and Elmer's Contact Cement are both available in hardware stores. The "Craftsman" Cement is available through all Tandy Leather stores. Epoxy cement does work on leather, but it requires mixing, and requires a bit too much fuss to work with compared with the other five.

Some type of leather cement or glue is used on almost every leather project; from laminating soles, to cementing seams, to cementing turned garment edges, to attaching parts, findings and embellishments. What are some of the things to watch for when bonding?

Is the cement or glue flexible? This is perhaps the first consideration in selecting a leather bonding agent, especially when using a bond on garments and footwear. If the cement does not flex with the fabric, it will crack and peel, breaking the bond. If the point of bond is required to bend with the fabric, then flexible cement must be used. Master's, Barge's, Craftsman, Goodyear, and Elmer's dry contact cements described above are all flexible bonding agents. Epoxy is not. None of the wet bonding agents is as flexible as the five dry agents just mentioned. Rubber cement is flexible, but is normally only used with leather when cementing garment seams and hems; it isn't strong enough for most other bonding demands.

And how strong will the cement bond be under stress? If you're glueing a bend or a fold in thick leather, the leather has a natural tendency to return to its flat shape. A bond of this type is therefore under internal stress. The laminated leather sculpture shown on page 137 was carved from eleven layers of laminated horsehide. These laminations were under severe stress while the piece was being carved. Goodyear Contact Cement was used on this particular piece. All of the glues and cements mentioned above create strong bonds on leather, except for rubber cement which is normally used only in leather garment construction.

Increasing Bonding Properties

How can the bonding properties of leather be increased? With both wet and dry bonding agents the bond can be strengthened by roughing up, or texturing, both surfaces of the leather pieces to be joined before the bonding agent is applied. Using a wire brush, coarse steel wool, sandpaper, or even scraping the leather rough with the edge of a sharp instrument are all methods of texturing leather to increase the strength of the bond. This surface roughness provides more area for the bonding agent to cover, and causes a deeper penetration of the agent into the leather fibers.

With dry bonding agents, the bond can be additionally strengthened by tapping the bond with a mallet or rolling it with an ordinary rolling pin. This eliminates air pockets and forces all surface areas to contact and hold. On wet bonding agents the bond can be strengthened by applying pressure or weight to the bond while it's drying. Pressure can be induced by weight such as that provided by heavy books, by a mechanical press, or by a vise or clamp arrangement.

Cleaning off Glue

Will the cement or glue stain the leather? And how well will it clean up? The dry bonding agents mentioned clean up beautifully and will not stain the leather. With these agents, excess can be rolled off in tiny balls as when cleaning up after using rubber cement. When bonding with wet bonding agents, however, you should be very careful in application to avoid excess. Excess oozing around seams with wet bonding agents is not only difficult to clean up, but the presence of dried excess will prevent dye from later penetrating the leather fiber. When using wet bonding agents I suggest you practice on scrap leather first to determine the minimum quantity necessary in order to avoid excess and still create a strong bond.

With several of the wet bonding agents, ooze that's not immediately removed will dry iron hard.

Avoiding Errors

What are the application problems with glues and cements? Glues and cements should be applied evenly with a flat–tipped brush. Many cans come with their own applicator brush. The one advantage to wet bonding agents is that they allow for adjustments when placing the two glued surfaces together. Dry bonding agents, on the other hand, bond instantly on contact. You cannot move the surfaces around when using dry bonding agents once you've placed them together. The point here is that when you use a dry bonding agent—when laminating the soles on sandals for example—you must be very careful that the two pieces of leather are placed together in the exact position you want them. If you don't hit it right the first time, you won't get a second chance. I've tested the strength of these dry bonds on leather. When you pull them apart, you don't pull the bond apart, you create a whole new tear. Another word of caution: many of these cements and glues are toxic. Use them in a well–ventilated room, and don't smoke a cigarette while you're using them. You should also wipe excess off the can cover before replacing the cap, otherwise it might become permanently bonded. And be sure to cover the cement when not using it. Air in the can will dry the cement.

Master's Quick Drying All Purpose Cement, Barge's All Purpose Cement, and Tandy's "Craftsman" All Purpose Cement are the most popular bonding agents used by leather craftsmen. But all of the glue and cement mentioned do work on leather within the limitations, and using the care, described. I recommend that you keep both wet and dry bonding agents on hand at all times. I'm always finding leather uses for both.

Construction by the author of cowhide laminated over wood. The round disks are circles of patent leather. Photo, Robert Estrin.

Leather knife sheath, using rivets and cobbling nails to laminate the two pieces of 8 ounce cowhide together. Made by Tom Tisdell, Cambridge, Mass. Photo, Dave Congalton.

CHAPTER ELEVEN

Findings and fasteners

Rivets, grommets, eyelets, snaps, zippers, buckles, nails, rings, hangers, locks, cleats, and spots are all grouped together into a category and called leather *findings.* Findings are the trimmings, the extras, the non–leather decorative or functional attachments which are necessary to leatherwork. This chapter will discuss findings and fasteners, and the tools that are required to install them.

Selection of Findings

The best time to select a finding is when you initially plan your design. Almost every functional leather project requires some type of finding, whether it's a fastening device, a cobbling nail, or a grommet. Don't wait until you get the project half completed before you begin to think about how to hold it together, or how to fasten it. Many findings serve exactly the same purpose, but with entirely different functional and visual results. For example, both a rivet and a snap will hold a buckle on a belt; a rivet is permanent, but a snap allows for interchangeable buckles.

Selection of the right finding, and the location of that finding on the particular project can very often either complement or destroy your visual result. For example, you might well design a sophisticated handbag, select just the right color and texture of leather, put the handbag together with impeccable craftsmanship and then visually wipe out the whole project because of poorly placed, gaudy findings that conflict with the over–all design. Take the trouble to select findings that complement your project, and then plan their placement so as to eliminate visual conflict within the design.

At this writing, brass findings, especially mellowed brass findings, are much more popular than nickel, chrome, copper, or colored findings. An unembellished antique brass is a complement to leather. And don't weigh the project down with brass just because it happens to be popular. Just a touch of brass in the right place is all that's needed. If you're in doubt as to the selection of the right findings at the right time, I suggest you look around in boutiques and small leather shops to see for yourself what young people are buying. More often than not, young people, especially college students, are the style setters. Find out for yourself what they like, and then work from there.

Metal findings very often come with a coating of high–gloss lacquer. If you want to tone down this gloss, begin by removing the lacquer with metal polish. Once you've exposed the raw metal the high gloss will tone down to a mellowed satin finish.

Many findings can be recessed into a leather, or completely hidden from view. For example, rivets need not be seen by the eye if you plan ahead of time how to position them so that they'll be concealed. And, if you're unable to locate tasteful manufactured findings for a given project, don't be afraid to let your imagination run free. If, for example, you need a fastening device for a handbag, how about an old brass lock, a wooden timber pin, a lock plate, or even an old bobbin? Taking the time to make your project unique and still tasteful is half the challenge.

Because findings are sold in a wide variety of sizes and colors, it's very difficult to describe them all in a text of this size. The text just can't function as a catalog. I suggest you send for one of the findings catalogs. listed at the back of the book, or else visit a findings supplier in person to see what's available. One final tip on the general subject of findings: don't install one until you've practiced on scrap leather ahead of time.

Rivets and the Rivet Setter

Rivets are metal fastening pins with either split ends or caps. Rivets are used to attach parts, or to add strength to stress points in seams. Rivets are sold in assorted sizes from small to extra large, and they're available in a variety of colors and metals, including black, brown, nickel, brass, and copper.

A small rivet has a post shaft approximately ¼″ long; a medium rivet has a post shaft approximately ⅜″ long; a large rivet has a post shaft approximately ½″ long; and an extra long rivet has a post shaft approximately ⅝″ long. Select the size of the rivet by length according to the thickness of the leather that it must pass through. Figure 51 illustrates a cap, or 2-part rivet and a rivet setter, and Figure 52 illustrates a split rivet.

Rivets are used in a number of ways. They can be used to strengthen seams, as at the top and bottom of handbag side seams; they can be used to attach straps; to fasten buckles in place; to add leather parts such as handbag flaps; or as purely decorative embellishment.

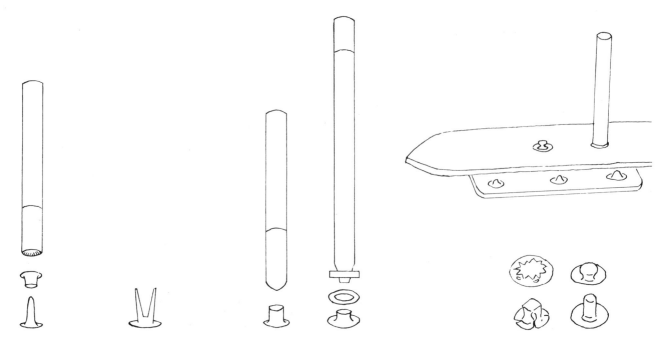

Figure 51.
*A two-part rivet,
and a rivet setter.*

Figure 52.
A split rivet.

Figure 53.
*(Left) an eyelet and its setter.
(Right) a grommet and its setter.*

Figure 54.
*A four-part snap, a snap setter,
and an anvil.*

Basically, a rivet is a holding device. Generally, they should be used sparingly, and only at points where they will have an essential function. For most craftsmen, the use of rivets is a matter of personal taste. I've seen the work of many craftsmen who prefer not to use rivets. These people prefer to hand sew everything, feeling that the presence of rivets violates the natural animal fabric. The only time that they might use rivets would be to strengthen seams, and even then they'll go to great pains to conceal the appearance of these rivets. The result is well worth it though; they end up with an all–leather visual product. Unless you feel equally as strong about rivets as these craftsmen, then I suggest you proceed to use rivets sparingly. There's no question that rivets save time and add strength to a project.

Setting Rivets

A split rivet is secured by merely punching a hole through the thicknesses to be joined (the hole size equal to the diameter of the rivet shaft), inserting the rivet into the hole and then bending flat the two split prongs in opposite directions, away from each other. The split end should normally be concealed from view.

The 2–part, or cap, rivet illustrated in Figure 51 can either be hammered together with a mallet, or set with a rivet setter. If the rivet head isn't going to show, then it doesn't make any difference if the cap is dented from a direct mallet blow. If, on the other hand, the cap is to be left visible to the eye, you'd be better off to set the rivet cap with a rivet setter; the concave tipped tool illustrated in Figure 51.

When setting rivets, you need a solid metal base against which to pound. You can either purchase an inexpensive anvil, or just use a piece of flat scrap iron.

A cap rivet is set by first punching a rivet hole equal to the size of the rivet shaft, shoving the shaft through the hole, and then pushing the cap over the shaft first with the thumb, and then setting it permanently on the shaft either directly with the mallet, or with the concave tip of the rivet setter which fits down snuggly over the cap. The butt of the shaft end should be placed flat against the metal surface when the cap is set. Forcing the cap onto the shaft with several hard strikes of the mallet or setter spreads the soft tip of the rivet into the cap space.

Eyelets, Grommets, and Setters

Figure 53 (left) illustrates an eyelet and an eyelet setter; Figure 53 (right) illustrates a grommet and a grommet setter. Both findings are tiny tubes that serve as reinforcement rings on leather lacing holes. Both findings prevent a leather lacing hole from tearing. They serve as a reinforcement sleeve through which lace is threaded. Because they are added to leather, they also have a decorative function in that they provide a tidy professional touch to the visual appearance of lacing holes. The most common use of these findings is on lacing holes in shoes, buckle holes in belts, lacing holes in vests and on drawstring holes in drawstring handbags. The boot illustrated on page 92 has grommets in the lacing holes; the vest illustrated on page 101 has eyelets in the lacing holes.

An eyelet is a single–piece finding; a single tube with a collar–like flange only on one end. A grommet, on the other hand, is a two–piece finding; it has a collar–like flange on the one end exactly as the eyelet does, it's larger than the eyelet, and it has a separate ring which is attached by means of a grommet setter to serve as an additional wide collar on the inside end. When an eyelet is installed, you create an inside collar by bending the eyelet tube lip over with an eyelet setter. You don't have to create an inside collar by bending a grommet tube because the inside collar comes as a separate part.

Because a grommet is larger than an eyelet, a grommet is usually used on heavier leather such as footwear. An eyelet is used on thinner leather such as garments. The use of these two findings is optional. Very often a grommet isn't necessary on heavy leather. The moc boot on page 89 laces without grommet reinforcement. On thin leather, especially on splits, the use of an eyelet does prevent a lacing hole from stretching and tearing in a situation where the lace is subject to a lot of tightening.

Eyelets and grommets are sold in a wide variety of colors, materials, and shapes. They're available in nickel, brass, and colored enamels over metal. They vary in shape from the standard tube shape shown here to a wide variety of novelty and specialty shapes. Eyelets and grommets are sold according to the inside diameter of the hole opening beginning at about ¼″ and working up.

Setting Eyelets and Grommets

An eyelet is set with an eyelet setter, illustrated on the left of Figure 53. A hole the size of the eyelet tube is first punched through the leather. The tube of the eyelet is pushed through the hole with the collar flange facing the grain side of the garment. The eyelet is then placed face down on a flat surface, preferably a surface that is both solid but buffered against scratching the eyelet. The eyelet setter has a tapered tip. This tip is placed in the open end of the eyelet and tapped gently with a mallet until the eyelet metal begins to spread into a lip or collar of its own. The taper of the setter forces the metal into a lip. As the lip forms it flops over and flattens out snug against the leather to hold itself securely in place.

A grommet is set with a grommet setter, illustrated on the right of Figure 53. The same procedure is followed as with setting an eyelet except that the additional inside collar ring is added. The ring fits down over the grommet tube and is tapped into place by spreading the lip of the grommet tube just enough to hold it tightly. As you can see from the illustration, the grommet setter is a two–part tool with a spreader punch and a small anvil. For each size grommet there is a corresponding size setter and anvil; a ¼″ grommet requires a ¼″ grommet setter, and so on.

Snaps and Snap Setters

Snaps are available in a wide variety of colors, metals, sizes, and shapes. Most findings catalogues break them down for specific projects, such as glove snaps, dot fasteners, belt snaps, and garment snaps. Again, this text isn't long enough to describe all the snaps available to the trade; I suggest you either write for a catalog, or visit a findings supplier for future reference in ordering.

Snaps are used to fasten flaps, secure garment openings, attach parts, or can be used to make strap and belt lengths adjustable. Since a snap gets a great deal of use, selection of quality snaps is important. Make certain the snap you select is sturdy enough to perform the fastening task that you require. Dot fasteners are the heaviest snaps. One guideline to quality is to test the snap on a scrap of the same leather as your project is made of. Open and close it a few times to make sure it's large enough and durable. When installing snaps (or other findings for that matter), one tip is to reinforce thin leather by cementing a double thickness of leather to the back side of where the snap will be attached.

Snaps come in four parts. There is the cap, the cap rivet, the snap and the snap rivet. Obviously, the cap rivet is set into the cap and the snap rivet is set into the snap. Once you have a snap in front of you, it's visually obvious which parts go together. Figure 54 illustrates the four parts of one type of snap.

Setting Snaps

A snap setter or dot fastener is required in order to secure snaps and dot snaps. As with a grommet setter, there is a specific size setter for the corresponding size snap or dot snap. The Tandy Leather Company sells inexpensive snap setting kits that come with a variety of setter sizes. The procedure for setting a snap is virtually the same as for setting a grommet except that there are two pairs of parts to be set instead of one. The trick in setting all of these findings which involve metal being spread is to create a consistent and smooth spreading pressure. Violent, off-center hits may split the metal, whereas weak hits may squish it out of shape. Again, practice setting snaps on scrap leather before you tackle the project itself.

For an extra heavy–duty reinforced snap, there's a bar snap that's set with a special bar snap setter. A bar snap is a snap head that's mounted within a flat, metal bar plate. The bar plate acts as a reinforcement around the snap, and stiffens thin leather to prevent it from tearing or stretching. A bar snap is a bit more expensive than an ordinary snap, but is well worth the extra investment on areas that must withstand extensive wear. Bar snaps are very often used on handbag flaps.

Zippers

The zipper is perhaps the most commonly used closing device available. It's used for garment openings on items such skirts, shorts, vests, and zip–out linings, and it's used on such articles as billfolds and briefcases. Why is a zipper the most commonly used closing device? Perhaps much of the reason is that, even though it's a durable closing device, it's the closing device that requires the least amount of imagination. It's ready–made, it can cover a long opening in a minimum of installation time, and it's a convenient and quick closing device for the consumer. A zipper seems to have everything going for it, but does it necessarily represent the ultimate in design?

A poet friend of mine recently was given a very expensive factory–made briefcase for his birthday. He had been coveting a thin leather envelope in which to carry his poems to readings. The briefcase he received had one of those garish zippers sewn all around the outside with heavy white thread. There was some excellent leather in that briefcase, but all you could really see was this glittery nickel zipper. He was so disappointed by the gaudy exterior of his briefcase that he gave it away, and I replaced it for him with a simple leather envelope that closed with a tuck flap.

My point here is that even though a zipper is quick, convenient, and readily obtainable, it also requires the least amount of design imagination. A leather craftsman produces handmade products; the consumer has a right to expect more from him than what is common by way of design. There are times when you'll want to use zippers, but please don't rely on them as closing devices. You can justify the use of a zipper on handmade garments if you can use it in a way that complements the design, as in the case of jumpsuits where the zipper is deliberately exposed for style.

Zippers are sold according to length and quality. They can be installed in a number of ways either by hand or on a sewing machine; slot–seam, lapped–edge, or invisible zipper seams. A sewing machine is the most uniform method of installing zippers.

Because our text space is limited, and because detailed step–by–step directions for installing zippers are readily available, I won't go into them here. Most sewing centers have pamphlets on the installation of zippers, and there are a number of texts available on the subject, including a very excellent chapter in, *How to Sew Leather, Suede, Fur*, by Krohn and Schwebke, published by the Bruce Publishing Company of Milwaukee, Wisconsin.

Before I leave the subject of zippers however, I'd like to challenge you to design other closing ideas before you depend on the "good old reliable common zipper." If something can be closed with a zipper, chances are it can be closed many other ways as well. Style very often evolves from trying the other ways first.

Buckles

A buckle is a fastening device that requires a belt or a strap to complete its function. Buckles are available in endless sizes, shapes, ornamentation, and material. At the moment brass buckles are the most popular. Other buckle materials include iron, bronze, nickel, plastic, wood, bone, and even ceramic. There are fabric covered buckles, buckles you can cover with leather yourself, plated buckles, novelty buckles and heavily ornamented buckles, such as cowboy buckles. Or, you can make your own buckles; carve them out of leather, wood, bone, or plastic. One of the handbags illustrated on page 109 has a leather buckle as a closing device.

The search for unique buckles, especially for belts, is one of the major pursuits of many leather craftsmen. I've met craftsmen who haunt old New England barns, antique shops, and even Salvation Army stores in search of harness brass and antique uniform buckles. Other craftsmen seek out sculptors and metalsmiths to design new and unique buckles for them. But the majority of leather craftsmen must rely on buckles manufactured for the trade, not so much from choice, but because of the law of supply and demand. The quantity they use just doesn't give them time for hunting.

Buying buckles in quantity gives you a distinct advantage in price as well as in selection. You can buy buckles directly from a manuaftcurer, or you can buy them from other leather craftsmen, shoe repair shops, or from retail outlets like the Tandy Leather Company. Most buckle manufacturers have at least a $20.00 minimum order requirement. The list at the back of the book includes several buckle suppliers. North and Judd Manufacturing Company of New Britain, Connecticut is one of the largest manufacturers of quality buckles for the trade. If you want to take advantage of manufacturer's prices and selection, then why not get together with several other craftsmen and submit one minimum order between you? Buckles literally set style, especially on belts and sandal straps. Before you pick out the first one you come to in the dime store, try finding something elegant.

Buckles are used on sandals, moccasins, vests, skirts, jerkins, handbags, handbag straps, belts, and many other projects. Buckles can be used both functionally and decoratively. Here are some examples of the choice of fastening device:

A skirt opening can be closed with snaps, a zipper, buttons, eyelets and lacing, hooks and eyes, or with straps and buckles. All of these devices function to close the skirt opening, but each closing device creates a unique garment style. A wrap–around leather skirt can be made to close with straps and buckles. The same is true with many other garments. If a vest is a pullover, it can be made with straps and buckles on the side seams; if it has an opening in the front, straps and buckles can again be used. A handbag flap can be snapped, fastened with a lock, left plain, weighted with an ornament like an old brass key, or it can be fastened down with a buckle and strap that loop over either the entire bag, or portions of it. The function of each closing device is the same; to make sure that the handbag flap stays down. But each closing device creates a unique design style. I could go on with similar examples of sandals, belts, moccasins and any number of other leather projects. It's enough to say that a buckle is only one way to fasten; there are many others.

Figure 55 illustrates several buckle styles: they are, top row, left to right—an ordinary, single bar buckle with a full–length, pivoting tongue; a center bar buckle, also with a full–length, pivoting tongue; and a single bar buckle with a loose roller to make the

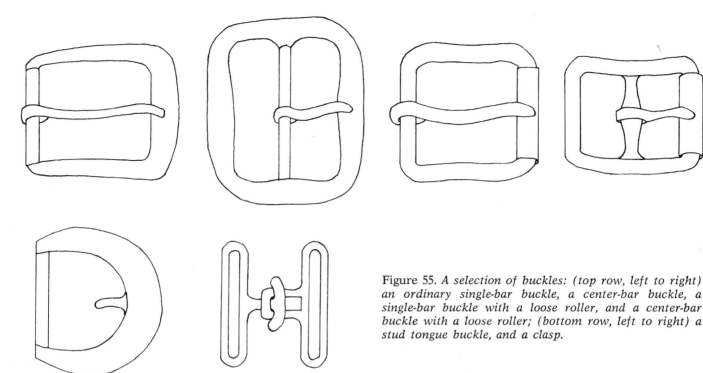

Figure 55. *A selection of buckles: (top row, left to right) an ordinary single-bar buckle, a center-bar buckle, a single-bar buckle with a loose roller, and a center-bar buckle with a loose roller; (bottom row, left to right) a stud tongue buckle, and a clasp.*

belt slide through the buckle hole more easily; and, a center bar buckle with a loose roller; bottom row, left to right— a stud tongue buckle where the belt doesn't pass through the buckle hole, but simply hooks into the belt hole by the buckle stud; and a single adjustment, clasp buckle used where only one length size belt is required.

Buckles come either flat or concave to fit the curvature of the waist. The single bar buckle usually requires the addition of a belt keeper (extra loop) to keep the belt end securely in place. The center bar buckle acts as its own keeper because the belt must bend up through the first hole and back down through the second hole. When using the stud tongue buckle, you can usually get along without a keeper because the buckle fastens in such a way that the extra belt end rests under the opposite side of the belt. The most commonly used buckle on footwear and garments is the center bar buckle. These five buckles are only a beginning of the styles available.

The procedure for securing buckles to straps and belts is virtually the same for all styles. The square end on the belt is looped over the buckle bar, front side out, and then bent under the bar, leaving enough extra length on the end to rivet, sew, or snap it in place. On thick leather, you might find that a shallow *U* groove cut across the width of the belt on the flesh side at the point of the bend will help keep the bend loop small and snug against the buckle bar.

On buckles with full–length pivot tongues, you'll first have to punch a hole equal to the size of the tongue in the direct center of the belt at the point of bend. As the belt is looped over the bar, the hole in the belt slips down over the tongue. If this seems difficult to follow, I suggest you look in your closet for a belt, and examine for yourself how the buckle is secured.

Once you've looped the buckle bar, I suggest that you cement the end to the belt proper. The cement will hold the loop in place while you sew, snap, or rivet the end permanently. How you finally secure this loop over the buckle bar is a matter of choice. As mentioned earlier it can be riveted, sewn, or snapped in place. Riveting is the quickest method, sewing or lacing eliminates hardware, and snapping allows for interchangeable buckles.

Loops, Dees, and Rings

Figure 56 illustrates, from left to right, a loop, a dee, and a ring. Loops, dees, and rings are manufactured in a variety of sizes, and are available in a variety of metals, including brass. These findings are sold by the width of the inside opening.

Loops, dees, and rings can be used in a number of ways on leather projects. An identical pair of loops, dees, and rings will make a self–adjusting belt or strap buckle. This type of buckle is popular on waist belts, moc boots, and sandals. This buckling device is very easy to install. Take the square end of the belt or strap, loop it through the hole in both findings, and then rivet, sew, or snap the belt end back against the belt as with regular buckles. (See moc boot on page 88) This adjustable buckle tightens by looping the belt tip up through the two rings from behind, and then tucking the belt tip back between the two rings in the opposite direction. Now, if you pull the belt tip, it slides between the two rings and tightens the belt.

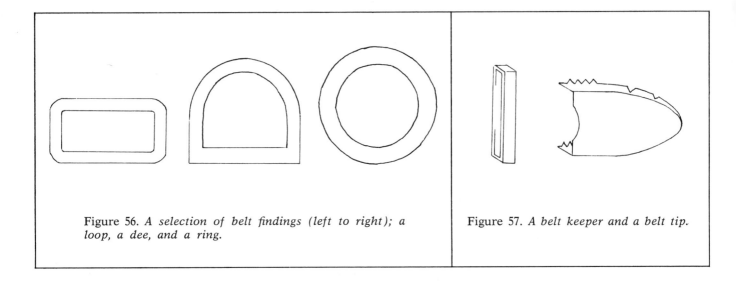

Figure 56. *A selection of belt findings (left to right); a loop, a dee, and a ring.*

Figure 57. *A belt keeper and a belt tip.*

Loops, dees, and rings are also used as hanging devices on leather relief, collage, and on such things as pipe and bottle racks (see pages 147 and 148). They can also be used as handbag strap hangers and as closing devices. The most widely used metal on this type of finding is again brass.

Keepers

A belt strap keeper is the extra loop that's installed on the belt to hold the belt tip close to the belt after it has passed through the buckle. Figure 57 illustrates a belt keeper. Keepers are available in metal, including brass, or they can be made out of scrap leather from the same piece as the strap or belt.

Whether or not you use a keeper is often a matter of choice. Most skirts, dresses and trousers already have enough belt loops on them so that a belt keeper is really not necessary. If however, the belt is to be worn on a garment without waist loops, a keeper is a must. Without a keeper, there would be no way to hold the extra belt tip length tight to the waist. Keepers are also handy on sandal straps where strap leather tends to stretch. I suggest you install a keeper whenever there's likely to be more than 2″ or 3″ of belt tip beyond the buckle.

Or, you can avoid a keeper altogether by using a buckle like the stud tongue buckle (Figure 56, bottom row center), or the clasp (Figure 56, bottom row right), where there's no extra belt tip.

Leather keepers are very easy to make. A ¼″ to ¾″ wide strip of leather is cut out of the scrap belt or strap leather. The width of this strip is a matter of choice depending upon the width of the belt proper. The strip is cut long enough to loop around two thicknesses of the belt or strap. This strip is then bent into a loop and the opposite ends are held together either by sewing, by snaps, by a heavy staple, or by skiving the ends, overlapping them, and then riveting them together.

A keeper can be installed on a belt or strap in the same loop as the buckle, or it can be slid onto the belt ahead of the buckle and left loose to slide along the belt at any adjustment. If it's installed within the same loop as the buckle, you'll have to allow a longer loop than you would without a keeper. The keeper can be kept stationary by a rivet on both sides; the same rivets that hold the buckle in place, but just placing the rivets one on either side of the keeper.

Belt Tips

Figure 57 (right) illustrates one style of a belt tip. This is an open–back, pointed belt tip. There are also square and flat tips in a variety of sizes. The belt tip not only ornaments the belt but gives the tip a dressed edge and additional body for feeding it into a buckle.

The use of a belt tip is optional. It does add more hardware to leather; many people, myself included, prefer keeping hardware at a minimum. The belt tip is secured by first cutting the belt to fit the shape of the tip. The tip is then slid onto the belt, turned over, and hammered tight by forcing the teeth of the belt tip tight against the leather. The hammering should be done on a cushion of leather so as not to dent the tip face.

Other Findings and Supplies

There are many other findings that can be used on a variety of leather projects. Most of these are specialty items like ear wires for leather earrings, or clasps for leather pendants, bracelets and watchbands. These are actually jewelry findings and can be purchased from jewelry findings suppliers.

There are also other items like handbag locks, cleats, spots, and billfold inserts. This text is not long enough to deal with each finding separately. We have discussed many of the major ones. If you want to explore other findings, I suggest you write for a jeweler's findings catalog.

CHAPTER TWELVE

Machine tools

For the purpose of this text, machine tools are defined as electrical tools. For the serious leather craftsman, especially one who hopes to derive an income from his labor, the use of machine tools has many advantages; they save time and labor, they allow the craftsman to produce in quantity, and they provide a uniformity in craftsmanship that cannot be duplicated by hand. The one drawback to using machine tools is that the finished product loses much of its handmade appearance; it takes on the flavor of a factory–made piece. Most craftsmen who support themselves through leatherwork are using machine tools. They find that in order to gain production, they must sacrifice a bit of the handmade appearance. This is one of the inherent evils of increasing production. But the evil isn't always that important; very often a machine tool can actually perform a specific task much better than the craftsman's own hands can.

Sewing Machines

There are two types of sewing machines used on leatherwork; the household sewing machine, and the heavy–duty, industrial sewing machine. Very few craftsmen I've interviewed are using household sewing machines. These machines are designed for weave fabrics. Leather is not a weave fabric. The household machine has only limited use on leather; it can be used for sewing lightweight leather garments, but is virtually ineffectual on anything heavier. An industrial sewing machine, on the other hand, will stitch through both thin and thick leathers. If you intend to buy a machine, I suggest buying a heavy–duty industrial machine.

A household sewing machine has only a single feed; the fabric is fed toward the needle only on the bottom. A single–feed machine is likely to cause the leather to bunch up at the needle. When this happens, there is an unevenness in the number of stitches per inch. A machine designed with a compound feed, on the other hand, feeds the leather toward the needle from both the top and the bottom. If you purchase a machine, I suggest you buy one with a compound feed. One particular industrial model that many leather craftsmen are using is the Singer Sewing Machine, Model Number 111, with a compound feed.

There's no need to buy a new machine. Used industrial machines are very plentiful; there's nothing much more obsolete, from the point of view of the commercial manufacturer of leathergoods, than a used industrial sewing machine. Most of these used machines still have hundreds of hours left in them, but they sell at a fraction of what a new machine costs. These machines are often available from manufacturers of leathergoods. A classified advertisement placed in one of the leather trade magazines should bring you quick results in locating a serviceable used machine. Here are three shoe trade magazines that accept classified advertising:

American Shoemaker, 683 Atlantic Avenue, Boston, Mass. 0211

Leather and Shoes, 10 High Street, Boston, Mass. 02110

Weekly Bulletin of Leather and Shoe News, 183 Essex Street, Boston, Mass. 02111

If you decide to purchase a used machine, I suggest that you talk the seller into giving you a couple of free lessons on how to use the machine, or at least get a hold of an instruction manual from either the seller, or the manufacturer of the specific machine. Machines do vary in style and you'll want to learn as much about your own machine as you can before you begin using it on a project.

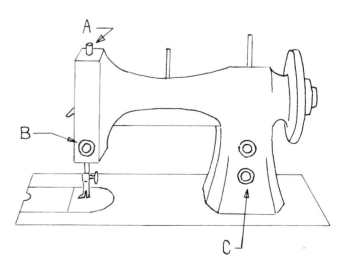

Figure 58. *A sewing machine: the pressure regulator (a); the upper tension regulator (b); the stitch regulator (c).*

Here are a few general suggestions that apply to the use of sewing machines on leather (see Figure 58):

1. Keep oil off of all exposed areas of the machine. Oil will stain leather.

2. For machine needles, see page 50, or consult your local sewing center.

3. The length of the needle stitch should be adjusted according to the thickness of the seam. This stitch regulator is usually found on the right hand, front side of the machine. The heavier leather, the fewer stitches per inch. As a general guide, heavier leather, over 6 ounces, requires somewhere between 6 to 9 stitches per inch; very thin leather, under 3 ounces, requires somewhere between 10 to 12 stitches per inch. You'll just have to adjust your machine stitch count according to the thickness of the given seam.

4. The pressure regulator (located on top of the machine, above the needle) should be adjusted to the thickness of the given seam. Less pressure is needed on leather than on other fabrics, as leather is a bit spongier than many other fabrics.

5. The upper stitch tension also needs to be adjusted according to the given seam thickness. The upper tension adjustment knob is located on the front of the machine, above the needle. If the thread breaks or forms a loop on top of the seam, the upper tension should be loosened. If thread loops on the bottom of the seam, the tension should be tightened.

6. Always test the stitch first on sample thicknesses of scrap leather.

7. I suggest you either mark the path of your stitch on the leather, or use the straight edge of masking tape as your guideline for sewing.

8. At points of heavy stress, for example side seams on handbags, avoid double stitching on leather seams, because sewing by machine twice over the same area has a tendency to cut the leather. If you need extra seam reinforcement, I suggest that you use rivets.

9. Stitch accurately, and not too fast. A heavy–duty machine has a tendency to whisk across a piece of leather. Don't work the machine too fast or you may lose control over your direction.

10. Check your machine thread against the thread suggestions on pages 50–51.

An alternative to buying your own machine is to bring the sewing project to a local shoe repair store, and have the repairman sew it for you on his machine. If you do this, bear in mind that the shoe man is used to sewing shoe soles. You'll have to give him instructions, slow him down and remind him that he's sewing a fine garment and not a shoe. Don't forget to tell him the approximate number of stitches per inch to use, and the color of thread, and it also helps to mark the line of your stitch on the leather with the edge of masking tape. If you follow all of these preliminary steps, he'll do the job you want and you'll have eliminated the possibility of error.

The Polishing and Sanding Wheel

An interchangeable polishing and sanding wheel, either portable or stationary, is one of the most useful and productive machines that a leather craftsman can invest in. Preferably, what you need in this department is a machine with an arbor that will accommodate a polishing wheel, a sanding wheel, and a circle edge slicker. A polishing wheel is no more than several layers of soft cloth sewn together into a disc. The sanding disc is a rubber backed wheel onto which is placed various grades of ordinary sandpaper. Both the polishing and sanding discs are available in hardware stores. The circle edge slicker is illustrated in Figure 31. Portable electric drills can be fitted with a polishing and sanding device by the addition of the interchangeable wheels. The Motor Tool Jigsaw has a side mounting power take-off that holds sanding and polishing wheels. Even a small portable Motor Tool (the kind that can be held in the hand) can be equipped as a polishing and sanding machine.

Leather edges sand easily with an electric sanding wheel. The sanding wheel can even up jagged edges, can bevel edges, and round off corners. The polishing wheel can add a professional touch to edges, make them glass smooth and evenly colored. Very often with dyeing, you're apt to be plagued with dye strokes from the dauber or dye brush. The polishing wheel can help to blend these visible strokes to give the leather an even, finished texture. The polishing wheel can also be used as a dye shading device in places where you might want lighter or darker dye tones.

If you intend to make sandals, an electric polishing and sanding disc is not only a time–saver, but the sanding wheel can first be used to trim the two sole laminations evenly, and then the polishing wheel used to develop a professional edge. Leather polish purchased in stick form, or paste polish can be applied to a polishing wheel, and then buffed onto leather. Most craftsmen have several interchangeable polishing wheels, each wheel working with a different shade of polish. This is an excellent method of finishing edges on belts, straps, bracelets, watchbands, leather sculpture, and even surface polishing to blend in dye strokes.

The Jig Saw, Band Saw, and Sabre Saw

It takes a good bit of heft to hand cut 12 ounce leather and up, especially to develop accuracy in cutting smooth edges. Most craftsmen do prefer cutting by hand, but if you happen to be a bit weak in the forearm, or addicted to labor–saving devices, a jig, band, or sabre saw will cut anything in leather from about 5 ounces up to the maximum in thickness. You can cut sandal soles, hair pieces, bracelets, handbag patterns, sculpture—just about anything with these saws. The only thing to watch for if you buy a jig or band saw is to be sure you purchase a machine with the maximum throat opening (the space from behind the blade to the back of the machine that allows swing room for turning the leather). This is where the sabre saw has an advantage over the jig and band saws;

there's no throat because the blade is powered from the handle. The sabre saw also allows you to plan and develop your negative waste, whereas jig and band saws will destroy negative patterns unless you take the trouble to drill holes in the leather and thread the blade through the holes at every new cut.

There's nothing esthetically wrong with cutting leather on a saw, especially if cutting by hand is difficult for you. It's the design and the finished product that count. I doubt that there's anyone who can visually distinguish between sandal soles cut by hand and sandal soles cut on a saw, as long as both pair are well made.

Dies and the Clicker

A die is a metal punch shaped in a specific pattern—in a shoe sole pattern, or a hair piece pattern, for example. A clicker is an electric machine that has a tremendous thrust to stamp a die through fabric. Generally, these are tools used by the trade; by leather products manufacturers. They're labor–saving machines. One man operating a clicker can die punch more leather soles in an hour than most craftsmen can hand cut in a day. Dies are made up on special order and can be manufactured into almost any shape from watch straps to handbag parts, to bows, to sculptural shapes, etc. There are many leather wholesalers and small leathergoods manufacturers who will do custom job clicking for the small craftsman. In other words, if you have plans of one day going into the retail leather business, but don't want to spend all your time cutting out sandal soles, you can have dies made of the sole sizes you need. Bring the dies and the leather to a firm that offers custom clicking and have the soles cut for you in quantity ahead of time. You can do this for almost every leather design; dies can be made of almost any shape and size. I'm not suggesting that you run out and purchase an expensive clicking machine, but I am exposing you to an idea. I know small leather craftsmen who do all their own clicking, and this has enabled them to go into the mail–order business with their leathergoods. It's been one way of doing something positive about the seasonal nature of leather retailing. If the day comes when you want to try something like this, you can try hiring custom clicking first, and build up to your own machine later. I also know small leather craftsmen who have cooperated in a given geographic area and have purchased a clicking machine cooperatively; each owning an interest in the machine, and each having his day of the week to use it. When you can cut as many sandal soles in an hour by clicker as you can in a day by hand, this is something to think about.

CHAPTER THIRTEEN

Basic odds and ends

There are a number of tools and supplies that are common to all leather projects; these are basic studio supplies. They're grouped here under the heading of odds and ends because, frankly, I haven't come up with a better title. These odds and ends are primarily used in the planning and preparation stages of leather design and include shears, the steel square, dividers, masking tape and pattern paper.

Leather Shears

Quality counts first when buying a pair of leather shears. It's possible to cut leather up to 5 to 6 ounces thick with an ordinary pair of household shears, but I don't recommend it. The leather trade produces a pair of shears especially designed for use on leather (see Figure 59). After you once compare the cutting ease and accuracy of a pair of household shears and a pair of leather shears, you'll never pick up the household shears again.

Leather shears will easily cut leather up to 8 ounces thick. This is an indispensable tool to the leather craftsman. Household shears will slip, twist, and often even spread its blades on leather. In contrast, leather shears will flow through leather with only a minimum of effort. A pair of leather shears has a ribbed cutting edge on one of the blades that firmly holds the leather. Leather shears are used for cutting patterns on leather projects up to about 8 ounces thick; above that you'll need a leather knife.

Steel Square and Straight–edge

A steel rule, or better yet, a steel square, is another indispensable tool for leatherwork. Not only does this provide an accurate measuring device, and a rigid, straight edge, but it also provides a permanent edge against which to run a knife blade when cutting straight lines on thick leather. For example, if you have to cut a straight edge on leather, you can place the leather, grain side up, on a flat wooden work surface, line up the rule edge, and then cut the line with a leather knife by holding the ruler firmly, and running the knife blade along the rule edge. The knife blade might accidentally cut into the edge on a wooden rule; it can't cut into the edge of a steel rule.

An added feature of the steel square on the rule is that it will give you perfect 90 degree corners. A flat steel square is easier to handle on leather than a carpenter's square with an adjustable, sliding side arm. A flat rule can always be held in place whereas an adjustable carpenter's square is wobbly, since only part of it rests flat.

Dividers

An inexpensive pair of adjustable wing dividers, as illustrated in Figure 60, is another helpful leather tool. Wing dividers can be used to create perfect circles of varying diameter, to plot curves, and to duplicate measured distances. I use mine to measure lacing hole distances, to duplicate button hole slits, draw button circles, plot cardboard pattern curves and even develop concentric circles like those of the mobile illustrated on page 136.

If you use the wing dividers directly on leather, remember that both ends are sharp. Unless you develop a very light touch, or place a buffer between divider tip and leather, the divider will leave a small prick mark on the leather surface.

Masking Tape

An ever–present roll of 1″ 3M Masking Tape has many uses for the leather craftsman. I use masking tape as a guideline when machine sewing seams. A strip of tape on leather will provide you with a straight line along which to sew; the straight edge of the tape acts as a sewing guideline. I use this when machine sewing shoulder and side seams on a vest, and on handbag seams, skirt seams, and even as a straight–edge guideline for hand punching when hand sewing and lacing. For example, if you're punching lacing holes on a billfold you can lay a strip of masking tape on the leather as a guideline for a straight line of punch holes.

Very often, when tracing a pattern on dark leather, it's difficult to see the tracing lines, especially on black. Here again I use masking tape along the straight edges of the pattern as my visual guideline in cutting. Masking tape is also excellent for temporarily holding down turned edge seams if you want to visually check evenness ahead of cementing and sewing.

Masking tape is also an excellent straight edge for dyeing. If, for example, you wanted a striped effect on leather with alternate tones of dye, you can use strips of masking tape to produce the hard edge of the stripes. If you want to use leather as an artist's canvas for dyes, you can create interesting optical patterns with the aid of masking tape as a straight–edge. These are but a few uses of masking tape on leather. I'm sure you'll find others. Keep a roll handy.

Tagboard and Paper Pattern Material

Each time you tackle a new leather project, whether you're jumping from one item to another or merely redesigning and updating an old standby, you'll need paper or tagboard on which to make your pattern. My own procedure is to keep a roll of 36″ wide brown wrapping paper on hand for working up patterns. The paper is thin enough so that it can be cut and trimmed easily to alter the design as it's being worked on. Once I'm satisfied with the design and am sure that it works, I transfer the pattern onto tagboard. Tagboard is an inexpensive, stiff paper product available through art supply stores. Once the pattern is transferred on to tagboard it's more or less permanent, and on this heavier material is not as apt to develop frayed edges from tracing.

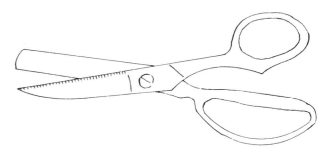

Figure 59. *A pair of heavy-duty leather shears with serrated blade edge for gripping leather.*

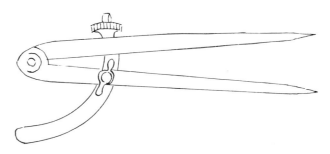

Figure 60. *A pair of wing dividers, for plotting curves.*

CHAPTER FOURTEEN

Dyeing, finishing, care, and cleaning of leather

To dye leather is to permanently change its color by means of a liquid colorant; the porous leather core fibers absorb and permanently hold the dye solution. Leather can either be dyed as a whole skin before it's cut into specific projects, or it can be dyed after it has been crafted into specific projects. In other words, if you were going to use a given undyed hide for handbags, you could either dye the whole hide before you made the handbags, or you could dye each handbag separately after it was cut from the hide.

There are advantages and disadvantages to both procedures. The procedure you select is a matter of experiment and personal preference. If a whole hide is dyed before it's cut up into specific projects, there's a much greater chance of controlling the evenness of dye penetration throughout the whole hide. On the other hand, the disadvantages are that you might find that dyeing a whole hide is too large an undertaking for your work space, that it involves buying quantities of dye larger than you can afford, or that you prefer varying the colors of the projects made from that one given hide.

Many craftsmen prefer to combine both procedures; they dye a whole hide first, and then later redye the specific projects in order to introduce shading and tones within the piece. I suggest you conduct your own experiments with procedures, but perhaps it's wisest to begin by dyeing one individual project first, and advance to the more difficult whole hide dyeing after you've had some experience.

Dye can be applied to natural undyed leather, or it can be applied over tannery–dyed leathers to strengthen or darken existing colors. Evenness of color is much easier to control on previously undyed leathers. Cowhide is the most commonly used undyed leather. Undyed cowhide has a light buff color, and will accept and hold just about every color in the dye color spectrum.

Characteristics and Properties of Leather Dyes

Undyed leather fibers are porous and will absorb just about everything in a liquid or semi–liquid state that has some kind of color in it. I've done some offbeat experimenting with colors on leather, and have tried such things as oil paints, acrylics, watercolors, wood stains, food coloring, and even All Purpose Rit fabric dyes. I've also experimented with wax resist dyeing, and even tried knot dyeing on leather. The techniques of experimental dyeing on leather are just now beginning to be explored. All of the above experimental techniques and colorants produce unique special effects on leather, but, for the most part, the small leather craftsman depends heavily on two basic types of commercial liquid dyes developed specifically for use on leather: water soluble dyes and oil and spirit solvent dyes.

There's nothing wrong with exploring ideas in experimental dyeing on leather and, in fact, let me encourage you to do so, especially in the area of staining leather as one would stain an artist's canvas. Experimental dyeing, however, is subject to a great deal of trial and error. Water soluble, and oil and spirit solvent commercial leather dyes, on the other hand, are both consistent and reliable. For this reason, this chapter will concern itself with acquainting you with these two basic leather dyes. I'll leave the trial and error of workshop experimentation up to you to pursue on your own time.

Water soluble and oil and spirit solvent dyes can be applied successfully to all leather projects. These two dyes are especially manufactured for the leather trade, and they have been proven reliable over many years of prolonged use. Most manufacturers sell these two types of dyes in both small and large quantities; 1 to 4 ounce bottles, and quart to ½ gallon containers. Because both dye types are liquid, they not only color the exposed grain surface on leather, but penetrate deep into the core fibers to produce permanent color change as well.

At this point, let's compare some of the likenesses and differences between these two dyeing agents. As one additional guideline for selection, I've found that most small craftsmen interviewed are using oil and spirit solvent dyes, especially Omega and Fiebing's leather dyes. The comparative chart on the opposite page was compiled by the Omega Chemical Company of Fort Worth, Texas, and Los Angeles, California, and I would like to thank them for help in preparing sections of this chapter.

COMPARATIVE QUALITIES	OIL & SPIRIT SOLVENT	WATER SOLUBLE DYES
Vivid Color	Excellent	Excellent
Fast Penetrating and Permanent	Excellent	Good
Quick Drying	Excellent	Good
Safe to Use	Excellent	Excellent
Non-toxic	Excellent	Excellent
Completely Water Resistant	Excellent	Fair
Dyes Evenly and Uniformly	Excellent	Excellent
Can Be Intermixed or Thinned	Excellent (Thinned with dye reducer)	Excellent (Thinned with water)
Perfect for Inlay	Excellent	Fair
Perfect for Over-all	Excellent	Good
Perfect for Shading	Excellent	Excellent (Plus)
Contains Beneficial Ingredients for Leather	Good	Excellent
Added to Antique to Strengthen Color	Poor	Excellent
Sealer Finish Adds Water Resistance	Excellent	Excellent (Only method that will give this dye water resistance)
Dye & Finish Coat Make Special Dressing	Good	Excellent

Caution: Oil and spirit solvent dye and water soluble dye will not mix together!

Equipment and Supplies for Dyeing

Here's a list of the things you will need for both individual project and whole hide dyeing:

Oil and spirit solvent, or water soluble dye

Dye primer and leather cleaner

Wool dye daubers for project dyeing (a scrap of wool fastened to the end of a wire handle)

Large, rectangular fine grain sponge for whole hide dyeing

Sheepwool scraps for dye applicators, for developing texture, and for buffing and finishes

An assortment of square and pointed tip ordinary artist's brushes (optional)

One small container (1 pint) of mineral oil

One stiff wire brush for induced texturing (optional)

A selection of finishes, sealers, and preservatives (to be discussed)

Newspapers to cover the work surface before dyeing

Rubber gloves to prevent hands from becoming dye stained

Dye reducer for oil and spirit solvent dyes

General Information

Dye always tends to stiffen leather. If there are holes to punch in the piece you're working on, I suggest these holes be punched before it's dyed, especially on belts, straps, and on leather beads. The holes are not only easier to punch before dyeing, but the dye will color and seal the hole edges, making them uniform.

When you dye, I suggest that you do your dyeing before the findings are attached to the project, whether the findings are snaps, rivets, buckles, or whatever. In the case of leather attachments—handbag straps, for example—I suggest these attachments be dyed separately and before they're finally attached to the bag. Projects should be dyed before they're laced.

Before applying one dye, the surface of the leather should be free from all foreign matter; it must be thoroughly cleaned if you expect to gain an even dye penetration. It's especially important to remove excess glue and cement. Dye won't penetrate hardened cement or glue. Inspect the surface carefully to make certain that all foreign matter is removed. To insure a clean dye surface, you can use either a commercially prepared leather cleaner, or you can mix a mild solution of oxalic acid with water (40 parts water to 1 part oxalic acid). This formula is approximately 1 teaspoonful to 1 pint of water. A gentle cleaning of the surface before dyeing will not only remove foreign matter, but will prime the leather to accept the dye more evenly and uniformly. Oxalic acid is available at most drugstores.

Another important thing to remember before you begin dyeing is that you should cover the work surface with newspapers, cardboard, or other absorbent material. If the work surface isn't free of foreign matter, a damp piece of dyed leather will pick up dirt and dust from the table. Newspapers or cardboard will provide a clean surface and a material to absorb excess dye to keep it from staining the table or running off onto the floor. I'd also suggest that you wear a pair of rubber or plastic gloves when you do your dyeing. If you don't, the dye will stain your hands; dye isn't the easiest thing to scrub off in a hurry.

Additional Dyeing Tips

The Omega Chemical Company has compiled a list of additional dyeing tips which are very practical for a beginner, and which are passed along here. After selecting your desired color or colors of dye, the following steps should be employed:

1. Check the shade of dye on a piece of scrap leather; all leather doesn't dye the same because of the various methods of tanning.
2. Place bottle conveniently so that you may dip applicator easily, and not have to reach across the leather.
3. Always begin dyeing with the lightest shade; end with the darkest.
4. Have only one color of dye before you, as this eliminates use of the wrong color if you're using more than one dye.
5. Never have a dye applicator overloaded with dye so that it will drip onto an undesired area.
6. Before the applicator is touched to the leather, it should first be gently touched on a piece of scrap to exhaust excess dye.
7. Either keep an ample supply of applicators around, one for each color, or else be certain to clean the applicator before using it for another color.
8. When dyeing, turn leather whenever necessary.
9. Relax, don't hurry your work; be deliberate.
10. Dark colors are generally better for over-all dyeing; they tend to improve and burnish with age. Light colors tend to fade unless a good finish is applied on top of them to seal in the color.
11. If you desire deeper tones after the first application, allow the first coat to set for about ten minutes, and then apply a second coat.
12. Allow the dye to dry thoroughly before applying a finish.

Project Dyeing

Always practice dyeing first on scrap leather. It not only gets the mind working in the right direction, but is a way of testing out both the applicator and the dye. It's much less costly to make mistakes on scrap, than on the actual project.

Begin by placing your project on a clean, absorbent material, such as newspaper or cardboard. The applicator dye strokes should either be back and forth from one end of the piece to the other (left to right), or in a circular motion, overlapping previous strokes as you progress into undyed sections. Full strokes from left to right along the whole length of the project tend to build an even graining effect, and at the same time keep the undyed areas of leather continuously in view so you can always see where you're going. Circular strokes tend to create an evenness in tone, and if the strokes overlap, the overlap redistributes any excess dye.

A piece of sheep wool works best on large surfaces, a dauber works best for edge dyeing, and a brush works best to get at hard to reach fussy spots. If you use a dauber on a large surface you'll be dipping into the dye so often that you'll tend to streak the leather. Despite the fact that you'll use up more dye, if you want an evenness in tone, I suggest you use a piece of sheep wool for surfaces over about the size of an armband or pendant. And, for maximum control when using a brush, be certain to hold the handle straight up and down, so only the brush tip touches the leather, not the side.

Whole Hide Dyeing

Whole hide dyeing, especially if it's as large as a single bend, requires plenty of work surface, dye, and a large applicator. You should be able to lay the whole piece of leather on a flat surface, leaving yourself plenty of room to get at all parts of the hide. For whole hide dyeing with oil and spirit solvent dyes, I suggest you use a large, fine grain rectangular sponge soaked first in a bath of mineral oil, and then blotted to wipe off excess. You'll also need a large flat container, such as a pie tin, into which to pour the dye and receive the whole flat surface of the sponge. Be certain that you've got enough dye on hand. It's utter chaos to overlook planning ahead and find yourself running out of dye in the middle of a hide.

Begin by saturating the sponge in the dye, squeezing out the excess, and then covering the hide with either whole sweeping strokes from left to right across the hide, or with a circular motion as with project dyeing. The procedure is exactly the same as for project dyeing, but you're using a larger applicator and covering a larger surface. Again, don't soak the dye applicator in mineral oil when using water soluble dyes!

Reverse Flesh Side Dyeing

Very often, when you purchase a tannery–dyed skin, the flesh side of the skin may be undyed. This may have been deliberate, or it may be because the leather was too thick to absorb the dye all the way through. On certain projects, you may want to dye this flesh side, especially if it will show, as on handbag flaps. The procedure for dyeing the flesh side is just about the same as for dyeing the grain side. You'll first have to try and match the grain side color on scraps. Once you've matched the color, it's essential, when using oil and spirit solvent dyes, first to soak your applicator in mineral oil. What you're trying to do here is to limit penetration to only the flesh side. Remember that the grain side is already tannery dyed and you don't want your own dyeing to bleed through. By making sure, when using oil and spirit solvent dyes, that the applicator is well bathed in mineral oil, and by lightly brushing the applicator across the leather, you'll be able to avoid the dye's bleeding through to the grain side. Don't rest the applicator on the leather; gently stroke it across the fabric just enough to induce a shallow surface coloring. You're not after depth, only surface coloring.

Evenness in Dye Tone

When using oil and spirit solvent dyes, the dye applicator should first be soaked in an initial bath of mineral oil. After the applicator has been soaked in the mineral oil, the excess should then be blotted off on scrap leather. This treatment provides a great deal more control when building up evenness in dye tones. An untreated dye applicator (one without mineral oil), tends to suck up unnecessary quantities of dye. When an untreated dye applicator first comes in contact with leather, the bulk of the dye is exhausted at the point of contact; the initial point of contact will have a heavier concentration of dye than the rest of the piece. This initial mineral oil bath prevents the dry applicator from absorbing excessive quantities of dye, with the result that dyeing can be much more accurately controlled. Do not use the mineral oil dye applicator treatment on water soluble dyes; this tip is only for oil and spirit solvent dyes.

Induced Grain Dyeing

If you deliberately want to create a grained affect with dyes, just forget about saturating the oil and spirit solvent dye applicator in mineral oil. An untreated dye applicator quite naturally tends to grain leather, or streak on its own.

One can also induce added graining by using a piece of heavy sheep wool. Pour dye into a flat dish or pan, and let just the tips of the sheep wool absorb the dye. If you then gently stroke the wool fiber tips across the leather, letting only the tips touch the leather, you can induce an artificial, almost wood–like grain. Still another way to induce grain is to take a stiff wire brush and stroke it across the leather in the direction you want the graining to appear. If you press down hard enough on the brush, the wire bristles will actually groove the leather into a textured grain. I've done this very successfully on waist belts. But before either of these induced grain techniques is tried on a project, I suggest you first practice on scrap leather.

Shading with Dye

Shading on leather is the process of building up tone differences within the same general color; for example, from tan, to light brown, to brown, to dark brown.

Shading is best accomplished within the same common base of color. Lighter tones should be applied first, and then toned darker in a graduated sequence from light to dark. Shading can highlight certain areas on a given design by making these areas literally stand out from the rest of the project.

The simplest method for producing graduated tones is to select, as an example, three basic dye colors: yellow, tan, and dark brown. First reduce or thin these full strength colors into a sequence of varying intermediate colors; light yellow, yellow, light tan, tan, light brown, and dark brown. To thin or reduce oil and spirit solvent dyes, you must use a commercially prepared dye reducer, and to thin water soluble dyes, water can be used as a strength reducer. A muffin tin makes an excellent mixing apparatus for reducing dyes. Reduce the three basic colors into a series of lesser strengths and then test them for tone build up on a piece of scrap. After you've determined the correct sequence from light to dark, I suggest that you label each color with a small piece of adhesive tape on the cup. Double-check your labeling on a piece of scrap. You should now have a whole series of tones from which to proceed in shading from light yellow to dark brown.

Shading should be done as quickly as possible so as not to let the dye dry out between tone build-ups. If you wait too long, you may end up with a slight line of tone difference between shades. If, on the other hand, you work quickly and in a sequence while the leather is still wet, you can feather any edges that might appear by using your index finger. Again, a series of dye applicators (one for each tone) first soaked in mineral oil for oil and spirit solvent dyes will be an added advantage in controlling tones.

Cross Dyeing

Cross dyeing is the process of obtaining colors that are not manufactured for retail sale by combining colors that are. Al Stohlman, in his book, *How to Carve Leather*, together with the Omega Chemical Company, worked up the following cross dyeing color chart. The author would like to acknowledge their help in supplying this chart.

CROSS COLORING CHART WITH BASIC COLORS

Red	over Blue	makes Purple
Red	over Dark Blue	makes Plum
Red	over Light Blue	makes Garnet
Red	over Brown	makes Henna
Red	over Dark Brown	makes Maroon
Red	over Purple	makes Wine
Red	over Yellow	makes Scarlet
Red	over Orange	makes Tangerine
Red	over Lavender	makes Rose
Red	over Gray	makes Taupe
Brown	over Orange	makes Havana Brown
Brown	over Yellow	makes Light Brown
Brown	over Purple	makes Seal Brown

Purple	over Green	makes Medium Blue
Purple	over Bright Red	makes Wine
Purple	over Dark Green	makes Navy Blue
Green	over Violet	makes Bright Blue
Green	over Orange	makes Olive Green
Green	over Light Blue	makes Peacock Green
Yellow	over Blue	makes Green
Yellow	over Dull Blue	makes Blue Green
Yellow	over Light Blue	makes Light Green
Yellow	over Green	makes Bright Green
Yellow	over Brown	makes Golden Brown
Yellow	over Purple	makes Green Brown
Yellow	over Orange	makes Orange Yellow
Yellow	over Salmon	makes Coral
Yellow	over Pink	makes Peach
Yellow	over Red	makes Bright Red
Dark Blue	over Dark Red	makes Plum
Dark Blue	over Orange	makes Dark Brown
Light Blue	over Dark Red	makes Garnet
Light Blue	over Yellow	makes Light Green
Pink	over Light Blue	makes Lavender
Pink	over Orange	makes Deep Orange

Laminated Dyeing

On projects such as necklace pendants, leather wall reliefs, and sculptured forms, where several layers of leather are laminated together and allowed to overlap, it's possible to create interesting dimensional effects by dyeing the separate layers different colors, or tones of the same color. In this case, dyeing should be done before the layers are laminated.

Lace Dyeing

Most lacing is already commercially dyed, but light colors can be dyed darker by hand. Obviously, lacing should be dyed before it's laced onto the project. The procedure for dyeing lace is very simple; two detailed procedures follow:

1. First cut the required length of lace from the spool. Next, place it, rounded side up, flat against a piece of cardboard or newspaper. Dip a dye dauber into the dye solution and hold it against the lacing. Now pull the lacing along under the dauber, from one end of the cut piece to the other.

2. Another method is to take the required length of lace and place it into a small jar partly filled with dye. Now replace the jar cover, tighten it securely, tip the jar on its side, and shake the dye solution around in the jar until it completely covers all the lacing.

Dye does stiffen leather, including lace. When you get around to actually tying the laces they'll have to be flexible. If the dyed lace should get stiff after it's dry, simply rub it down with either saddle soap, or Vaseline Petroleum Jelly, being sure to remove all excess soap or Jelly before beginning to lace.

Caring for Brushes, Daubers, and Other Dye Applicators

Dye applicators can be reused dozens of times if you take the trouble to clean them off between dyeing projects. Dye applicators used in water soluble dye can be rinsed clean in warm water. Dye applicators used for oil and spirit solvent dyes can be rinsed clean in a mild alcohol solvent. After the applicators have been rinsed clean, they should be washed in soap and warm water, and then blotted dry.

Bleaching

Bleaching is the process of removing color in leather by means of special bleaching agents mixed with water. The Tandy Leather Company stocks a bleach made especially for leather, and the supply list at the back of the book lists other bleach producers.

Bleach is tough on any fabric, including leather. It's especially hard on fabric if the fabric is not thoroughly rinsed after the process of bleaching is finished. Bleach can be used to remove color from a skin in order to begin the whole dyeing process over again. It can be used in small quantities for reverse tone effect in shading, and it can be used to capture surrealistic effects when using leather as a skin covering around sculptural form. Bleaching is mentioned here only as a possibility for further exploration in special tone effects.

Finishes

The finish is the final protective film applied to leather; a coating of one of many commercially prepared finish products. Most craftsmen use some type of finish coat on all projects, excluding leather where there's a nap, such as suedes and splits. As long as there's a hard surface to the leather, the fabric will accept a finish coat. A finish coat not only lubricates the leather core fibers to give them longer service, but also reduces the chances of color fade, and the possibility of discoloration caused by stains. A finish coat is therefore beneficial not only to the leather, but to the final visual product as well.

A finish can be applied over undyed leather, hand-dyed leather, or over tannery-dyed leather (for example when you want to restore color fade). There are dozens of commercial leather finishes and many of them overlap in function. Generally, finishes can be grouped into the following categories: *Conditioners, Soaps and Cleaners, Waterproofing Agents, and Polishes.* Many of the products available in each category come as either a liquid, or a semi-liquid, paste-like compound. The following section will discuss finishes by category, and a number of specific brand names will be mentioned within each category. No one brand name is necessarily any better than another. Many craftsmen have developed a personal preference, but even this is not consistent between craftsmen. The finishes discussed can be purchased from a variety of sources including wholesalers, luggage stores, shoe repair shops, saddle and harness suppliers, and from retail outlets such as the Tandy Leather stores. I suggest you consult the suppliers list at the back of the book for more information on names and addresses.

Leather Conditioners

Generally, a leather conditioner softens and nourishes leather. It provides a protective coating over leather which helps it to resist scuffing and color fade. A leather conditioner will also produce some degree of surface luster when polished, and many conditioners temporarily tend to darken leather, at least until the conditioner has thoroughly soaked into the fibers. A good conditioner is one which leaves no residue. The following conditioners meet this requirement:

Goddard's Saddler's Wax is a conditioner, made in England, which nourishes, cleans, and polishes leather. It's used mostly on saddles, boots, shoes, handbags, and leather of similar quality. It can be applied with the fingers, a cloth, a brush, or a damp sponge.

Melo-Wax is a conditioner in a liquid form that's neutral in color. It's used for cleaning, polishing, and softening smooth grained leather. It can be applied with a cloth or the fingers, allowed to dry, and then polished with a soft cloth.

Kiwi Leather Conditioner is a liquid conditioner that cleans, mellows, softens, and preserves smooth grained leather. It can be applied with a cloth or the fingers and then polished gently after it has been allowed to dry.

Meltonian Shoe Cream is an English product that's used widely in this country by leather craftsmen. It nourishes, cleans, and softens leather, and is used on belts, handbags, billfolds, watchbands, bracelets, hair ornaments, and other small leather items. It's applied in the same manner as Goddard's Saddler's Wax.

Lexol is a liquid conditioner which penetrates deep into the core fibers making them supple while at the same time providing a preservative finish. On new leather Lexol develops a deeper, more mellow color. Several light applications of Lexol are better than one heavy coat. Lexol can be used on all smooth grain leather projects. It's applied in a thin coat with a sponge, a cloth, or the fingers, and then allowed to soak in for about ten minutes before being polished with a soft cloth.

Adams Tax Wax is an English leather dressing and conditioner similar to Goddard's Saddler's Wax. It's normally used on heavier leathers with a smooth grain surface. Adams Tax Wax is applied with a cloth, the fingers, or a brush, and then allowed to dry, and finally polished lightly with a soft cloth.

Omega Finish Coat is a wax base dressing with the consistency of a creamy liquid. It can be applied with a cloth, a scrap of sheep wool, or with the fingers. This finish polishes to a gloss, and provides a protective coat over the leather grain surface while at the same time acting as a preservative. It can be applied

as often as necessary, and can be mixed with water soluble dyes for deeper, more vivid colors. It can be used on all leather projects with a smooth grain, and is especially good over lacing.

Omega Carnauba Cream cleans, preserves, and restores leather. It's applied in the same manner as Omega Finish Coat. It has a neutral color, and is especially good on heavier leathers.

Fiebing's Tan Kote gives leather a clear, moisture–resistant finish that won't crack. It's applied with a dauber or brush. Its properties are very similar to Omega Finish Coat, and it can be used on all smooth grained leathers.

Vaseline Petroleum Jelly is used as a conditioner by many craftsmen to soften leather, bring back color, and provide a protective coating to resist scuffing. It's a bit messy to work with, but is well worth the effort. It can be used on all smooth grained leather. It's applied with the fingers and rubbed onto the leather. It should be allowed to stand for 15 to 20 minutes and then wiped off with a soft cloth. It's commonly used on belts and handbags. If you try it, I suggest you invest in an economy size jar.

The above conditioners represent only a few of the brand names available on the market. There are many other conditioners that work equally well. Just remember to stay clear of any conditioner which tends to leave a residue.

Saddle Soaps and Cleaners

Saddle soap is used as a cleaner on smooth grained leather surfaces. It also conditions leather as it cleans. In general, a saddle soap shouldn't be allowed to settle into cuts or impressions on leather because it has a tendency to leave a white residue. This residue can be avoided by carefully wiping away excess after the leather has been cleaned. Saddle soaps are applied with a wet sponge or brush, worked into a thick lather, wiped off with a dry cloth, and then polished to a soft luster. Most saddle soaps have some type of tallow base and they do actually clean leather. There are many brand names available on the market. A few of them are listed here, but again, the list doesn't include every brand name. The brands identified by name are the most commonly found in retail outlets.

Kiwi Saddle Soap
Belvoir Glycerine Saddle Soap
Belmont Saddle Soap
Propert's Saddle Soap
Castile Soap
Blue Ribbon Saddle Soap

Waterproofing Agents

Waterproofing agents are available in both a liquid and a paste–like form. They're used primarily to produce a water repellency on smooth grain leather surfaces, especially on boots and shoes. Most of these products also tend to ˙soften leather, and many of them will produce a light luster when polished. These agents are applied either with a cloth, a brush, the fingers, or a scrap of sheep wool. Again, many firms manufacture waterproofing agents. A few of the more common brand names are listed below:

Fiebing's Neatsfoot Oil
Propert's "Dubbin"
Lecton Leather Care
Blue Ribbon Neatsfoot Oil

Polishes

Leather polishes are available in an almost endless number of brand names. They are used on smooth grained surfaces to produce a luster. Many of them are completely unsuited for use on anything but shoes. The reason for this is because they tend to leave a white residue within any surface cracks or impressions. And then too, most of them, like the self–polishing liquid varieties, tend to produce such a high gloss that the leather looks almost too plastic. I suggest you keep away from the self–polishing variety that's sold with the applicator dauber attached to the top of the bottle. There are, however, several brands which do produce a mellow luster, and if the excess is carefully wiped out of impressions there'll be no residue. Propert's make an excellent polish sold as a boot cream, and the Kiwi Company also makes a fine neutral polish. Before trying other brands on a project, I suggest you try them first on scrap.

Antique Finishes

Several firms manufacture a finish coat called an "antique" finish. This type of finish is advertised as a product that produces an "early American" look on leather. What I think this means is that the finish tends to mellow the color of leather, to give it a sort of nutmeg look which amplifies all the natural markings on the grain pattern; something similar to that produced by the stains used on early American furniture. Antique finishes produce a satin luster rather than a high gloss. This type of finish is sold in colors; all of them producing a rich wood–like appearance. The finish is applied with any type of applicator; it doesn't streak or cake, and the longer it's left on the surface without wiping, the deeper the color becomes. It can be used on all smooth grain leathers. The Fiebing Chemical Company manufactures one excellent type of antique finish which is readily available through most retail outlets.

The Care and Cleaning of Leather

Most of the articles and pamphlets that have been published on the subject of the care and cleaning of leather sound as if leather were the eggshell of the fabric industry. These articles go into all sorts of tiptoe procedures that generate the impression that leather is fragile, that it must be handled with extreme care. This approach, in retrospect, tends to frighten off the consumer, especially in the case of garments. One ends up feeling that leather would be a lovely fabric to have for a garment, but hardly worth the effort in upkeep.

As the author of this book I'm going to emphatically take exactly the opposite stand, stick my leather neck out, and tell you that there's absolutely no truth in the impression that leather, in garments, or in any other project, is a fragile substance. We've spent part of a whole chapter discussing its strength and durability; we've comparatively proved its core structure as a fabric leader. So don't worry about leather. It's not fussy. It's not difficult to care for, and it's the strongest garment fabric in the industry.

You can walk on it, throw it in the bathtub, bang it around, and even slosh it in a mud puddle, without really damaging the fabric (although, of course, I don't recommend this kind of treatment). Step–by–step you've seen how it goes through the tanning process, how it's tumbled in drums, soaked in chemicals, stretched, dried, and then resoaked. Leather is a powerful fabric, so don't worry about a little dirt. If you make a leather garment, then relax; you're wearing the next best thing to an iron shield.

How to Clean Deerhide, Buckskin, and Elk

One of the easiest ways to clean a garment made out of deerhide, buckskin, or elk is to chuck it in the automatic washer, dump in some mild soapsuds, and turn on the button. But turn the washer off before it gets to the spin cycle. Spinning a buckskin garment doesn't hurt it, but it does crease it with all sorts of wrinkles. Take the garment out before the spin cycle, hang it on a wooden coat hanger, and let it drip dry to avoid wrinkles. Deerhide, buckskin and elk can be washed in mild soap and water. The only precaution is not to squeeze or wring it dry. Squeezing and wringing presses in wrinkles. Avoiding wrinkles is for the benefit of the consumer, not because the fabric can't stand the abuse. On the contrary, wringing doesn't hurt leather at all, but it does affront the esthetic sense of the consumer. Smaller buckskin articles can be hand washed in a solution of mild soap and water.

How to Clean Suede

A stiff bristle brush (non-wire), or fine sandpaper can be used to clean away dirt, and most spotting on suedes and splits. Simply brush the fabric vigorously until the dirt disappears and then gently wipe it with a damp sponge. An artgum eraser can also be used on suede for removing dirt. If you want the nap to look more uniform on suede, you can brush it all in one direction. There are also a number of commercial suede cleaners available, and many commercial dry-cleaning establishments that specialize in the cleaning of suede.

How to Clean Smooth Surface Leather

Any number of commercial leather cleaners can be used to clean leather with a smooth surface, including saddle soap, Omega Carnauba Cream, and leather conditioner. The procedure for using these cleaners has already been discussed under the section on finishes.

You can also send a smooth-surfaced leather garment to one of the dry-cleaning establishments that specialize in this type of service. A little dirt on leather doesn't hurt it a bit, in fact most people who are really close to leather as a garment fabric find a bit of dirt a mellowing, or ageing influence.

Touching up Spots and Stains

I think we've established just how tough a fabric leather is. But what do you do if you should spill grease or paint on a leather garment? The answer is that you do just about the same as you'd do with any fabric. You'll just have to risk a commercial spot remover on the fabric and hope it doesn't remove too much of the dye. Once the spot is out, you can then re-dye the spot with either of the two dyes discussed in this chapter, and try your best to match the color, working up in tone from light to dark. If you work at it carefully, you should be able to match the color with a minimum in tone difference. The only danger in using commercial spot removers is that you might remove the dye color or create a ringed effect. If this happens, you'll just have to carefully build the color back over the spot. If the final result still shows a color variance, you can't criticize the fabric any more than you could criticize cotton or wool.

In preparing this text, I've done some experimenting with unconventional cleaning and dyeing procedures. I just wanted to test for myself whether the so-called "fragile" nature of leather was a fact or a myth. I've dyed cowhide leather jackets in a bathtub filled with liquid All Purpose Rit, and I've scrubbed sueded garments in a laundry tub with mild soapsuds. I've tried all the things one is *not* supposed to do. And what happened? Almost nothing. The garments did not shrink. I was able to avoid wrinkles by letting them drip dry. The nap on suede and split garments did get a bit stiff from washing, but after brushing them down, and wearing them for awhile, I couldn't tell that anything had happened. My point here is that most of the so-called "fragile" talk about the care and handling of leather garments is a myth. No garment looks new forever, whether it's made out of wool, cotton, or leather. Nobody is critical of a wool garment when it begins to show its age, so why all the concern over the mellowing of leather? If you demand that a leather garment always look new, you're demanding a miracle. As long as you keep leather from drying out, from cracking, and from extremes of temperature and moisture, you've got a fabric that you'll get bored with long before you'll wear it out.

Removing Wrinkles

Leather can be ironed if a pressing cloth or a piece of heavy brown paper is used between the iron and the leather. You shouldn't use steam on leather. Simply set the iron at its lowest temperature, and then keep it moving across the fabric to avoid overheating.

Additional Tips

Don't store leather garments in tightly sealed plastic bags. Leather garments should be stored in an area where there's both ample space and circulation. Plastic bags tend either to stick to leather or to discolor it. Finally, don't use commercial moth-repellent sprays on leather; many of these commercial sprays contain chemicals which may discolor it.

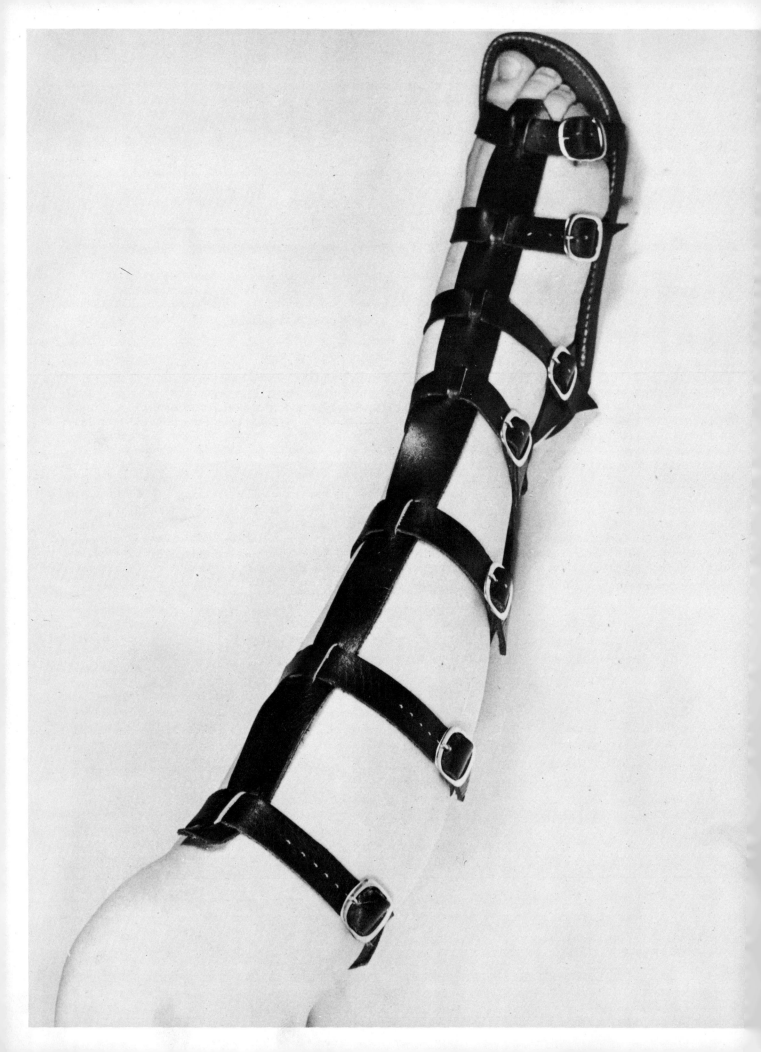

CHAPTER FIFTEEN

Sandals

Sandals are unquestionably the bread and butter item of the small leather craftsman. In most instances, the demand for handmade sandals far exceeds the supply. Therefore, the man who takes the time to develop his skill as a competent sandalmaker, is the man who protects himself against risks in the leather business. The craftsman's skill as a sandalmaker provides him with a built–in insurance policy against consumer style and taste changes; sandals seem to be a steady sales item, no matter what else happens in the leather business. Even if you don't plan to go into the leather business, the ability to make a few pairs of sandals for friends each season will quickly return more than was expended in your investment in tools, supplies, and leather.

This chapter, then, will discuss many of the techniques used in making sandals. Sandals come in an enormous variety of styles and designs. In a text of this size, it's virtually impossible to provide an illustrated step–by–step demonstration of how to make sandals. If I did this, I would be providing a step–by-step procedure for only one style or design, and the strap arrangement on that particular sandal may have nothing at all in common with the next sandal. However, the text does provide you with many close–up photographs of sandals; the styles vary greatly, but the techniques used in making them are common to all sandals. This chapter will therefore concentrate on techniques. Along the way, if you have any questions, I suggest that you examine a pair of your own sandals as you read. Or, better yet, if you have an old, worn pair of sandals around the house, take them completely apart, examine the technique used in making them, and then compare your discoveries with this text for further assistance.

Before we begin to examine how to make sandals, I should tell you that among leather craftsmen there's a running controversy over which is the best way. The controversy centers around the methods used in securing the two laminations of sole leather, and around the use of the arch. There are those who insist that the only way to make quality sandals is to wet the soles, and then bend in an arch by hand. Then, there are those who insist that cork, rubber, or composition material arch cushions should be used as sandal arches. These people argue that hand–built arches flatten out with wear. On the question of laminating soles together, there's one persuasion that insists that the best sandals are sandals in which the sole laminations are cobbled together with cobbling nails. The opposing view insists that sole laminations should be machine stitched. This then, completes the entire range of different opinions.

As your author, I've done my best to examine all types of sandals, both for quality in craftsmanship and for style design. I feel that I can now take sides in the matter and pass along my own observations for your consideration. It's my opinion that the best sandal technique thus far developed is the technique in which the sandal is made with a hand–built wet and bent arch, and a sandal in which the soles are permanently laminated with cobbling nails as opposed to being machine sewn. There's no question in my mind, that as far as design is concerned, the cobbled sandal with a hand–built arch is far superior to the sandal displaying a border of white thread all around the circumference of the sole and having an arch cushion that interrupts the flow of the design lines. And then, too, I believe that a sewn sandal sole will break down and pull apart much more quickly than a cobbled sandal will. It's not unusual, especially with cork arch cushions, to discover that the cushion breaks down organically after prolonged wear, or, in the case of rubber and composition material cushions, that they'll slip out from between the laminations if the machine thread ever gets loose or begins to rot from contact with moisture. (The technique of cobbling is described in detail in the section on cobbling in this chapter.)

Because this controversy is so strong among sandalmakers, and even though I've asserted my own preference, I'll cover these other sandal making techniques in order to provide the reader with a choice. Hopefully, in this way, the reader can discover for himself which technique he finds the most attractive, both in design and in quality.

Roman-style ladies' sandal. There are many variations of this Roman-style sandal. The leg straps give limited support and are primarily for design purposes. The two laminations of sole leather were first cemented together, and then stitched on a machine. Made by Justis Taylor, Bennington, Vt. Photo, Larry Hyman.

Wedged heel ladies' sandal. The heel was made by laminating layers of leather together in the form of a heel, then attaching it to the sandal with long cobbling nails driven up from the bottom. Notice how well dressed the edges of this sandal are; the entire sandal, including the heel, was edge-dressed on a sanding and buffing wheel. Made by Tom Tisdell, Cambridge, Mass. Strap arrangement designed by Roger Rello. Photo, Dave Congalton.

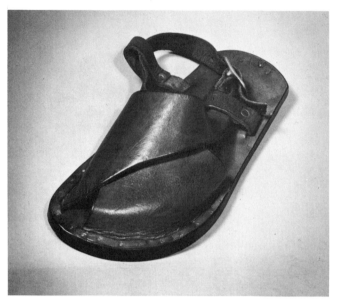

Men's sandal. On this sandal, the top sole lamination was made from 7 to 8 ounce cowhide, and the bottom sole lamination from 12 ounce cowhide. This sandal was nailed from the top because of the particular design; the edges were dressed on a machine. Made by Tom Tisdell, Cambridge, Mass. Photo, Dave Congalton.

Wet and bent arch sandal. Notice that the sole is bent up slightly at the toe and the heel to insure that the foot stays in place. The edges here were edge-dressed on a sanding and buffing machine. Made by Tom Tisdell, Cambridge, Mass. Photo, Dave Congalton.

Toe strap sandal. With a close look, you can see that the toe strap runs between the laminations all the way to the front edge of the sandal. Made by Tom Tisdell, Cambridge, Mass. Photo, Dave Congalton.

Design

Most sandals are basically the same, but one structural makeup of their design differs greatly. Sandals consist of two layers of laminated sole leather, plus some type of strap arrangement at both the toe and the heel. The ankle strap which holds the sandal to the heel is common to almost all sandals, but there are several methods used to hold the front of the foot to the sole. Basically there are three types of front strap arrangements: the toe loop, the toe strap, and the arch strap. And there are still other combinations and variations within these three front strap styles.

Figure 61 illustrates these three basic front strap styles in addition to one illustration showing a combination style using both toe loop and toe strap. The toe loop is nothing more than a thin strap of leather, about ½″ wide, which loops over the large toe on each foot in order to hold the front of the foot down on the sandal. The toe strap is a thin, but strong, piece of leather that extends from the sole to the ankle strap, and runs between the first and second toes on each foot. And the arch strap is very similar to a leather pocket which loops over the top of the foot so that the whole foot slides in under it. The combination toe loop and toe strap sandal illustrated in Figure 61 indicates one of several ways in which strap styles can be combined for an even more secure grip on the foot. All of the straps on sandals begin and end between the layers of sole lamination, and are first cemented, and then either cobbled or sewn in place. Throughout this chapter you'll find a number of sandal styles illustrated. I believe all of these illustrations show enough close–up detail for you to quickly follow the techniques used in their design.

Tools

To cut sole leather from a hide by hand, you'll need either a square point leather knife or a round knife. If you haven't the necessary strength to pull one of these knives through the leather, then you can use a band, sabre, or jig saw. And if you're dealing with sandals at a production level, you can have metal cutting dies made of the various sole sizes, and use these dies with a leather clicking machine to cut soles. It's also possible to buy ready–made soles, or even to have them custom cut for you. The most common method of cutting soles is to use either the square point knife, or the round leather knife. This is the procedure followed by most small craftsmen.

To cut sandal straps, you'll need either a draw gauge or a plough gauge, mentioned in the chapter, *Knives and Gouges*. While on the subject of straps, you'll also need a selection of buckles or, if you prefer, you can use loops, rings, or dees in place of buckles. Remember that it takes two loops, rings, or dees used together to take the place of one buckle. The most common material currently being used on sandal straps is brass. The most common size for buckles, loops, rings, and dees used on sandal straps is ½″ to ¾″ in diameter. Because sandal straps withstand a great deal of stress, strap buckles are normally secured with rivets. If you use brass buckling

Figure 61. *A selection of basic sandal strap styles: toe loop, toe strap, combined toe loop and toe strap, and arch strap.*

81

devices on these straps, then I'd suggest you also use brass rivets. When setting strap rivets, I'd suggest the use of a rivet setter in order to prevent denting the exposed rivet caps. You'll also need a revolving punch to punch buckle tongue holes in the straps.

The neatest way to cut strap holes in the top sandal sole is to use the oblong, or bag, punch. The punch method is much simpler and more exact than trying to whittle, drill, or cut the holes. You'll also need a supply of leather contact cement to initially bond the sole laminations, plus heavy paper for making patterns and a ballpoint pen or scratch awl for tracing patterns.

As mentioned earlier, the top and bottom soles can be either cobbled or sewn together on a heavy-duty sewing machine. If you prefer cobbling, then you'll need a supply of cobbling nails, preferably flat-headed brass nails, a tack or heel hammer to drive the nails with, a piece of solid iron to pound the nails against in order to bend them over, and a mallet to tap the sole laminations together with once they've been cemented. If you prefer using a machine to secure the two soles, you'll need the heavy-duty machine plus a supply of beeswax, and at least a 5-cord polyester dacron thread.

If you wet and bend in the arch by hand, you'll also need a source of water and a bucket large enough to soak the soles in. For trimming, sanding, and polishing the sole edges, you'll need an electric sanding wheel, preferably equipped to accept an interchangeable polishing disc. And then too, you'll need the usual supply of dyes and finishes once the sandals are made.

Leather

Much of the skill in sandalmaking is in the proper selection of leather. The Berman Leather Company of Boston, which supplies many small New England craftsmen, has kept an accurate account of the most common leather thickness purchases for sandals. For bottom soles on women's sandals, Berman recommends 9 to 10 iron (or about 12 ounce) leather, and for bottom soles on men's sandals, he recommends the use of 10 to 11 iron (or about 14 ounce) leather. For top soles on both men's and women's sandals, Berman recommends the use of 6 iron (or about 8 ounce) leather. Many craftsmen prefer using sole leather with a cod oil tannage, and others prefer using a leather that combines a vegetable and chrome tanning. Vegetable tanning tends to soften leather, and chrome tanning tends to make leather strong.

What's needed, especially for top soles, is a soft, yet durable leather. The sole weights above are fairly thick, and will provide a lasting and durable sandal; this is why it's especially important that the sole leather be soft in order to eventually conform to the shape of the foot. For further recommendations, I suggest you consult your local source of leather supply.

There well may be readers who don't want sandal soles quite as thick as the above recommended weights. In fact, many sandalmakers prefer using a lighter weight leather. If this is your own preference because of a desire to limit the weight on the foot, then at least stick with the tannages recommended

above. In support of thicker soles, I believe that most craftsmen using them will vouch for the fact that their sandal soles, especially at the heel, will far outlast the sandal made with thinner soles. A thicker sole does present more of a break-in problem to the wearer, but I feel the effort is well worth it. If the customer is required to pay a good price for a handmade pair of sandals, he certainly ought to have the security of knowing that his investment will last more than one summer.

Industrial belting makes the best possible sandal strap leather. Many novice sandalmakers, who really don't know any better, are using a latigo tannage on straps. Latigo stretches and will not keep its shape. An industrial belting leather of about 6 ounce weight, on the other hand, is curried especially to minimize stretch. When selecting strap leather for sandals, I recommend that you insist upon industrial belting. Often this comes already cut to strap size, and is available wrapped around a spool. Whatever you do when buying sandal leather—insist upon only the best.

Selecting a Style

Before you even begin to make a pattern for your sandals, you'll first have to decide upon a style. Style is not only a matter of design, but of foot comfort as well. For example, many people can't stand the feeling of a toe loop around their large toe or, for that matter, the feeling of a strap between their first and second toes. These people would therefore prefer selecting a sandal style with an arch strap. Still another individual might have some type of foot deformity that will necessitate the selection of one style over another. As the reader can clearly see from the several photographs in this chapter, sandal straps can be designed in any one of dozens of styles.

One of the advantages to wearing sandals is that the strap can not only be designed to conform to the esthetic taste of the buyer, but can be designed to accommodate peculiarities in size, or even deformity in foot shape. For example, an individual with severe bunions can select a sandal design with an arch strap, and therefore eliminate the possibility of the leather rubbing against the tender spot. As a matter of fact, arch style sandals are often said to be a form of corrective device for people suffering from bunions. Whereas a shoe will often squeeze the width of the foot and irritate the bunion, an arch strap sandal will produce no pressure at all, and allow the foot to regain its normal health. Therefore, wearing a sandal should be the next best thing to walking barefoot.

Notice the illustration of the Roman-style sandal where the strap continues on up the leg. In this chapter, there are also illustrations of a ladies' sandal with a wedged heel, and men's and women's sandal styles using a single lamination of leather as a heel to take the place of an arch. There are many variations in all of the above styles, including several variations of the Roman style. There's even a new style that has no sole at all. This sandal consists of only toe and heel straps, and was designed for women who prefer walking barefoot, but can't get into certain suburban shopping centers without something on their feet.

If you're in doubt as to which sandal style to select, I suggest you take a sample strap, tie it around your foot in several of the ways suggested by the photographs, and then select the style that provides maximum comfort. Again, the important point is to know exactly what you want before you even begin to make a pattern. You'll have to decide upon style, arch, heel, and strap arrangement.

How to Make a Sole Pattern

In order to make a sole pattern, simply take off your shoes and stockings and stand barefoot on a piece of heavy pattern paper, and then trace around both feet with a ballpoint pen. As you trace, keep the pen tight up against your foot, and when you reach the area of your arch, tip the point in toward the center of your foot, and trace just the part of your foot that's touching the paper. If you curve the pattern slightly in toward the center of your foot as you pass the arch, you'll eliminate excess sole leather from the pattern. There's no advantage in wearing sandals with huge soles much bigger than your feet; you'll just have to carry all of this leather around on your foot if you do. And as you trace, be certain to put all your weight on your feet, and keep your feet perfectly flat.

After you've traced both feet, you can then even up the toe lines on the tracing in order to add a uniform shape to the sole. As you trace, the pen will sort of bounce down your toes like a ball bouncing down stairs. This line will be irregular, and that's the line to repair by making it a uniform curve. The next step is to add about ¼″ to ⅜″ to the circumference of the tracing in order to allow for a sole that is a bit larger than the foot.

Many people prefer making soles so small that none of the sole shows from above. Others prefer to allow between ¼″ to ⅜″ all the way around the tracing circumference to provide room for straps and to give the craftsman just a bit of elbow room to work with. If the sole is too small, you can never enlarge it, and you may end up partly walking on the straps as they come up from between the laminations. If it's too large you can always trim it down. I think you'll find the ¼″ to ⅜″ addition to the circumference to be satisfactory in most instances.

Next, cut out the two sole patterns with a pair of scissors, and then stand on them again to double-check a perfect fit. If the pattern size is accurate, you can then mark the location of your straps directly on the pattern. The straps should come up through the top sole lamination between ¼″ and ⅜″ in from the outside edge of the pattern. Once you've marked the location of all the strap holes on the sole pattern, including toe strap holes, you can then punch these holes right out of the pattern in exactly the same way that you'll eventually punch them into the top sole. This is the place where it's best to use the oblong, or bag, punch mentioned in the section on tools. If you've accurately measured the location of these holes on the pattern, and if you've punched them accurately, then you can take a piece of extra strap leather and try out your strap arrangement on the paper pattern

Archless sandal without a toe strap. Mr. Carleton doesn't wet and bend his arches, and uses a single lamination of 12 ounce leather for the heel. The strap leather is made from 6 to 7 ounce curried and pre-stretched industrial belting. The sole leather has a cod-oil tannage. Made by Bort Carleton, Boston, Mass. Photo, Dave Congalton.

before you cut out the actual sole. If your checking has been accurate, you're now ready to cut the soles.

When making a pattern, you may discover that your feet are not exactly the same size. Don't be alarmed; this doesn't mean that you're eligible for a circus sideshow. Many people have feet of slightly different sizes. Unless the size difference is enormous (which is highly unlikely), I'd suggest retaining that size difference right on the pattern, rather than trying to make both feet the same by reversing the pattern of one foot and trying to use it on the other foot. Unlike factory-made shoes, sandals should be designed to fit your feet, not some mythical average American foot size which certainly doesn't exist anyway, except in the charts on manufacturer's walls.

If you ever plan to sell sandals, it's a good idea to record the name of your customer on the pattern in the event that the customer ever wants another pair made, or wants to refer to that pattern at some other time. You can then file the pattern away alphabetically, knowing that you can quickly refer to it if the need ever arises. Another suggestion on the subject of selling sandals is to provide your customer with either sample styles made up ahead of time, or illustrate your styles on a wall chart. This is a much easier means of communication than trying to wave your arms around describing styles in the air. It's also basic to salesmanship.

The Arch

The use of an arch is a matter of personal preference. Many sandalmakers feel that arches are a wasted effort and either pull the sole laminations apart or, in case of wet and bent arches, they claim these arches will flatten out once they are wet. Other sandalmakers insist upon arches as the only means of achieving real foot comfort. And then there's something like the middle road between the two extremes, illustrated in the last three photos on page 80 where a single heel lamination is added to provide at least a minimum elevation to the sole. If you do decide to use an arch, there are several methods of building one.

Precut, ready–made arch cushions can be purchased from many shoe trade suppliers. (A few of them are listed in the back of the book.) These arch cushions are small, half–moon shaped pads that fit between sole layers to permanently elevate the arch. They're available in a variety of materials including composition material, rubber, and cork—and they can be hand carved from thick pieces of scrap leather. Precut arch cushions are fitted in place by cementing them between the sole layers, and then either sewing or cobbling them permanently in place. As mentioned earlier, I don't recommend the use of these arch cushions, even though many sandalmakers will disagree with me. I feel strongly that a hand–built, wet and bent arch is far superior to the arch cushion, both in terms of design and durability.

Wet and Bent Arches

Wet and bent arches are formed right into the sandal soles by forming the sole leather with the thumbs and heel of the palm when the leather is wet. A well formed sandal sole should not only have an arch, but should be slightly cupped at the toe and the heel. (The word "cupping" in this reference means that the outside edges of both the toe and heel are slightly raised, as if to form a rim.) This cupping at the toe and heel tends to hold the foot within the length of the sole; it prevents the foot from slipping off the sole, both front and back.

After the pattern is cut, trimmed, and accurate to the foot size, you must then trace it onto the hide. Four sole pieces are needed; a right and left foot bottom sole in thick leather, and a right and left foot top sole in 8 ounce leather. Most sandalmakers prefer tracing onto the hide so that when the laminations are placed together, the two flesh sides will face each other. The grain side on the top sole must face the bottom of the foot. Trace the four pieces accurately onto the hide; use a ballpoint pen or a scratch awl, and be sure to also trace the strap holes on for the top lamination only. The soles can now be cut from the hide, and then the strap holes can be punched out in the top soles by using the oblong, or bag, punch. Place the two sole layers together for each foot as they'll finally appear, and double-check to see that they match. You're now ready to form the soles.

Begin forming the soles by first soaking them in water. Because the top soles are thinner, they'll take less time to soak than the bottom soles will. It takes from between 10 to 20 minutes to soak the bottom soles and 8 to 10 minutes to soak the top soles. The bottom sole must be formed first, and then the top sole formed to the curvature of the bottom sole. If the leather is too spongy when you first remove it from

soaking, you'll just have to let it begin to dry out a little. You'll know if it's too spongy by the fact that when you try and bend it, the leather will flop back into its flat plane. If it holds its shape, the leather is ready to mold.

The most successful way to form sandal soles is to exaggerate all three bend areas; the toe, the heel, and the arch. In other words, create bends that are slightly more pronounced than is actually necessary. In this way, you'll produce enough of a bend in each instance to allow the foot to eventually mold itself to the sole. If you make the bends too small, the foot then has nothing to work against.

What you're after in the bends, is a more or less elongated, open, and curved W form where the heel and toe are both bent up, and the arch is humped up in the center. Begin forming with the bottom sole first. Bend up the heel by either applying thumb pressure to the flesh side, or by pressing the flesh side of the heel against the palm of one hand. It makes little difference how you hold the leather as long as you come up with the right results. Once the leather begins to bend, you must then cup the outside heel edges even further up to form a slight outside lip around the heel area. Now repeat this same procedure with the toe. Next, bend in the arch by applying thumb pressure against the flesh side of the sole. As you apply pressure with your thumbs, the motion is to stretch the leather into shape by firmly pressing your thumbs across the leather and working toward the outside edge of the sole. When the sole looks like an elongated W, you've reached the right shape. With this exaggerated shape, it might look like your foot will never fit, but you can be assured that once you put your weight on this strange shape, you've given the leather liberty to form itself to your foot. The arch bend should be slightly higher than the bend in both the heel and toe; about half again as high.

Once the bottom sole is formed, you can take the top sole, place it above the bottom sole, and duplicate the form by working the soles into each other: the top sole should be worked into the bottom sole and they should eventually fit snugly one into the other. Slight differences in shape can eventually be trimmed off after the soles are permanently laminated, but keep working the two soles into each other until they duplicate each other's bends. The last step in forming is to let the leather dry thoroughly.

Preparing Straps

Straps on women's sandals are usually between ⅜" to ½" wide; straps on men's sandals are a bit wider, from ½" to ⅝" wide. The width of the strap must be equal to the width of the strap holes already punched into the top sole. Straps are cut either with a draw gauge or a plough gauge. Be sure you cut enough strap to allow for both the right and left foot on the sandal style selected. The buckle and buckle tongue holes are added to the straps after the straps are permanently secured between the sole laminations. The length of the straps should account for both the buckle, and the area of the strap that's laminated between the soles. Toe straps, toe loops, arch straps, and heel straps should be long enough to allow at least one full inch to extend between the sole laminations.

The next step is to square off the ends of the straps; those ends that will fit into the top sole strap holes and be laminated between the soles. Insert these square ends into the strap holes on the top sole; this process will vary greatly according to the sandal design being used. Some craftsmen prefer to skive thickness off the portion of the strap that extends between the laminations in order to make the lamination less bulky. Once the straps are arranged according to the style you've selected, slip your foot into the straps and adjust them as tightly as possible on your foot. Once the straps are in place, and are comfortable on the foot, you're ready to cement the strap ends to the flesh side of the top sole. Cement just those strap ends which run between the laminations. On toe straps, the leather that runs between laminations should be allowed to run all the way to the point of the toe and beyond. Excess that might hang out beyond the toe can be trimmed off flush after the soles are permanently secured.

Once the strap ends are cemented to the flesh side of the top sole, you can then generously spread leather contact cement over the entire flesh side of the top sole and bottom sole. Remember that contact cement bonds instantly and doesn't give you room for adjustment once the two surfaces are placed together. When the cement is thoroughly dry, I'd suggest giving the sole a second coating, and then allowing this second coating of cement to thoroughly dry also. Next, carefully place the two laminations together in exactly the position that you want them, making certain that all strap ends that are supposed to run between laminations are properly in place. To make the sole laminations even stronger, I'd also suggest that you lightly tap the bond together with a mallet to eliminate the possibility of any air pockets. You're now ready to either cobble or sew the laminations together.

Cobbling

One of the ways of permanently laminating sandal soles is to cobble them. Cobbling is the technique of laminating layers of leather together by using cobbling nails. The cobbling technique dates back several centuries—it consists of driving small nails completely through layers of leather until they strike a solid surface and then bend back on themselves to form a *U*, or hook. The cobbling technique is used primarily when making heels and soles on footwear, especially on sandals. It can also be used as a purely decorative technique.

Although the usual method of laminating is to cement layers of leather together, in the case of heels and soles on footwear, cement alone is just not strong enough to create a permanent bond. This is when cobbling nails are used—they create an almost indestructable bond which does in fact resist the normal stress and strain placed against layers of leather on soles and heels.

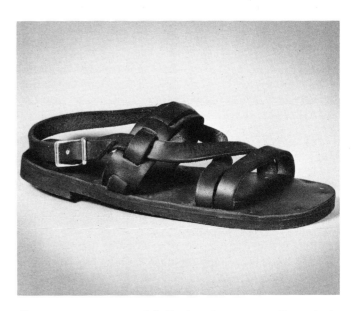

Front arch strap sandal. Notice the woven effect of the arch strap. Made by Bort Carleton, Boston, Mass. Photo, Dave Congalton.

For cobbling, you'll need both soling and cobbling nails and some type of metal surface against which to nail. Cobbling nails are especially designed for leather. They have a serrated edge which allows them to bend back on themselves into a hook when they strike metal. The nail is hammered through the layers of leather until it strikes metal. It then bends back into a hook, burying the hooked end in the leather. Cobbling nails are available in a variety of lengths, they come with either flat or round heads, and they're available in either steel or brass wire. The length you buy will depend upon the thickness you have to go through. The nail should be at least 1/8″ to 3/16″ longer than the thickness of leather.

The most popular nail is brass, preferably with a flat head. A flat head is much less noticeable on leather, and brass seems more complementary to the dye tones used on sandals.

The most expedient place to get a small sample of cobbling nails is from the nearest shoe repairman. If you want to order more, he can probably get them for you, or you can write to one of the suppliers listed at the back of the book. W. W. Cross and Company manufactures one brand of soling nails called Klean-Kutt soling nails.

The normal procedure is to cobble the laminations together with the nails set in about 1/4″ to 3/8″ from the outside edge of the sandal and spaced about 1″ apart. Many sandalmakers prefer using a minimum of cobbling nails and only set them at stress points, for example, across the heel, toe, and wherever straps run between laminations. My own preference is to cobble about 1″ apart, and to also make certain that at least one nail pierces each strap as it runs between laminations. This keeps the strap from ever slipping out. Cobbling nails can either be cobbled from the top through to the bottom, or cobbled in reverse:

from the bottom through to the top. The nail heads will not show if the nails are set from the bottom through to the top. On the other hand, many craftsmen prefer to leave the flat-headed brass cobbling nails showing on the top sole as a part of the sandal design. For the most part, these nail heads won't be seen anyway once the sandal is being worn on the foot.

The important part in cobbling is to get the nail to run straight through both laminations and then bend back on itself when it hits the iron plate placed under the soles. Always cobble against a piece of hard metal. This is the only way that the nail will bend back on itself. The nails used should be at least ¼″ longer than the thickness of the sole.

I begin placing my nails by hand by jabbing them into the leather just enough so that they stand on their own. I then use a heel hammer to drive them through until they strike the metal plate and *U* back on themselves. If the nail begins to head at an angle, I've found that if you turn the whole sandal around and hit the nail from the opposite side, you can then straighten its path through the leather. After you've driven in all the nails, double-check them on the opposite side to be sure all nail points are headed back onto the leather.

Heels

Heels should be an integral part of the sandal, added at the same time the cobbling is done. Three of the photos in this chapter illustrate a single heel lamination which was first cemented to the bottom sole and then cobbled right onto the sole laminations. The wedged heel sandal illustrates a heel which was built up by laminating layers of leather together with cement, then shaping the heel on an electric sanding wheel, and finally cobbling the heel to the sole with long clinching, or cobbling, nails that extend from the bottom of the heel all the way up through both sole laminations; this heel is therefore an integral part of the sandal sole, rather than having been tacked on

afterwards. In other words, the nails that hold the sole laminations together at the heel are the same nails that run all the way up through the heel itself. Heels are normally cut from the same leather thickness as the sandal's bottom sole.

Bottom Sole Variations

There are a few sandalmakers around who use composition material for their bottom soles. These composition soles can be purchased directly from shoe trade suppliers in pre–cut sizes. I've also seen sandals that use tire tread rubber as a bottom sole. These soles are cut out of discarded tires and then cemented and cobbled to the leather top soles. Then too, a few craftsmen have tried wooden soles as the bottom lamination, and then there are sandalmakers who prefer using heavy–duty rivets with which to laminate soles together, rather than cobbling nails.

Putting an Edge on Sandals

After the soles are permanently laminated, you may find a bit of unevenness along the edges where the two laminations come together. This unevenness can be sanded off on an electric sanding wheel using a fine grade sandpaper. Once the edges are even, they should be dyed, and finally burnished smooth on a polishing wheel. As you can see from the photos on page 80, the edges on these sandals have a smooth, professional finish.

Dyeing and Finishing

The final step in sandalmaking is to dye the leather, apply a finish coat, and add the buckle and buckle tongue holes to the strap. It's also a good idea to occasionally apply a preservative to the sandal leather to keep it from cracking. If the sandals are constantly subjected to moisture and then to extreme heat, the leather will dry out quickly. You can use either Lexol, or a neatsfoot oil for this purpose.

CHAPTER SIXTEEN

Moccasins, slippers, and moc boots

Walter Dyer (whose moc boots are illustrated in this chapter) boasts that his handmade footwear creates "happy feet and smiling toes." No matter how corny this bit of New England wit may sound to the sophisticate, it does contain one truth that every craftsman about to undertake the construction of footwear should keep in mind. Handmade footwear must be, first and foremost, the most comfortable experience feet have ever encountered. The hand craftsman's responsibility is to produce footwear that surpasses the quality of factory-made footwear. In addition to se-selecting only the most supple leather, developing unique style design, and exercising meticulous craftsmanship, the hand craftsman has an added advantage over the factory; he's able to produce footwear sized to the measurements of a given individual's foot, as opposed to producing standard sizes. The hand craftsman must perform as a custom footwear maker.

This chapter doesn't give step–by–step construction procedure for footwear, because footwear styles vary so greatly, and the construction of one style may be quite different from another. However, I'll attempt to provide the reader with construction principles that are applicable to all types of handmade footwear.

Tools

To make footwear patterns, you'll need light, pliable tagboard (something similar in thickness to the leather you intend using in the footwear). Most slippers and lightweight moccasins can be cut from the hide with a pair of leather shears, but on moc boots using heavy leather, you'll need a square point leather knife. Depending upon the style used, you may also need a revolving punch, and certainly a curved awl to punch lacing or thread holes. Again, depending upon the style, you may also need rivets, a rivet setter, or eyelets, and an eyelet setter. And if the design requires it, you'll need closing findings such as buckles, loops, rings, dees, or even snaps.

If you're making moc boots, you'll require the use of a last, tacks, a pair of lasting pincers, and some type of last jacket. For stitching or lacing, you'll need thread or lacing, needles, and some type of thimble arrangement. (The chapter on sewing and lacing provides detailed instructions on all of these items.) And finally, if the design and the leather require it, you'll need the usual dyes and finishing supplies.

Leather

Leather which is used for footwear must be supple, therefore it should have an oil base tannage. An ideal tannage is one that is not only supple, but that has a minimum stretch (just enough to conform to the foot, but not so much as to make it lose its shape). For footwear designed to be worn outdoors, the leather should be somewhere in between the extremes of latigo and oak; latigo stretches too much, whereas oak is too rigid, is likely to crack, and is entirely too dry. With these basic requirements in mind, you and your supplier should be able to make intelligent leather selections. I've seen very successful moccasins and moc boots made from leather with cod oil tannage, aniline tannage, chrome tannage, vegetable tannage, and leather tanned with special animal fats such as a mutton tallow base. Just stay clear of dry and super stretchy leathers.

Slippers will require only a lightweight leather, about 3 to 4 ounces thick. Moccasins will require leather a bit thicker, something from about 4 to 6 ounces thick, and moc boots and outdoor footwear should be made from thick leather, from 12 to 14 ounces thick.

Many craftsmen prefer lining certain styles of moccasins, slippers, and moc boots with undyed sheepskin. This not only provides added warmth, but a luxurious softness to the foot. Sheepskin is simply cut and cemented to the flesh side of the footwear leather.

A natural sheepskin will very likely cause feet to perspire, and unless sheepskin lined moccasins are given a chance to air out once in a while, they can become quite rank. (This is added as a postscript in the event that you do elect to use sheepskin along with other leather.)

Selecting a Style

This chapter illustrates several styles of footwear, from low Oxfords, to moc boots, to wrap–around boots, to fringed boots. If you take the time to study the illustrations, you'll notice the variety of closing designs—from rawhide lacing, to loops, to zippers, and even to leather buttons. What's photographed here is only a small fraction of the footwear designs available to you. Before you worry about a pattern, you'll have to first select a style.

For handmade footwear, I suggest you select a style

Avant-Garde moc boot, unlined; made from 14 ounce, imported English cowhide. This moc boot is entirely handmade, and was sewn with 8-cord polyester dacron thread. It was first cut from the pattern by hand, then tacked to a last and sewn with a locking stitch, using two needles and two lengths of thread. Notice that the heel seam is raised up enough to prevent the wearer from walking on it. (I have a pair of these moc boots and can honestly say that they're the most comfortable things I've ever worn on my feet.) Made by Walter Dyer, Rockport, Mass. Photo, Dave Congalton.

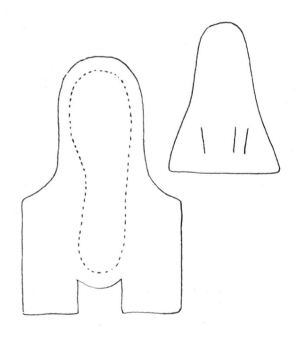

Figure 62. *An approximate pattern for a moc boot (the dotted line indicates actual foot size).*

with a minimum number of seams, preferably a two–piece construction. Most moccasins are of two–piece construction. They consist of the lower, one–piece wrap–around sole, and the vamp, or top, that usually extends from the toe to the ankle. The moc boots illustrated in this chapter are both two–piece constructions. Two–piece construction requires a minimum in seams—two—the vamp seamed to the lower portion, and the heel seamed up the back.

Most handmade footwear is designed with a wrap–around, one–piece sole which is an integral part of the design, and serves as both the two sides and the sole. A few craftsmen, but not many, prefer adding a manufactured composition material sole, especially on footwear intended for outdoor wear. Mr. Dyer, who's opposed to the use of composition material soles on handmade footwear, has developed a double, wrap–around sole that is hand–stitched over the first sole. This technique doesn't invade the delightful leprechaun lines developed in the design of his footwear. Most craftsmen feel (and, I think, rightly) that the use of these flat composition soles is a violation of the tradition of handmade footwear. Like Mr. Dyer, they prefer saving the design, and the handmade look, as opposed to slapping on a composition sole in the name of longer wear. These same craftsmen achieve their longer wear by carefully selecting leathers which provide maximum durability. As a last word on this subject, let's say that an extra sole is acceptable only when it complements the lines of the design, as in the case of the wrap–around extra sole.

One fast way of introducing yourself to the techniques involved in making footwear is to try making a two–piece construction moccasin. For study purposes, you can pick up one of the inexpensive, Tandy Leather Company moccasin kits. For the beginning craftsman, the kit is a quick teaching device; but once you've done the kit, put it away for good, and spend your energies designing your own footwear.

Because this chapter illustrates only a small fraction of footwear styles, I suggest that you spend some time looking at as many styles as you can find in shops, catalogs, and on people in the street. Keep a notebook handy to record construction techniques, and when possible, I'd suggest that you make rough sketches of what you see for memory recall. The more styles you can come up with, the more exciting will be your involvement in footwear. One designer I know spends a great deal of time in museums studying and sketching antique footwear. He's come up with a number of very successful contemporary adaptations of some of these antique styles.

An important consideration in footwear design is the proper location of the seams, especially the heel seam. Many craftsmen and, in fact, many manufacturers, fail to properly design moccasins and moc boots so that the seams are raised up far enough off the walking surface to protect them from being walked on. If the seams are not raised up off the sole at least ¾″, the consumer will more than likely wear the thread or lacing out by having to walk on it. This isn't the consumer's fault, but the fault of the designer. The heel seam on the Avant-Garde boot and the Oxford tie moccasin is a full 1″ up from the sole surface.

The Pattern

There are several ways to overcome the pattern problem in making footwear. The quickest and simplest procedure is to take a worn pair of old moccasins in your own size, rip them apart at the seams, flatten the leather out over a piece of pattern tagboard, and simply trace the pattern for each piece. Many leather craftsmen who eventually branch out into footwear often come up with patterns by buying footwear styles they like, deliberately taking them apart at the seams, and then adding their own improvements to the basic style. For example, they might extend the vamp, put a flare in it, or introduce a unique new closing device, or piece of hardware.

Another way to lick the pattern problem is to purchase patterns already made in the size desired. Many craftsmen will sell you the use of their patterns in given sizes, and there are a number of firms listed in the *Shoe Factory Buyer's Guide* that sell ready–made footwear patterns.

Making Your Own Pattern

If you prefer making a pattern from scratch, you should begin by knowing exactly what style you want. The most accurate way to make a pattern is to use a pliable tagboard with a thickness equal to the thickness of the leather you intend using in the footwear. Again, I'd recommend beginning with a simple, two–piece construction.

There's a great deal of trial and error involved in making a pattern from scratch. You'll have to be willing to rework your pattern a number of times until you get it exactly the way you want it. You can begin by tracing your foot onto the pattern tagboard in the same manner as when tracing your foot for sandals. The next step is to extend the circumference of the

Oxford tie moccasin, unlined; made from 15 ounce, imported English cowhide tanned with mutton tallow. This moccasin was hand sewn from a one-piece vamp, with 8-cord polyester dacron thread. It was sewn over a last with the aid of a last jack. Made by Walter Dyer, Rockport, Mass. Photo, Dave Congalton.

Wrap-around two-tone boot. This boot was entirely hand-made, and was sewn over a last with 8-cord polyester dacron thread. The side fastenings are made from rolled pieces of leather. Made by Walter Dyer, Rockport, Mass. Photo, Dave Congalton.

sole tracing outward to account for the wrap-around sides and heel design. Figure 62 indicates an approximate shape for the pattern of the Avant-Garde moc boot; the dotted line within the pattern represents the original foot tracing. By simply measuring the height of your foot according to the style that you're trying to develop, you can add to the circumference of the original tracing. Once you think you've gotten the pattern reasonably close, you can retrace it onto fresh tagboard, cut it out, bend it to form, and actually sew the tagboard pieces together into a paper shoe in order to try it out for size and style. The more pains you take in insuring accuracy, the less likely you'll be to encounter problems when graduating to the actual leather. It's much cheaper to make your mistakes on paper than it is to make them on leather.

Cutting

After the pattern is in order, you can then trace it onto the leather, making certain that you've traced it so that the grain side of the leather faces the outside of the foot. On slippers and lightweight moccasins, there's no particular trick in cutting out the pieces, but on moc boots using thick leather, the seam lines should be cut on both the lower or body pattern and on the vamp so that the outside leather edges along all seams are beveled 45 degrees in toward the center of the boot. This bevel can be cut with the same stroke you used to cut the pattern from the hide, simply tipping the blade of the square point knife to the required 45 degree angle. Moc boot leather has a thickness of over ¼″ and this beveled edge along the seam is necessary in order to insure evenness when the seams are sewn together, much in the same manner as one would bevel 45 degree corner on the four pieces that make up a picture frame. Only the seam areas require beveling; the other edges can remain perpendicular at 90 degrees. If you can't manage this bevel in the same cutting stroke as when cutting out the pattern, then cut the bevel in afterwards; but just make certain that it's there.

Sewing Slippers and Moccasins

Slippers and moccasins should be sewn together with either thin strips of rawhide, latigo lace, or with polyester dacron thread with a cord count of from 5 to 8. You won't need a last when sewing moccasins made out of thin leather, but it does help to retain the inside shape of the moccasin if you at least try to form the toe around some type of padding as you sew. You might try stuffing the toe with rags and then temporarily holding the toe pieces together with safety pins at about six points along the seam.

When sewing moccasins and slippers, many craftsmen prefer to punch lace or thread holes ahead of time, and others prefer to punch only one hole at a time as they progress along the seam. There are advantages and disadvantages to both procedures, especially when using lightweight leathers. Punching ahead of time will insure an even spacing between stitches, but is not as likely to gain as tight a stitch as when punching one hole at a time. Whichever

method you use, make certain that the punched holes are no longer than the diameter of the lacing or thread; the lace or thread should fit tightly into each hole. A simple loop stitch, a running stitch, or even a baseball X stitch can be used to sew the vamp to the sole, and can also be used to sew up the heel seam.

The circumference around the outside edge on the sewn portion of the vamp is always less in length than the circumference around the corresponding matched portion of the lower sole. In other words, the lower sole piece, as it bends up to form itself to the vamp, ends up being slightly puckered, or gathered, in order to use up this excess circumference. What all this means is that the spacing between the punch holes on the lower sole must be further apart than the spacing between the punch holes on the vamp. You'll need the same number of punch holes on each piece, but the distance between them is greater on the lower piece than on the vamp. The vamp remains a flat plane of leather, whereas the lower sole must bend up and form itself to the vamp. This difference in distance between punch holes (greater on the sole, lesser on the vamp) is what allows you to pull the excess circumference of the sole up to meet the vamp. On all footwear, the lace or thread holes should be set back from the edge of the leather at least 3/16″.

Sewing Outdoor Footwear

In order to sew moccasins or moc boots (outdoor footwear) made from thick leather (12 to 14 ounce), you'll require the use of a last. The last functions as an inside core form around which the article of footwear is built; the finished piece of footwear ends up with inside dimensions equal to the outside measurements of the last. In other words, the last equals the measurements of the foot that will eventually fill the moccasin or boot. The chapter on sewing and lacing explains the function and use of both the last and the last jack, and contains a suggestion of how to hold a boot for sewing without a factory–made jack.

In order for the reader to follow the procedure in sewing outdoor footwear, I'll describe in detail the procedure used by Mr. Dyer in making the Avant-Garde boot illustrated in this chapter. Mr. Dyer's lasts range in sizes from 6 to 13 and in widths from A to EEE. The pattern is cut from the hide and all matching edge seams on the lower sole and on the vamp are beveled. Mr. Dyer's workbench is equipped with a United Shoe Machine last jack; this last jack serves to hold the last in place while the boot is being prepared for sewing. The jack is constructed so that it can be tipped or swung for convenient access to all parts of the boot.

The first step is to begin tacking the lower sole to the last. Mr. Dyer uses small cobbler's tacks and drives them through the leather and into the last with the hammer on the lasting pincers. The leather is bent up around the last and held in place with the tacks. The vamp is then tacked in place to match edges with the lower sole. He first sews the toe seam, and then sews the heel seam. The tacks are driven into the leather close enough to the outside edges so that the

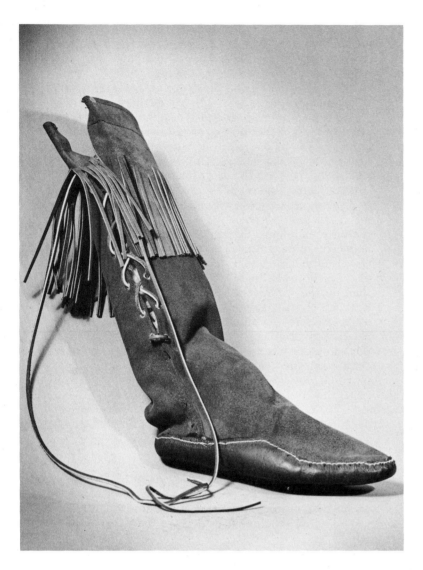

Fringed boot with rawhide side lacing. The one-piece sole of this boot was made from 12 ounce cowhide, and the top was made from 5 to 6 ounce cowhide. A last was used to sew the two pieces together. Because the leather for the body of the boot is thin, eyelets were used to reinforce the lacing holes. Made by Tom Tisdell, Cambridge, Mass. Photo, Dave Congalton.

Smooth grained fringe boot. This stovepipe-style boot made with the aid of a last and a last jack by Tisdell, Cambridge, Mass. Photo, Dave Congalton.

eventual thread will cover up the marks left by the tack holes. As the lower piece forms up around the last to meet the vamp, he checks to see that excess lower leather is left at a minimum in order to avoid excess pucker. If there's too much of an indicated pucker, he then trims off a thin strip of the lower sole at the point of excess, and then retacks the leather to the last.

Mr. Dyer uses an 8-cord polyester dacron thread treated with beeswax to sew all of his boots. He also uses two straight needles and two lengths of thread which are constantly opposing each other as he stitches. In this way, he has a double weight of thread as opposed to a single thread, and each stitch is locked in place as the boot is sewn together. The lock is obtained by simply looping the threads after each stitch; this lock prevents the whole seam from pulling apart in the event that a section of the thread breaks during the lifetime of the boot.

A curved stitching awl is used to pierce the holes for the thread, and Mr. Dyer pierces one hole at a time ahead of the stitch, rather than piercing all the holes ahead of time. The thread holes are pierced from the lower sole up through the vamp keeping the curved awl blade angled as it passes through the thicknesses of the leather; in other words, rather than piercing straight through the leather, he pierces at an angle toward the vamp. This angle keeps the eventual seam much tighter.

He begins stitching at the beginning of the seam by running one needle through the vamp to the sole and the other needle in the opposite direction from the sole up through the vamp; the two needles pass each other in opposite directions as they run through the same hole. In order to drive the needles through the leather, Mr. Dyer wears a ring of leather around his finger as a thimble. By using two threads and two needles, he can pull each stitch tight by applying pressure from opposite directions. He simply repeats this process with each stitch as he advances around the seam. The Avant-Garde moc boot uses a running stitch. As he advances, he pulls out the next tack with the lasting pincers, runs the awl from bottom to top to pierce the thread hole, and then passes the two opposing needles through each hole. The stitches are closer together at the point of the toe than they are along the side seams. At the points of greatest stress (the beginning and end of the seam) he quite often will run a loop stitch back over the regular running stitch. If he sews on a double sole, he prefers using a baseball *X* stitch, making certain to lock each stitch in place before advancing to the next. The tighter each stitch is pulled, the less likely the boot will be to lose its intended shape. Exactly the same procedure is followed when sewing the heel seam. After the seams have been tightly sewn, the last is removed, and the boot will hold its shape permanently. The secret of quality handmade footwear is in learning to control the amount of pucker when stitching around the point of the toe. This takes a great deal of trial and error, and comes only from experience.

Finishing

Most craftsmen dye footwear leather before sewing the individual pieces together, or else they purchase leather which is already tannery dyed. If you wait to dye after the seams have been sewn together, you'll have difficulty controlling dye penetration along the seams and the dye will stiffen and dry out the thread.

Moccasins, boots, and moc boots should be cared for with the same degree of attention as dress shoes. Just because this type of footwear is worn with casual dress is no justification for neglecting its care. I suggest that you regularly clean handmade footwear with saddle soap, and occasionally give it a thorough treatment of Lexol or neatsfoot oil.

CHAPTER SEVENTEEN

Garments

This chapter introduces the techniques involved in leather garment construction. A garment is simply any article of clothing worn as a covering. Don't for a minute think that leather garments are limited to women's fashions, or men's vests. Leather garments include the whole spectrum of apparel: skirts, hats, coats, jackets, jerkins, trousers, capes, and whatever else can be loosely defined as a garment. And leather garments aren't restricted to any one type of person or to any one sex; leather is worn by children, teenagers, men and women of all ages; by thin people, fat people, short people, and tall people; by everyone who wears clothes. Whatever can be made from a conventional weave fabric, can also be made from leather.

But what type of garment is the more complementary to leather? Because leather isn't as pliable as a weave fabric, it therefore adapts itself more successfully to garments that hang loosely. A good example is a leather cape. Still another example is a garment that doesn't require "tucking in," as one would tuck in a blouse or a shirt. A leather garment is the most attractive when the leather is allowed to maintain a maximum in natural flow. I suggest you keep this in mind before selecting the style of your first garment project.

Leather is a special garment fabric—one doesn't see it being worn everyday by everybody. Yes, it's a bit more expensive than some of the weave fabrics, but it's actually no harder to make a garment out of leather than out of cotton. Leather doesn't require complex garment construction to show it off; in other words, leather lends itself to simple construction—a construction that uses simple patterns, and avoids as many seams, darts, puckers, and gathers as possible.

Garment Leather

The most common leather weight used in garments runs from 2½ to 3 ounces. There are of course exceptions to this weight recommendation, depending upon the particular garment. For example, a heavy vest, or leather used in an outdoor, unlined jacket might be as heavy as 5 ounces. For the most part, indoor garments such as skirts, jerkins, vests, and dresses, turn out best with 2½ to 3 ounce leather in either smooth grains, splits, or suedes.

The basic requirement for garment leather is that it be soft and pliable. Leather from several animal species is regularly used in garment construction including goat, calf, cow, horse, steer, sheep, and deer skins. Again, as mentioned in the chapter, *Selecting, Buying and Storing Leather;* the pelts of smaller animals are sold by the full hide, whereas the pelts of larger animals are sold either by the full hide, or by the side (half of the pelt).

Most suppliers stock leather which has been especially tanned for use in garments. I suggest you use these leathers rather than trying to adapt some other tanning process. The Tandy Leather Company especially recommends the use of a cowhide tanning process called "Softan" for garments. For approximate hide sizes, and definitions of some of the terms used in describing garment leathers, see *Selecting, Buying, and Storing Leather.*

The pattern comes before the leather; in other words, don't buy leather until you know exactly what your pattern requirements are. If you buy leather in person, bring the pattern along with you and test it out on the hides to insure proper footage. There's no point in buying excess leather, and if you underestimate quantity, you may have trouble duplicating color from the same tannage lot. Before you buy leather, examine the skins closely for imperfections. If there are imperfections, make sure these don't fall within the pattern requirements. Garment skins must have uniform weight and color. Make sure the skins come from the same tannage lot if the garment requires more than one skin. Simply lay out the pattern pieces right on the skins at the supplier's place of business. If you follow this procedure closely, you'll have no trouble making leather purchases. The most uniform skins should be used for fronts and sleeves. This suggestion is made for the sake of appearance. If you buy through the mail, then follow the procedures recommended in the chapter *Selecting, Buying and Storing Leather.*

Before discussing the specifics of garment design and construction, I'd like to suggest that you do some additional reading on this subject. Several of the national pattern companies, including Simplicity, pro-

Suede dress, lined with bridal satin. This dress was hand cut from a re-made pattern, and machine sewn. Courtesy of Poor Richard's, Denver, Colo. Photo, Don Engel.

Safari jacket, unlined; made from split cowhide with deer antler bone buttons. Courtesy of Poor Richard's, Denver, Colo. Photo, Don Engel.

Trousers, unlined; made from cowhide. The smooth side of the hide is on the inside and the rough side is on the outside, making these trousers easy to get in and out of and eliminating the need for a lining which would inhibit the natural "breathing" and ventilating qualities of the leather. Courtesy of Poor Richard's, Denver, Colo. Photo, Don Engel.

vide excellent pamphlets on garment construction in leather. The Tandy Leather Company also sells a fine little pamphlet "Sewing with Leather," and, for in-depth detail, there's Krohn and Schwebke's book *How to Sew Leather, Suede, Fur.* These additional sources all contain detailed step–by–step illustrations on elementary and advanced sewing techniques.

Ready-made Patterns

All of the major pattern companies provide an enormous selection of patterns in every style and type of garment, and many of them have patterns especially designed for use on leather. These ready–made patterns are inexpensive, cover a wide variety of garments and styles, and contain excellent step–by–step instructions. One way to carry through with your own garment designs is to buy a commercial pattern in the correct size that most corresponds to your own idea, and then restyle and adapt that pattern to fit the design innovations you originally had in mind. In this way, the garment design will still be uniquely your own.

Every major city and almost every small town in America has a store that sells garment patterns. All of these stores not only sell stocked patterns, but most of them provide catalogs from which to order patterns not stocked. If, for some reason, your town doesn't have a pattern store, the major pattern companies are listed below. I've contacted them all, and they're more than willing to handle mail-order business.

Vogue Pattern Service, P. O. Box 200, Canal St. Station, New York, N.Y. 10013

Simplicity Pattern Company, Inc., 200 Madison Ave., New York, N.Y. 10016

McCall's Pattern Service, 230 Park Ave., New York, N.Y. 10022

Butterick Pattern Service is a less expensive line of Vogue patterns, and can be obtained by writing the Vogue Pattern Service address listed above.

Original Patterns

But what about the reader with his own ideas? Suppose he can't find his ideas converted into a commercial pattern? We can't neglect him, so let's look at an example of how he can follow through with his own designs. Let's say that this reader saw a vest somewhere that had a pocket on each side of the front vest panels, and had a crew neck. He's looked everywhere, and can't find a commercial pattern with pockets and a crew neck. But he did see several vest patterns in his size that had the same front opening.

A pattern is meant to be only a general style in a specific size. There's no rule that says patterns can't be changed. Our reader with the problem can buy the front–opening vest pattern in his size, design pockets out of paper or inexpensive muslin, sew them together, see how they work, adapt them to leather, and then repeat the same procedure for the crew neck. His design adaptations can be constructed right into the commercial pattern as long as he has the right size and a front–opening style. This same problem of restyling is true with every garment, so don't abandon your own ideas just because you can't find them duplicated in a ready–made pattern.

Pattern Reminders

When buying a commercial pattern, check the back of the pattern envelope for fabric and yardage suggestions. Patterns call for fabric requirements in yards—leather is sold by the square foot. To convert the pattern yardage to square feet, see the *Garment Conversion Table* on page 22 in the chapter, *Selecting, Buying, and Storing Leather.*

Check the pattern envelope to make sure that the given pattern is suitable for use on leather. Don't try to adapt a pattern intended for use on a lightweight fabric to leather. If you have any questions about a particular pattern's suitability for leather, then ask the sales clerk, or better yet, write down the pattern number, the pattern manufacturer, and write directly to the company.

Figure measurements vary even within the same size number. For example, Mary and Jane may both wear a size 12 dress, but Mary might have larger hips than Jane, and may even be an inch shorter than Jane. For this reason, on women's patterns, many pattern companies sell their patterns according to one of five basic figure types: teen–size, miss–size, half–size, junior–size, and women's–size. The pattern store should have a chart illustrating basic figure types. Before buying a pattern, I suggest that you compare your own figure (or the person for whom the garment is intended) with the figure types on the chart, and then make your pattern selection accordingly.

The Simplicity Pattern Company uses a special black diamond shape which is printed along the cutting edges of the pattern. Other companies use similar markings. These markings are called *notches.* The notches are numbered, and joined to corresponding numbers in the order of their use as the garment is constructed. When you encounter one of these notch markings along a pattern edge, the notch should be cut outward (never in). Cutting the notches outward not only makes them easier to see, but keeps the seam allowances exactly as called for in the pattern.

As mentioned earlier, you may want to deviate from the commercial pattern in order to develop your own design. If you elect to do this, or if you make any alterations in the original pattern, don't wait and make these changes on the garment. The changes must first be made on the pattern, so that they will properly fall into place on the garment. All seams on the paper pattern should be trimmed to ⅜″ before you begin working. This reduces leather waste, and also eliminates bulk later on in the sewing.

For a beginning craftsman, it's an excellent practice to try the pattern out on an inexpensive muslin (minus the facings), before graduating to leather. This does require a bit more time, but you'll eliminate mistakes on the leather, and be able to familiarize yourself with the construction techniques of the pat-

Wrap-around leather skirt, lined with a floral print; machine sewn. Made by Justis Taylor, Bennington, Vt. Photo, Larry Hyman.

Suede skirt with patch pockets; machine sewn. Made by Justis Taylor, Bennington, Vt. Photo, Larry Hyman.

tern, as well as to discover ahead of time any changes or alterations you'll want to make on the garment. You can then transfer these changes to the pattern before you begin working on the leather. The Simplicity Pattern Company recommends that all craftsmen make this muslin procedure a regular working *rule*. Whether it's a hat, a skirt, or a vest, you can always eliminate problems if you first make the garment out of muslin.

Interfacings on leather garments are important to shape retention, especially if you're using a lightweight leather. Canvas or non-woven fabrics are suitable for use on medium weight suedes and grained leather. On very lightweight leather, you can use an interfacing material such as the brands Interlon or Pellon, which are non–woven fabrics. Pellon is also available in an iron–on variety which works on leather. The Simplicity Pattern Company recommends that the front section of the interfacings be extended to garment armholes for additional shape retention.

Facings on most leather garments are made from the same leather as the body of the garment. Facings are attached to the garment according to the instructions enclosed with the pattern. The Simplicity Pattern Company recommends the use of ribbon (such as grosgrain ribbon, similar to what's normally used on sweaters) for waistband facings. You can also use a rayon or silk bias tape with leather facings in order to hand sew them to linings.

Laying Out the Pattern

Leather has a grain which runs lengthwise along the backbone of the animal from head to tail. Pattern pieces should be placed on the hide so that they run *with* the grain. This insures a proper drape to the eventual garment. Never place the pattern across the grain—or from side to side. It makes no difference which end of the hide the pattern pieces face as long as they run *with* the grain. For example, if you're working with a dress pattern, you would place the neck of the pattern lengthwise along the hide. This is also true of garments with sleeves; the length of these sleeves should run *with* the grain, as well as all other pattern pieces.

Always place the pattern on the flesh side of the hide—this minimizes damage to the exposed surface. Check to see that there are no thin spots or imperfections falling within the pattern pieces (thin spots can be strengthened with iron-on tape as mentioned earlier).

There are many ways to attach the pattern to the hide. You can use masking tape, mending tape, Scotch tape, or even the new spray material which, when applied to the back of the pattern, will make it pressure sensitive. You can also use paper clips if you're careful not to mark the leather. And then, it's also possible to use pins, as long as the pins fall within the seam allowances and don't poke holes in any exposed area of the leather. Once the pattern is attached to the hide, you can trace around it with chalk, a pencil, or a felt-tip pen for additional placement insurance. A good rule to follow throughout the construction is to

protect the leather from pin holes, dents, and scrapes. Leather is not a weave fabric. If it's marked, especially on smooth grains, the mark will show. You don't have to be quite as fussy with suedes and splits, but it still helps to keep this rule in mind.

If the pattern requires two of any single pattern piece, and only one pattern piece is included in the package, as for example with sleeves, be sure to make an extra sleeve out of brown paper and place it on the hide along with all other pieces. When laying these duplicate pattern pieces on the hide, be sure to reverse the second, or duplicate, pattern piece. This reversing of the pattern pieces will insure that you don't end up with two right sleeves, or two right front garment panels.

Leather pattern pieces aren't cut on the fold (by folding the material in half as with other fabrics), they are all cut on the flat of the material (as the material is spread out flat on a table). On some pattern pieces, you may find markings on the pattern requiring that certain pieces be cut on the fold. To cut on the fold means to fold the material. *Do not follow this procedure on leather.* When encountering these fold markings, simply cut another duplicate pattern piece out of brown paper, tape it to the original pattern piece along the edge that had the fold marking, and then lay it out on the hide along with the rest of the pattern. Before you begin cutting anything, all garment pieces must be accounted for, laid out on the flat of the material, and then attached to the hide.

When laying out the pattern on the leather, you may run into weak or thin spots in the hide. Many craftsmen reinforce these weak or thin spots by simply using a standard iron–on tape pressed to the flesh side of the leather over the thin spot before cutting out the pattern. In ironing this tape to the leather, follow the usual ironing procedure for leather—use no steam, and press over brown paper or a pressing cloth.

Linings are another important thing to consider when constructing leather garments. Leather against bare skin, or even against other material, has a tendency to cling. Because of this, linings are an important part of many leather garments, especially jackets, trousers, and coats. As for leather skirts, a lining can be omitted by wearing a half–slip, or by stitching a half–slip permanently in place at the skirt waist. Lining fabrics recommended for leather should be colorfast, such as satin, taffeta, and rayon twill. These are the lining fabrics normally used in any garment construction; lining leather is the same as lining any other kind of fabric.

If you want less leather waste, you can always increase the number of seams on the garment in order to make smaller pieces. This should only be done, however, after you've gained some experience and con-

Suede dress, lined with silk. A darker suede was used on the hem and on the cuffs. The zipper extends 1/3 the length of the dress in an implied jumpsuit or coat-dress style. Courtesy of Ted St. Germain, Nantucket, Mass. Photo, Sy Lippman.

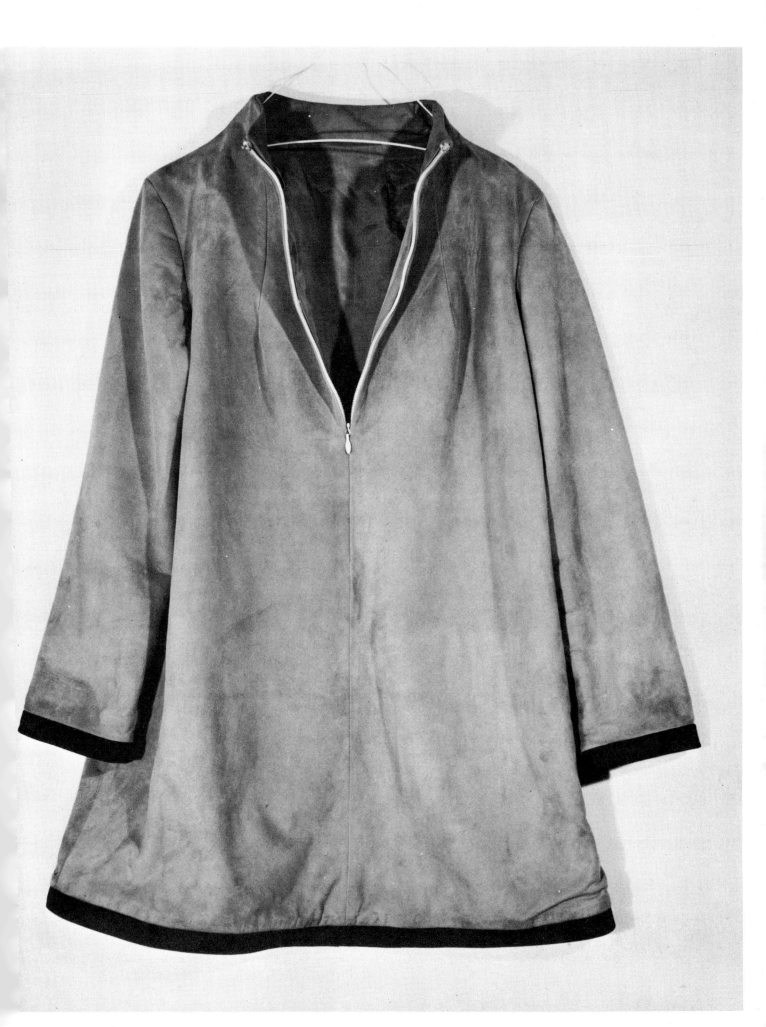

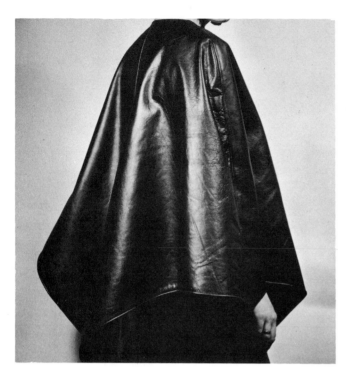

Black leather cape, made from four pieces of leather; machine sewn. Made by Bill Rowe, courtesy of The Crafty Seaman, Cambridge, Mass. Photo, Dave Congalton.

Figure 63. *A selection of vest styles: a front opening style using buckles and straps as a closing device; a double-breasted vest with handmade, round buttons; a pullover vest with a crew neck; and a pullover vest with open sides and double straps.*

fidence. For example, it's possible to seam a vest up the center of the back even though the pattern may call for a single piece across the back. Two pieces instead of one would give you more area on the hide to work with.

Leather can also be combined with other garment materials such as wools, knits, and other equally heavy fabrics. If you plan to make combinations, I suggest you do it sparingly and in good taste so as not to clutter a garment with all manner of complex construction. One can either trim other garment materials with leather, or trim a leather garment with other fabrics. For example, collars, cuffs, buttons, and sometimes even front panels can be tastefully interchanged either as a complementary fabric on leather, or by using leather as the trim fabric.

Beginning Leather Garment Projects

Begin with simple garments and then advance to the more difficult constructions after you've established a rapport with leather. A good place to begin is either with a man's or a woman's vest. Figure 63 indicates four basic styles, and then, within this chapter, there are additional photographs showing variations in vest styles.

Basically, there are only three pieces in most vests —the two front panels and the back. If you prefer making a pullover vest, there are only two pieces. Most men's vests don't need darts (unless a form fit is desired), but women's vests do require darts, at least one on each side, to allow for the bustline. It's possible to leave garment edges raw, or unturned, but most craftsmen feel that turning all garment edges not only creates a much more professional edge, but the ribbed effect created by a turned edge, tends to highlight the leather texture.

Other than the side darts on a woman's vest, the only other seams are at the shoulders and the sides. These can be treated in a variety of ways: the side seams can be *X* stitched with rawhide and eyelets, machine sewn, and fitted tight to the contour of the figure, closed with buttons and side straps, buckles and side straps, or one of several other style variations.

Front closings on vests can be treated in as many style variations as side seams can. Again, the illustrations and photographs in this section suggest a number of ways to design front openings. I suggest you also reread the chapter on findings and fasteners for additional ideas on closing styles.

Another garment which is fairly simple to construct is a leather cape. The photograph of the black leather cape on this page illustrates a cape made from four pieces of leather seamed down the front center, the back center, and along both shoulders. This same cape could have been constructed with only two seams and two pieces of leather—a front and back piece seamed along the shoulder. A cape is one of the most successful garments for allowing leather to show itself off in a natural drape.

Ladies' leather vest, lined. The three pieces of this vest are held together by rawhide lacing threaded through eyelet holes. The vest has two darts in each of the two front pieces to insure a snug fit. Courtesy of Ted St. Germain, Nantucket, Mass. Photo, Sy Lippman.

Men's lined, front-opening vest. The use of front darts creates a close fit. The vest was designed in such a way that it would hang open; the edges are turned, and sewn by machine. Made by Tom Tisdell, Cambridge, Mass. Photo, Dave Congalton.

Ladies' hat, made from five pieces of English tanned 4 ounce cowhide; machine sewn. Notice the decorative use of machine stitching around the brim. The hatband is secured with thread. Courtesy of Button's Buckskins, West Danville, Vt. Photo, Phil Grey.

3-piece men's leather vest with a front opening. This vest is held together by rawhide lacing and has a front buckle closing arrangement. Notice that the edges aren't turned, but are left as they are after being cut. Made by the author. Photo, Larry Hyman.

Advanced Leather Garment Projects

Hats, skirts, coats, jackets, dresses, trousers, and jerkins should be tackled after you've gotten the feeling of leather garment construction. Throughout this chapter you'll find illustrations of many garments in leather; all of these garments were made by hand by individual craftsmen.

Don't hesitate to take on a more involved garment construction. This chapter has given you the basic technical information which pertains exclusively to leather, as opposed to other fabrics. If you've sewn with other fabrics, and you apply the techniques in this chapter, you'll have no trouble with even the most complicated constructions. For every garment illustrated in this chapter, you'll be able to find ready-made patterns of nearly equal style for use on leather. And then, if you do take the time to read the additional pamphlets and books recommended, you'll prepare yourself with full confidence.

For Men Only

In almost every leather shop I've visited while researching this book, I've found that the male proprietor shies away from garment construction in favor of employing women to handle this aspect of his business. Something's happening to the tradition of men performing as tailors. The "something" has got to stop!

For the males who read this book, I have a few brave and private comments to make. I've found that constructing a woman's skirt from leather is every bit as challenging as cobbling a pair of sandals. I'm altogether aware that the prospect of mastering the techniques of hand and machine garment construction seems terrifying to many men. Many of us look upon garment sewing as some sort of mysterious female secret—something akin to what some men consider to be the mysteries of cooking, kitchens, and aprons. Well, I'm here to tell you that garment construction, and the ability to handle patterns, as well as a sewing machine, is no different from setting the carburetor adjustment on the lawnmower; it takes a basic mechanical skill which most men seem to have a surplus of anyway. There are courses in sewing and garment construction being offered by almost every high school, college, agricultural extension service, sewing machine manufacturer, and even by church groups throughout the country.

Procedural Reminders

The following is a list of procedural reminders gathered with the help of practical experience, and the assistance of the Simplicity Pattern Company, the Coats and Clark Thread Company, and the Tandy Leather Company.

Cut the pattern pieces with a leather shears, double checking that all seam allowances are trimmed to ⅜".

All corners should be cut round—not square.

When sewing, double-check the machine setting on scrap. Use a size 14 or 16 needle with either silk or heavy–duty mercerized cotton thread. The machine tension should have a slightly loosened balance, and you should be stitching (for garments) at approximately 8 to 10 stitches per inch. If your machine has an adjustment for the presser foot, adjust the presser foot to the weight or thickness of the skins and let the leather ease through the machine—don't stretch it. For more information on thread, needle, and machine techniques—see the chapters, *Sewing and Lacing* and *Machine Tools*.

If you feel you need a guideline on the leather in order to produce a straight path in stitching, use the straight edge of masking tape.

As you begin to assemble the garment pieces, it helps to press as you sew, but remember not to use steam. Simply iron over brown paper or a pressing cloth on the flesh side of the hide.

Elk and buckskin are a bit stretchier than other leathers. When using these leathers on slacks or trousers, and in order to avoid baggy knees, it's recommended that before the hide is cut, you soak the hide in water, and then tack it to a wall or board and stretch it tightly as you tack. This sounds a bit unorthodox, but many craftsmen using these two leathers follow this procedure. This homemade prestretching technique eliminates the problem of knees stretching and becoming baggy.

After the pattern pieces are cut out, any construction details from the pattern that you want recorded on the leather should be recorded on the flesh side with chalk.

Darts: Press or tap slash darts open, and cement them down with rubber cement, tapping them flat with a mallet after they are cemented. If cut edges appear too bulky, these can be beveled. See Figure 64.

Seams: Figure 65 illustrates the technique of stitching, cementing, and pressing seams by tapping them with a rawhide mallet. For shape retention on seams, it helps to sew rayon seam tape the full length of the seam. Cut the tape to the exact length of the seam, paper clip the tape over the center of the seam, and then stitch. After stitching the seam, press or tap it open with a mallet, and then rubber cement the excess, and tap it flat again as illustrated in Figure 65. This procedure should be followed on all seams: front and center back seams, shoulder seams, and sleeve seams. After the seam is cemented and pounded flat, lift it up again and let it fall back into a natural fold. This helps to eliminate excess tension.

Curved Seams: After stitching curved seams, remove excess bulk by cutting notches along the excess, as indicated in Figure 66. When cutting the notches, be careful not to cut into the stitch.

Always tie thread ends—never back–stitch.

Hems on leather garments are never hand sewn. The usual procedure is to make them 1" to 2" wide, press or fold them over, and then cement the upper half of

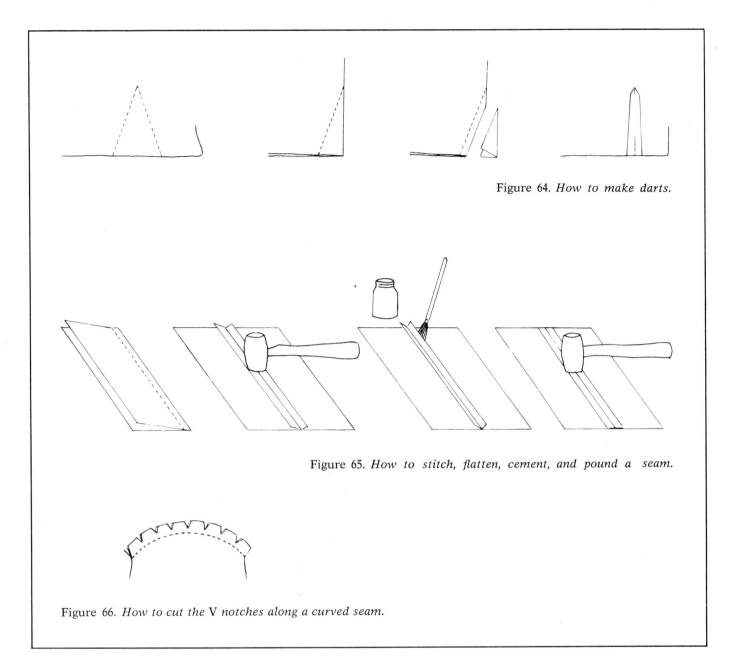

Figure 64. *How to make darts.*

Figure 65. *How to stitch, flatten, cement, and pound a seam.*

Figure 66. *How to cut the* V *notches along a curved seam.*

the hem width, and pound it flat in the same manner as with seams. On the hem of a flared skirt, you'll have to cut slits every 6″ to 8″ along the hem excess in order to keep it flat when you turn and cement it down.

When attaching a fabric lining to a leather facing, you can either glue the lining under the edge of the facing, or bind the facing by slip–stitching the lining to the binding.

On sleeves, follow the procedure normally used in the construction of any fabric sleeve; except where the sleeve is normally basted in place on other fabrics, it can be cemented in place with leather, again using rubber cement. Once the sleeve fits properly, it can be sewn in place in the same manner as with other leather seams.

Sleeve linings are treated in the same manner as with other fabrics—they are attached by stitching them in at the neck and cuff by hand.

On buttonholes, try the construction method out ahead of time on scrap. Lightweight leather can have either machine or hand bound buttonholes.

Rubber cement is recommended for all garment seams because of its flexibility. A small brush, or even an ear syringe (which can be purchased in a drugstore) is recommended for an applicator.

Use a ball of dried rubber cement (pour some out on glass to dry) to remove excess rubber cement on leather. You can also use benzene or carbon tetrachloride.

For greater detail on any of the above procedures, I suggest you read Krohn and Schwebke's book, *How to Sew Leather, Suede, Fur.*

CHAPTER EIGHTEEN

Handbags

Rather than provide step–by–step instructions on how to make a handbag, this chapter will discuss materials, techniques, and design suggestions applicable to all handbags, regardless of style. As one can see from quickly browsing among the photos in this chapter, there are an almost endless number of handbag styles—to select only one of them, for the purpose of providing step–by–step instruction, would be entirely misleading to the reader. If the reader learns to understand the principles of handbag design, he can then use these principles in the construction of every bag style.

To work as a total design, a handbag must create a harmony between style and function. A unique handbag style, no matter how attractive or innovative it might be to the eye, is of little value to its owner if it provides difficult access, is clumsy to wear, or is shaped in such a way that it has no value as a container or receptacle. The primary function of a handbag, after all, is to serve as a container in which objects can be conveniently carried.

Unfortunately, with styles as they are, women aren't blessed with the male convenience of pockets in their garments. Moreover, women have been known, not infrequently, to lug around a few more personal objects than the average male does. The point I'm getting at is that many handbag designers are men, and men aren't confronted with the task of having to cart a handbag on buses, into shopping centers, or phone booths. The handbag is exclusively a female accessory. The designer is well advised to keep this in mind at all times. He must consider the problem of access (how easy is it to open and close the bag), the problem of transporting the bag (does it conveniently fit over the arm, rest in the hand, or remain up on the shoulder, as the case may be?) and the problem of how well the bag functions as a container.

It would be a valid exercise for every male who anticipates designing a handbag to take the time to unload the contents of one in order to discover for himself just exactly what most women demand from the bag as a container. You're likely to find an over-abundant supply of tissues, a billfold, a key case, a can of hair spray, a brush, a collection of jewelry, a pair of gloves, a child's toy, a number of small bottles containing either pills or cosmetics—and the list goes on. At the same time, a potential handbag designer would do well to place the average "loaded" handbag on the scales in order to discover just how much stress is being applied to handbag seams and straps. The result of such an experiment would be to discover that most women use a handbag as a substitute suitcase, and no matter how small or large the bag is, it's more than likely to be filled to capacity at all times.

What all this means in terms of design is that a handbag must do the tasks every woman expects of it and, above all, it must be constructed with the expectation that it will encounter maximum abuse and maximum internal stress. A handbag, then, is definitely not an item of frill. It has a very specific and practical function, but it can still be designed as a visually attractive object.

Styles

Basically, there are three general types of handbags—the clutch bag, the arm bag, and the shoulder bag. The type of bag in each instance is determined by how the bag is carried—in the hand, on the arm, or from the shoulder. And then, within each general type, there are a number of variations. For example, a clutch bag can be designed for either formal or informal wear; the arm bag can be designed to be worn either on the arm, or carried in the hand when suspended from a handle or strap; and the shoulder bag can either be exclusively a shoulder bag, or it can be designed with an adjustable strap that makes it both an arm bag and a shoulder bag. And then too, the shoulder bag can be designed as a double-pouch saddlebag where there are actually two smaller bags joined together by a saddle–like shoulder strap.

The type of handbag is in direct proportion to the size of the bag. The clutch bag is the smallest; it's used primarily for special occasions when a woman wants to carry along only a bare minimum—perhaps a billfold, lipstick, and comb. The arm bag is usually an intermediate–sized bag, and is restricted in size by the fact that its weight must be carried from the hand or arm. The shoulder bag is generally the largest of the three bag types inasmuch as it has the strongest body position of support. Although there are exceptions to these general size and type relationships, every exception is still made within a framework; in other words, a given shoulder bag might be only small–to–medium in size, but a clutch bag will never be large.

Within each of the three general bag types, there are a great many bag styles. Several things determine style: the type of leather, the way in which the bag is constructed, whether or not the bag has a fringe, whether the bag closes with a flap, or closes with a drawstring, the type of findings and hardware used

Shoulder bag, duffle style; with a leash-type shoulder strap. Made by Tom Tisdell, Cambridge, Mass. Photo, Dave Congalton.

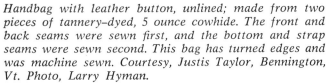

Handbag with leather button, unlined; made from two pieces of tannery–dyed, 5 ounce cowhide. The front and back seams were sewn first, and the bottom and strap seams were sewn second. This bag has turned edges and was machine sewn. Courtesy, Justis Taylor, Bennington, Vt. Photo, Larry Hyman.

Handbag with leather button, lined. The flap is smooth grained on both sides, and the button was punched out with an arch punch. Courtesy of Justis Taylor, Bennington, Vt. Photo, Larry Hyman.

on the bag—and so on. Style, then, is a specific consideration which applies to one given bag, whereas type is a general category applying to all bags.

In recent style trends, there's been a flurry of smaller bags—bags of about clutch size—even though these bags may end up as arm or shoulder bags. This flurry, although it may last a while, is a deviation from traditional bag sizes. As a general rule of thumb, the clutch bag is used by all ages of women because it serves a specific function; the arm bag is used by older women and working girls; and the shoulder bag, in terms of sales statistics, seems to be more popular with younger women. These are important considerations to keep in mind when designing bags.

Tools

Leather for handbags can be cut with a pair of leather shears. Most raw leather edges on handmade bags are turned under ⅜″ to ½″. You'll need contact cement, a skiving tool, and either a mallet or a rolling pin to flatten the turned edges. Bag seams are either sewn on heavy–duty sewing machines, or sewn by hand. Depending on how you sew your seams, you'll either need access to a machine or you'll need thread, lace, and a needle. Straps and flaps can be riveted, cemented, snapped, or sewn in place depending upon the designer's preference. The strap and flap arrangement will therefore require the use of planned findings, including such considerations as strap rings, strap hangers, and flap locking devices. A Tandy catalog, or one of the other findings suppliers listed at the back of the book will provide information on these findings. And then too, depending on the style, you may require the use of a revolving punch, or the oblong, or bag, punch. Unless you purchase tannery-dyed leathers, you'll also require the usual dyes and finishing supplies. (See the chapter, *Dyeing, Finishing, Care, and Cleaning*).

Leather

Of all the leather accessory items available as projects, the handbag is subjected to the most use and abuse. Handbag leather should therefore be of fine quality, and be able to resist scuffing and wear. There's no point for the hand craftsman to design handbags on the principle of planned obsolescence. The woman who wears a handcrafted bag pays more for it than she would for a factory bag, and she therefore has every right to expect that the leather in that bag will last.

You can of course design suede bags, and bags made from splits, but you must keep in mind that once the bag leaves your studio, it may well end up on the floor of a car in the middle of winter—with dirty, melting snow staining the surface. If you use suedes or splits, then the design of the bag should indicate bag type, or that it's intended for use on special occasions or when dressing up. I'm not trying to degrade suedes and splits as a material for handbags, but only trying to point out that this leather should blend with bag type and use.

The most common leather weight used in handbags runs between 5 to 6 ounces. Most craftsmen purchase handbag leather which is already tannery dyed. There's an abundance of rich shades in browns, greens, tans, and even embossed grains in cowhide and other leathers. I suggest you purchase leather especially tanned for use in handbags; leather that has a special tannery finish to provide maximum scuff resistance while at the same time being supple. There's no point in trying to take belting leather, or a dry, oak tanned leather and adapting it to use in handbags when tanners have already perfected a quality especially for handbags.

Most craftsmen make the bag straps and the pocket flaps from the same leather as the body of the bag. In order for a strap to have strength—at least when it's made from the same leather as the bag body—it must be turned under at the edges to provide a double thickness. This involves either cementing or sewing. Some craftsmen prefer to avoid this labor when making bags, and for that reason, they use a round, industrial leather belting for straps and handles. Belting is sold on spools, and runs from ⅜″ in diameter and up. One variety is sold by the United Shoe Machine Company listed at the back of the book under *Suppliers*.

Bag Patterns and Construction Techniques

The usual procedure in making a bag pattern is to work up the style in a sketch, determine the bag size, number and location of seams, method of construction, number of parts, and then begin a pattern on either brown paper or a light tagboard. I suggest that before you complete a pattern, you actually make a finished sample bag out of pattern paper, including sewing together the paper parts. This way there'll be no guesswork when it comes to transferring the paper pattern onto the leather.

The simplest bag is the bag with the least number of seams, perhaps only two side seams, or at most, a bottom seam and two side seams. A bag with a minimum number of seams will of course consume the greatest quantity of leather from the hide. For example, with shoulder bags, such as the handbags with leather buttons illustrated in this chapter, you may only be able to get two bags from the hide. If the use of this much volume seems too expensive for your pocketbook, I suggest that you design your bags with the maximum number of seams and parts. In this way, you'll be able to work with smaller pieces; but of course, you'll run into more labor, and the number of seams may have an effect on the design unless they're placed to blend with the lines of the bag. For example, a bag pattern can be designed to include the flap and bag body in one piece of leather, leaving only the strap as a second piece. To cut down on the volume of leather consumed by two–piece bag construction, you can design the bag so that the flap is a separate piece which is sewn or riveted onto the body of the bag during construction.

Of the many bags illustrated in this book, perhaps the bag with the simplest pattern construction is the

Mexican leather handbag illustrated on page 150. This design, or an adaptation of this design, might be a good place for a beginner to start. The bag consists of nothing more than two leather circles cut from 5 to 6 ounce smooth grain tannery–dyed cowhide. The bag is unlined. The circles have a 14″ diameter. The strap hole is cut from within the circle by cutting the hole out of one circle, and cutting just the matching arc line on the other circle; the arc line on the second circle becomes the flap of the purse when folded through the hole in the first circle. The two circles face each other (grain side in), and are held together with a ½″ strip of the same bag leather that has been laced in a web–style around the circumference of the bag. This bag does not even require the use of cement. The lacing slits were measured at equal intervals around the circumference of the circle, exactly duplicated on each piece, and were cut through with an X-Acto knife blade. The band of webbing was then laced in place tightly, and the two webbing ends tucked on the inside of the bag. The bag was then turned inside out, and the webbed ends were tacked in place with cement. A simple method of construction, but an effective design.

Lining

Many craftsmen prefer to line at least the underside of handbag flaps, while others prefer to line the whole bag. A flap lining is simply cut from the same leather (or if you prefer, from a lighter–weight leather in the same color) to the size of the flap (ending at the flap bend line), and then sewn to the flap by hand or machine inside out—grain side to grain side. You can either sew the lining close to the edge, leaving almost no margin, or you can run the stitch as much as ¾″ in from the edge in order to fold the excess back on itself and cement it down. The flap is then turned right side out and is complete. If you decide to fold the excess edges back on themselves, you should cut out V notches along the circumference, as described in detail in the garment chapter. Folding and cementing is really no better than sewing close to the edge, except that you'll eliminate more pucker in the circumference when the parts are turned right side out.

The point in lining any part of a bag is to give that part more body. Lining the flap will give it added physical weight and will naturally make it hang closer to the bag.

Lining a whole bag simply requires facing each piece of outside leather with a piece of lining leather, flesh side to flesh side. Most craftsmen simply cement their bag lining in place with contact cement. Once the pattern pieces are lined as you want them, you can then proceed with the final construction.

Dividers

A few craftsmen insist upon incorporating a divider into their handbags. This divider separates the inside of the bag into sections. A divider is cut as a matching piece to the bag and sewn into place at the same time the seams of the bag are sewn. You must be careful to see that the divider piece is placed properly—so that it will end up as a center piece, and not be left hanging outside the bag after it's sewn together and turned right side out. If you have any doubt about the placement of a divider, I suggest you make a miniature bag out of onionskin paper, staple the parts together inside out as you'd sew a bag, and then turn it right side out to check proper placement.

Seams

Most bag seams are sewn inside out by sewing grain side to grain side either by hand or by machine, and then turning the bag right side out. The seam construction is the same for bags and garments. As when lining a flap, you can either sew your seams close to the edge so there'll be no excess to later cement, or you can sew them ½″ to ¾″ in from the edge and then cement down the excess. The further in from the outside edge you sew your seams, the more you'll accumulate excess bulk leather, and the more you'll reduce the inside dimensions of the bag.

If you don't use a flap lining, I suggest you plan to turn down and cement all exposed raw edges such as the flap edges, and any other unsewn edges. This gives those edges more body, and a much more finished look. If you do turn raw, unsewn edges, you of course will have to allow for this extra leather in your original pattern.

Side and bottom seams should never be double stitched, as this has a tendency to tear the leather. I suggest you use inside rivets as reinforcements at the points of greatest seam stress; where the straps attach to the bag, and at corners. The rivets should be set in place along the seam line toward the edge side of the stitching before the bag is turned right side out. In this way the rivets won't show. The more you can bolster up the stress points on seams, the longer the bag will last. Don't forget that the bag will most likely be used as a small suitcase when it comes to actual container weight.

Curved seams should be treated in exactly the same manner as when sewing curved seams on garments. This involves cutting the small V notches along the curve in order to reduce leather bulk.

There are so many variations in bag styles, that it's impossible to lay down hard and fast rules as to construction procedure. Very often, a baseball X stitch is used when hand lacing bag side seams, and in most cases where this stitch is used, the side seams simply overlap one another and the stitch runs through two thicknesses of leather. Again, if you have the slightest doubt as to construction procedure, make the whole bag up ahead of time in paper as a trial run.

Fringe

In several areas of the book, including this chapter on handbags, you'll find photos of projects trimmed with a leather fringe. This fringe is nothing more than a separate band of leather sewn into the project after it's been fringed into strips with a pair of leather

Handbag, belt-style; machine stitched. Made by Bort Carleton, Boston, Mass. Photo, Dave Congalton.

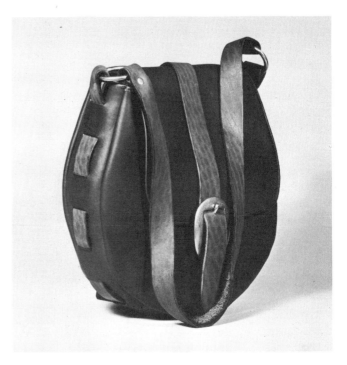

Handbag with a brass buckle, incorporating two colors of leather; dark brown for the body of the bag, and a mottled hemp color for the strap. The buckle is made by North & Judd. Made by Bort Carleton, Boston, Mass. Photo, Dave Congalton.

Handbag; belt is nonfunctional and was added only for the sake of design. Made by Bort Carleton, Boston, Mass. Photo, Dave Congalton.

Handbag with saddlebag-style flap. This bag is made entirely of leather and is completely free of metal hardware. The flap resembles a saddlebag and is a mottled, hemp-brown color, while the body of the bag is a darker, chocolate brown. Made by Bort Carleton, Boston, Mass. Photo, Dave Congalton.

Fringe bag made from split cowhide. Notice how the shoulder strap was turned over and cemented. Made by Tom Tisdell, Cambridge, Mass. Photo, Dave Congalton.

Handbag with a strap made from industrial belting; when the center loops are pulled tight, the bag closes. Made by Bort Carleton, Boston, Mass. Photo, Dave Congalton.

shears. Simply lay the band out on the work table, measure and mark the location of fringe widths (they should be equal), and then cut the strips with the shears.

Straps

There are several variations in strap styles and in the method in which straps are attached to, or become part of, the bag. Arm or hand bags normally have round straps; shoulder bags normally have flat straps, like a belt—but this isn't a hard and fast rule, and there are always exceptions. The round strap is designed for minimum thickness so that it can be conveniently carried in the hand; the flat strap, on the other hand, is wider in order to provide surface area and an even weight distribution when it rests on the shoulder. Arm or hand bag straps usually run from 14″ to 18″ in over–all length. 3″ to 4″ of this over–all length is used up inside the bag when the strap is fastened to it. In other words, 1½″ to 2″ on each end of the 14″ to 18″ strap is used up in securing the strap to the bag. Straps on shoulder bags usually run from 32″ to 36″ in over–all length with the same amount of strap length (3″ to 4″) being used up in attaching the strap to the bag.

A round strap for use on arm or hand bags can be made from industrial belting, or it can be made by wrapping a strip of leather around a strap filler cord and sewing the two sides of the strip into a seam around this filler cord. A filler cord is actually a stuffing that creates the roundness in the strap; it can be ordered from handbag suppliers. Using filler cord requires much more labor than using round industrial belting does. If the bag has a top opening without a flap, two straps are usually used (one on each side of the opening) to give the bag balance. If the bag has a flap, or is light in weight, one strap is usually enough. The clutch bag may not need any handle, or at most, a single handle.

A flat strap is cut with either a draw gauge or a plough gauge in the same manner as one would strip a belt. If the leather is thick enough (from 5 to 6 ounces), the edges have enough body without being turned. On the other hand, if you use a lighter weight leather for straps, you should plan to turn the length edges under along both sides of the strap and either cement these turned edges down, or stitch them down by hand or machine. Turning the edges on thin leather adds body to the strap and gives the edges a finished appearance. As an example when using thin leather, if you wanted a finished strap width of 1½″, you would cut a strip 3″ wide, and then turn under ¾″ along each edge.

Obviously, handles and straps on handbags need not be made of leather. Many other attractive materials are regularly used by craftsmen—from braided rope, to wood, to solid and chain–link brass. There are also dozens of ready–made handles sold by handbag suppliers. As long as the strap complements the bag design, and is convenient to carry, it makes little difference what it's made of. Straps allow for a great deal of design innovation and very often set the style for the bag. There are all kinds of strap possibilities; recently, I've seen some very attractive shoulder bags with straps made from factory–made dog leashes tipped with brass findings. Still another possibility is to design the bag in such a way that the strap is not an attachment, but is an integral part of the bag—one piece of leather for combined bag and strap.

Straps can be attached to the bag in several ways: to the outside of the bag, to the inside of the bag, or they can be run from the outside to the inside through holes punched into the sides of the bag with an oblong, or bag, punch; the strap ends can be riveted to the bag, sewn or laced to the bag, or mounted through strap hangers such as rings, dees, or rectangular metal keepers that run through both the bag and a loop made at both ends of the strap. Whichever method you use to secure the strap to the bag, you must always remind yourself to arrange the strap for maximum strength. Don't be afraid to cement leather reinforcement swatches to the inside of the bag to give the bag a greater thickness where it joins the strap. And don't hesitate to use concealed rivets as additional reinforcement.

If you browse through the photographs in this chapter and study the construction of the bags pictured, you'll be able to see for yourself the many variations in straps and methods of attachment.

Flap Closing Devices

If the bag has a flap, you can either let it hang loose, or you can design a closing device (Figure 67). Oh yes, there are all sorts of commercial "ticky–tacky" brass closing devices sold by handbag suppliers, but these are for factory–made bags, not for handmade bags. The consumer expects more from the hand craftsman.

The flap lock is where you can let your imagination run wild. You can loop the bag with a belt, make your own buttons to close the flap, or you can use one of hundreds of antique hardware pieces to make your bag a one–of–a–kind item.

One word of caution; just don't overdo the amount of hardware you hang on the bag. As mentioned earlier, many craftsmen hate to see any kind of hardware on a bag; they feel that it violates the esthetic appeal of leather. Others, who do use unique hardware, do so with good taste. Just don't try to substitute hardware for bag design; the bag should be able to speak for itself; the closing device should be a savory complement.

Care of Handbags

Suedes and splits can be brushed clean with a suede brush or with fine–grain sandpaper rubbed gently over the bag surface. If you try one of the many commercial suede cleaners, be sure to test it first on an inside section of the bag in order to make sure that the cleaner doesn't remove the dye color.

The leather on smooth grained bags can be kept rich and supple by regular applications of a leather conditioner, such as saddle soap, Meltonian Shoe Cream, or even Vaseline Petroleum Jelly.

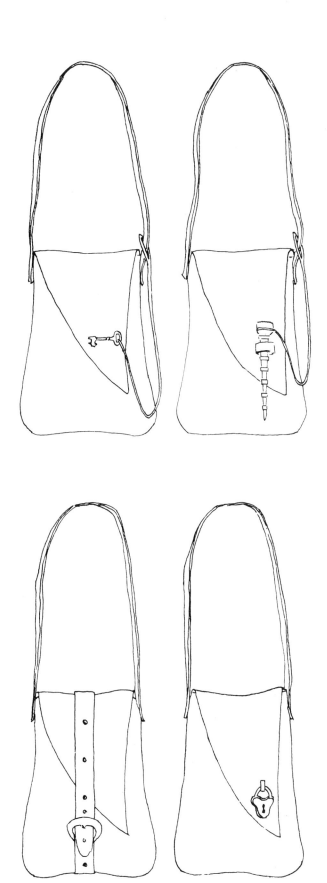

Figure 67. *A bag showing a variety of possible closing devices: a brass key, a wooden bobbin, a belt riveted around the bag, and an antique lock.*

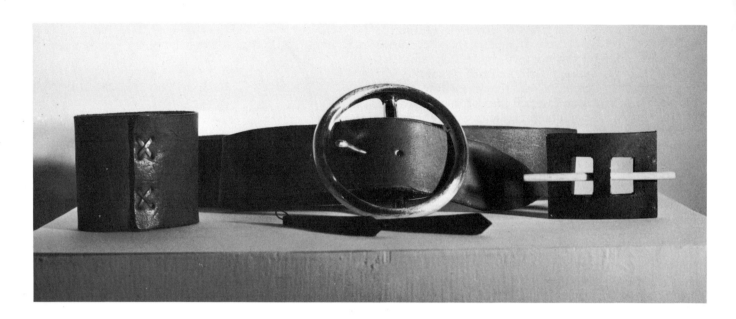

(Above) Belt, armband, earrings, and hair piece. Photo, the author. (Below) Three belts made from 8 ounce bridle back. The belt on the far left has a brass ring buckle; the center belt has a standard, North & Judd brass buckle; the belt on the right has a handmade buckle. The belts and the keepers were sewn entirely by hand. Made by Tom Tisdell, Cambridge, Mass. Photo, Dave Congalton.

CHAPTER NINETEEN

Belts, billfolds, watchbands, and other small accessories

The craftsman who's willing to explore the application of leather in its widest capacity of esthetic and functional use is the craftsman who'll benefit the most, not only in terms of monetary return, but also in terms of design discovery. Exploring the many uses of leather has a boomerang effect on the craftsman; the more he explores, the more he discovers. No matter how elementary a project may seem, there's still room for discovery—new techniques, new designs, and improved adaptations of existing designs. It's never the object that's the visual bore—it's the design of that object which makes it tiring. A necklace pendant, a billfold, or even a leather bracelet might sound like an elementary project, but believe me, it's far from elementary if the craftsman takes the time to use his mental wheels of originality. This country needs more designers who care about the visual appearance of the objects which we take for granted. I'll give you one good example of the reincarnation of one of these traditional leather items.

The watchband has been around since the invention of the watch. Until recently, all leather watchbands looked pretty much alike—they consisted of a simple straight strap with a buckle on one end. For generations, the watchband has looked exactly the way most people assumed a watchband should. The watchband was one of those small objects taken for granted by the design industry; as a straight leather strap with a buckle, it was assumed to have reached its peak of perfection.

Recently, a group of contemporary leather designers resurrected the design of the watchband. Watchbands, from sophisticated to zany, are now available in almost every drugstore and department store in this country. The leather craftsman started the move; he began to design wide straps, double–mounting straps, interchangeable straps, and then began laminating brightly colored patent leathers to produce psychedelic watchbands. The straps available today are a far cry from the straight leather straps which were available only a few short years ago. This same transformation has taken place in the construction of leather belts, leather bracelets, leather pendants for both men and women, and in a number of other, similar, leather items. The potential for design and redesign in leather is unlimited.

The point here is that nothing currently being made from leather is a visual bore. The entire leather industry is on fire with new ideas. The leather crafts-man's visual perception and awareness are now in their maturity. There's no longer any room for the summer camp leathercraft mentality that sets children to snapping together loop belt kits, or lacing the edges of prepunched comb cases.

The items covered in this chapter are all in the process of design rebirth; and this rebirth is just beginning. There's still a great deal of room left for each of my readers to make his own contribution. Don't, for a single second, make the false assumption that any of the items covered in this chapter are too "craftsy" in the negative sense, or too elementary. Again, no matter what the item is, if it seems to be too elementary for you, the fault lies with the designer, not with the project. I challenge you to accept the responsibility of improving even what you find in this book!

As a final note of introduction, many of the projects covered in this chapter, with the exception of belts, can be made out of scrap leather. Don't throw away scrap—even the smallest piece of leather can be worked up into attractive necklace beads or earrings.

Belts

A number of belt styles are illustrated in this section—belts using manufactured and handmade buckles, a braided belt, an all–leather belt using slots as a closing device, and belts using novelty closing devices (Figure 68). For additional information on the construction of belts, I'd suggest you re–read sections of the chapter on findings and fasteners where buckles, loops, rings, clasps, keepers, dees, and belt tips are discussed and illustrated, and the chapters on edging, folding, and creasing, where detailed instructions are included on how to put an edge on leather, using a belt as the example.

Basically, a belt is a leather strap that girds the waist. It used to be that belts were worn in order to hold one's trousers up, but this is no longer the literal truth. Belts are now an item of apparel—they're a distinctive design accessory—the job that they do in holding up one's trousers has become a secondary function. Clothing styles (skirts, slacks, jeans, jumpers, and even overblouses), are now designed which use belts as purely a decorative accessory. The revolution in belt design has even forced manufacturers to enlarge the size of the traditional belt loops on slacks and skirts. Most men's slacks will now accommodate

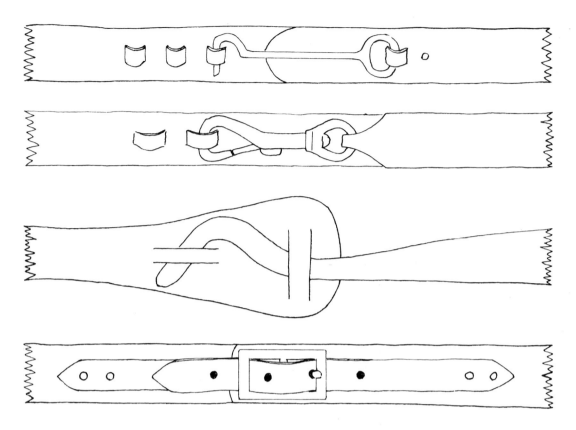

Figure 68. *A selection of belt fastening styles: a brass door hook with leather loops; a boat clasp purchased from a marine supplier; an all-leather belt with no hardware; and a double-strap belt.*

belts up to 1½″ to 1¾″ wide, whereas a few years ago these loops would accept nothing wider than 1″ belts. Hip–hugger styles, both men's and women's, often eliminate belt loops altogether, and are designed to be worn with loose belts as wide as 2½″ to 3″.

At the moment, clothing designers have gone a bit belt mad; anything and everything seems to go. I've seen belt buckles made from bull rings, from harness brass, from sailing boat hardware, from keys, from door latches, from fishing hardware; I've even seen belts braided into rope–like leather riding crops. Then there are belt keepers, belt tips, and even belt eyelets. Freedom in belt design is unlimited.

If the proper leather is used in making belts, the leather will usually conform and adjust itself to the circumference of the wearer's waist. This fact eliminates the necessity of having to cut belts to special order—or cutting them wider at one point along their length than another. For the craftsman who hopes to sell belts, I suggest that unless belts are specially ordered by a specific individual, they be left untrimmed at the tip end. This makes it possible for every customer to be a potential buyer for each completed belt. To conclude a final belt sale, all you have to do is measure the customer, cut the tip end to size, dye the tip edges, burnish them, and punch in the buckle tongue holes. Most leather craftsmen follow this procedure in their shops. The excess which is eventually cut off the belt tip can later be used in making watchbands or bracelets.

Belt Tools

Belts are stripped off the hide with either a draw gauge or a plough gauge. To get a straight edge started on the hide, you'll also require the use of a steel–edge ruler (preferably at least 4′ long), and a square point leather knife. Depending upon the closing device, you'll need a supply of rivets, a rivet setter, snaps, a snap setter, or lacing, and a lacing needle. And you'll need a revolving leather punch to punch out the belt tip buckle tongue holes. For edging belts, you'll need one or more of the following: rough canvas, an edge beveler, an edge cutter, an edge creaser, a circle edge slicker used by hand, or a circle edge slicker mounted on an electric wheel. For dyeing and finishing, you'll need the usual supply of dyes, as well as Lexol, Meltonian Shoe Cream, Vaseline Petroleum Jelly, or a similar product for the final finish.

Belt Leather

The kind of belt leather you use will determine the finished quality of the belt. There should be no substitute for using only the best belt leather. Most craftsmen use 7 to 8 ounce cowhide for belts—either English bridal backs, or bridal butt ends. A few craftsmen use the less expensive belly section, primarily from horsehide. When selecting belt leather, keep away from both latigo tanned leather, and oak tanned leathers—latigo is too stretchy and oak is too stiff.

Belt leather should be supple. Good belt leather is sold by suppliers at a premium price. Don't be afraid of paying the premium price—you'll more than make up the difference in the quality of the finished belt.

Stripping a Belt from the Hide

The chapter on edging, folding, and creasing tools describes the procedure for stripping a belt with either the plough gauge or the draw gauge. You must begin by first making a straight edge across one side of your hide. The belts should run along the hide from head to tail. As you strip, I'd suggest you strip the whole length of the hide so as not to interrupt the straight edge. Belt widths vary from ½" up to 3" to 3½". If you go beyond 3" to 3½" wide, the consumer will encounter discomfort in wearing the belt, because it will begin to dig into the flesh of the hips and upper torso.

Belt Styles

The belt end designed to be used with a buckle can be secured around the buckle in several ways. It can either be riveted in place, sewn in place with an *X* stitch, using lacing, or it can be snapped in place in order to allow for interchangeable buckles. The section on buckles in the chapter, *Findings and Fasteners*, provides many technique pointers in attaching buckles.

A belt without a buckle is illustrated in Figure 68. The tip and end of this belt are designed so that the belt tip loops through the belt end in such a way that it becomes its own closing device. This style eliminates the use of hardware.

Another simple tip in making belts is to give the belt a trimmed edge by using either the edge cutter, or the edge creaser. This adds a trim line to the belt edge, making an inner border around the belt circumference. To use one of these tools, simply wet the belt, and carefully run the tool along the edge. When the belt dries, the edge line remains permanent. Be sure you press hard enough on the tool to make a distinctive line. This extra bit of effort is well worth it in terms of final professional appearance.

Braiding a Belt

The photograph of braided leather illustrates the technique of belt braiding. This belt braiding always looks mysterious to the consumer, as if it were one of the technical wonders of leathercraft, but in reality the technique is very simple. It can be used on belts, bracelets, and I've also seen it used on leather handles for ceramic teapots. Braiding is the last step in the normal construction of a belt. In other words the actual braiding is done after the belt has its buckle, its tip, is dyed, and is finished. But before the belt is dyed and finished, you'll first have to cut the braiding strips into the belt.

First decide where you want the braiding to appear—just on either side of the buckle across the front, or across the sides, or all the way around the belt. Mark with a pencil on the raw leather whichever section of the belt you want braided, then simply divide that section into three equal parts. The separate parts should not exceed ½" strips, otherwise the braiding gets a bit tough. In other words, you can successfully braid a belt that does not exceed a 1½" over-all width. Using a ruler, draw two penciled lines along the length of the belt in order to divide the width of the belt into three equal strips. Now lay the belt flat on your workbench, place a steel straight-edge along the first line, and cut that line all the way through the leather thickness. Repeat this procedure for the second line. You should now have a continuous belt that has a center section consisting of three, independent equal strips.

At this point the belt should be dyed and finished, making certain that the inside edges of the braiding strips are also dyed and finished along with the outside edges of the belt. When this step is completed, you're ready to braid the belt.

The technique is exactly the same 3-strand braiding technique used by every child who wears a pigtail—it begins by placing the left strip over the center strip, and then right strip over center strip—and so on. As you braid, the other ends of the three strips will tangle; simply untangle them as you go along. In other words, if you braid from one end and untangle the other end, you'll eventually braid the full length of the

Braided leather, showing the technique of belt braiding. This is a close-up of a belt made from 8 ounce bridle back. Courtesy of the Om Leather and Sandal Shop, Aspen, Colo. Photo, Chuck Askren.

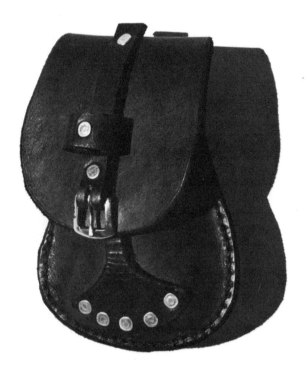

Belt bag, 8" long; made from undyed, 8 ounce cowhide, and hand sewn with the aid of a lacing pony. This type of bag is worn on the belt. Courtesy of the Om Leather and Sandal Shop, Aspen, Colo. Photo, Chuck Askren.

Belt bag with side pocket, unlined, 8" wide x 10" long; designed to be worn on the belt as a carry-all. Courtesy of the Om Leather and Sandal Shop, Aspen, Colo. Photo, Chuck Askren.

braiding strips. When the three strips are braided as tightly as possible, you can then even out the braid pattern along the length of the belt so that no one area is tighter than another. This is done simply by loosening the braid and adjusting the tightness evenly along the entire length of the belt.

Finishing a Belt

For additional tips on dyeing, graining, and finishing belts, I suggest you again refer to the chapter on dyeing and finishing. A belt should end up being very supple—the more supple it is, the more comfortably it will fit, and the more quickly it will sell. Many craftsmen finish a belt by giving it a final coating of Vaseline Petroleum Jelly. They rub Vaseline into the leather with their fingers, let it soak in for perhaps half an hour, wipe away the excess, and then wrap the belt around something like a wooden stairway rung and work it back and forth across the rung in order to induce additional flexibility. This final step requires extra time, but is well worth the finished results.

Billfolds

Basically, there are two types of billfolds in both men's and women's styles: the regular folding billfold and the pocket secretary billfold. The regular folding billfold normally runs from 9" x 3" open, to 9½" x 3½" open. The pocket secretary billfold normally runs from 7" x 7½" open, to 7½" x 8½" open (these are outside edge measurements). These are the sizes normally considered adequate to conveniently hold the variety of cards that one is required to carry around. If you want to make larger sizes for the he–man, or for the truck driver, you can of course extend these standard sizes.

For many years, handmade leather billfolds were stereotyped into the "tooled" western look category. By now, I think I've made my point quite clear that cowboy motifs in contemporary leather design have finally joined the era of the hooped skirt. Contemporary leather craftsmen are now devoting their energies toward new designs in billfolds, from the belt bags illustrated in this chapter, all the way up to experimenting with abstract dye colors, and even laminating tannery dyed colors and textures to exterior billfold surfaces. The billfolds in this chapter illustrate what can be done using rich, full grained cowhide in both the folding and pocket secretary styles. These examples, although very plain, come through loud and clear by virtue of their expressing the quality of the leather, rather than by doodads tooled onto the surface.

Billfolds allow for experimentation in lacing styles. The several laminated leather layers that make up billfolds create thick edges. These edges can be dressed with several of the lacing styles illustrated in the chapter, *Sewing and Lacing*, from the simple running stitch, to the loop or whip stitch, to even the popular double loop stitch.

There are a great number of accessory parts that are available for use on billfolds. I'm not sure these add much to the design, but they do accommodate the

(Above) Three billfolds. The lacing is round and is looped over the edges rather than used in a running stitch. Made by Tom Tisdell, Cambridge, Mass. Photo, Dave Congalton.

(Left) Two billfolds, pocket-secretary style; made from 5 ounce cowhide, and hand sewn on a lacing pony with 5-cord dacron thread. Courtesy of the Om Leather and Sandal Shop, Aspen, Colo. Photo, Chuck Askren.

(Below) Men's billfold. In order for this billfold to bend easily, it was necessary to cut the inner layer about ¼" shorter than the back piece. Courtesy of the Om Leather and Sandal Shop, Aspen, Colo. Photo, Chuck Askren.

man who is a card carrying organization joiner. The Tandy Leather Company supplies billfold backs, dividers, liners, prepunched kits, and several varieties of the plastic card-case insert.

Billfold Tools

Leather for billfolds can be cut with a pair of leather shears. If you'd like to dress up the edges on the inside compartment pieces, you'll need an edge creaser. To temporarily hold billfold parts together while punching lace holes, you'll need a supply of contact leather cement, and for punching lace holes you'll need thonging chisels and a rawhide mallet. Lacing used on billfolds is usually either flat or round, and most craftsmen prefer using the strong latigo lace. When lacing, you'll also need a lacing needle. And to complete the billfold, you'll need the usual supply of leather dyes and finishes.

Billfold Leather

Leather used in billfolds usually runs in thickness anywhere from as thin as 2 ounces up to as thick as 5 ounces. The billfolds in the photographs were made from 5 ounce cowhide. This is about as thick as one dare go without encountering problems in folding. Perhaps the most common weight used in billfolds runs from 3 to 4 ounces. The thicker the leather, the less likely the billfold will be to need any sort of lining to bolster up the thickness.

All types of leather are used for billfolds including splits, suedes, embossed grains, and smooth grains. And there are a great many hide species used as well, from deerhide to goat, from calf to pig, and from lamb to leathers tanned with the hair left intact. The two most important considerations in selecting leather for use in making billfolds is that the leather be supple enough to bend easily in half, producing a minimum bulk, and that the leather have a surface that will resist scuffing, because, don't forget, a billfold is subjected to continual sliding in and out of pockets and handbags.

Billfold Styles

A billfold can contain as many compartments as the craftsman is willing to design. Each additional compartment will add another layer to the thickness of the billfold. Compartments can be as simple as flaps, or as complicated as separate pockets, and then there are a great many ways to design flap or compartment edges; V shapes, straight edges, curved edges, and square edges. You can design a simple billfold like the ones illustrated here, or you can design complicated billfolds complete with key cases, stamp cases, and built-in coin snap purses. Generally, you must have one compartment for paper money, and at least two compartments for cards and licenses. Before you tackle the construction of a billfold, you must first decide on style—style in this context means number of compartments, design of compartment edges, and the type and style of lacing you intend to use. A Tandy

catalog will provide photographs of just about every billfold style ever designed. Use these Tandy photos to determine style; however, I don't recommend using the kit construction advertised on the same pages. Design your own billfolds; kits are for tired minds.

A billfold pattern can be made from lightweight tagboard and then traced from the pattern onto the leather. The section on folding and creasing in the chapter on tools will give you some additional pointers on why it's essential to make your inside money compartment piece a bit shorter than the outside billfold back piece—you must take into account the folded area, and the fact that the fold does consume length. To avoid problems, you can work the whole pattern up in tagboard, and then test the fold ahead of time on the pattern rather than on the leather. If the thickness of the tagboard equals the thickness of the leather, and the pattern works, then the billfold will also work.

Before you begin to lace, it's generally recommended to cement the parts of your billfold together with an edging of contact cement. Having the parts firmly secured will assist you in the punching of lace holes and in the actual lacing.

Watchbands

Watchbands are one of the simplest leather projects to make. The important point to remember is to dress the edges carefully, and if you prefer, to also run an edge creaser around the band edges for an added professional trim.

The photographs in this chapter illustrate a number of watchband styles. If a band is designed to be permanently attached to one watch, it can be secured with either rivets or laced in place with an X stitch. If you prefer using several interchangeable bands on one watch, you must then secure the band to the watch with small snaps.

At the moment, the most popular watchband styles are those incorporating the double strap idea—one thin strap mounted over a wide bracelet strap. These styles range in over-all widths of from 1½" to 3". The construction of the bands shown here should be self-explanatory. Buckles on men's bands usually run about ¾" wide, and on women's bands, from ⅜" to ½" wide.

When making a double watchband, the lower band should be made from something equal to belt leather —from 6 to 7 ounce cowhide is generally recommended. The top strap can be made from 4 to 5 ounce leather. On these double strap bands, the lower strap acts as a bracelet and a space of about ½" is usually left between the ends on the under side of the wrist. The top strap contains the buckle and therefore holds the lower strap in place. When attaching the buckle, I think it looks neater if it is placed so that it falls in the center of the lower strap division.

Another popular technique used on watchbands is to laminate patent leather as a veneer over thicker cowhide. Patent leather comes in an endless variety of bright colors, and many craftsmen design these patent veneers with snaps so that colors can be interchanged.

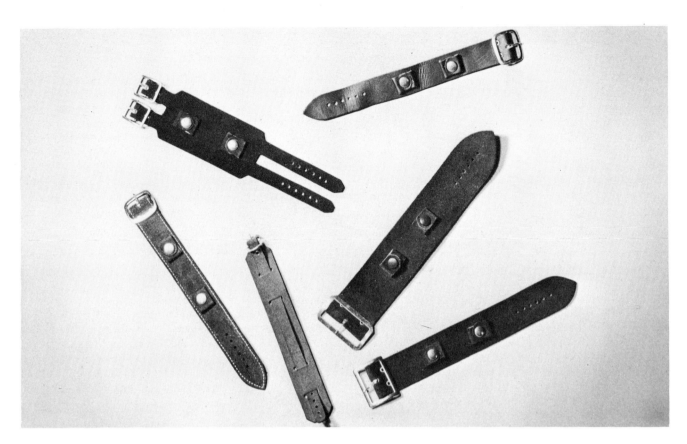

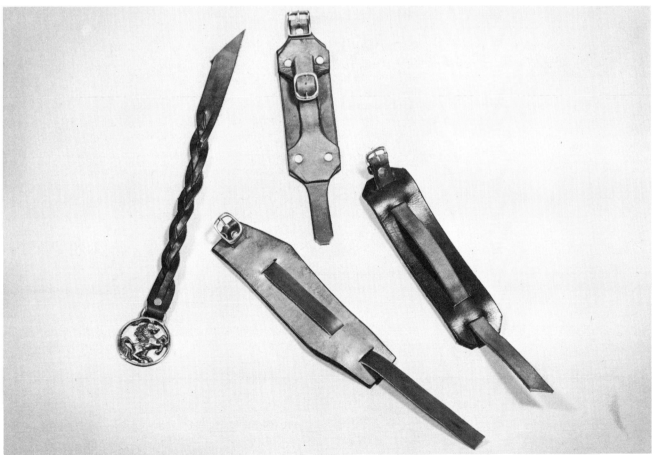

(Above) Selection of watchband styles. All but the top band were made from split cowhide. Made by Bort Carleton, Boston, Mass. Photo, Dave Congalton.

(Below) Three watchbands and one leather watch–fob; made from 7 to 8 ounce, hand–dyed belt leather. Made by Tom Tisdell, Cambridge, Mass. Photo, Dave Congalton.

(Above) Three leather bracelets made out of 8 ounce cowhide. All three show what can be done in the way of contemporary tooling design. The bracelet on the left was incised with a square motif and then roughed. The bracelet in the center and the one on the right were engraved with an awl blade after the leather had first been wet. Made by Tom Tisdell, Cambridge, Mass. Photo, Dave Congalton.

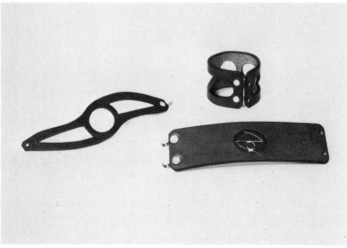

(Left) Three styles of leather bracelet; two use negative space to create the design, and the third incorporates brass wire into the design for an abstract motif. Courtesy of Justis Taylor, Bennington, Vt. Photo, Larry Hyman.

Bracelets

Leather bracelets are constructed in the same manner as watchbands; they're closed with either snaps, buckles, or rawhide. Bracelets are usually cut from belt scrap. One technique is to use cutouts, another is to develop abstract incised motifs with an awl, and still another technique is to braid a bracelet in the same manner as one would braid a belt. The trick to making an attractive bracelet is to take the extra time to burnish the bracelet edges to a fine, smooth surface. Leather bracelets provide an excellent outlet for experimentation in dyes, textures, tooling, and style.

Hair Barrettes

The illustrations in this chapter show a wide variety of styles in hair barrettes. Very often barrettes can be made from pieces of scrap leather, especially bottom sole leather on sandals. The dowel holes punched in barrettes are made with either an oval drive punch or a round drive punch. The trick to making barrettes so they won't slip is to make certain that the dowel holes are properly spaced. One way to determine proper spacing is to make a cardboard pattern of the barrette ahead of time and test the spacing with an actual dowel.

Two of the barrettes shown have a handmade brass dowel. The other barrettes illustrated use dowels made from ¼" round wooden dowels, the type sold in most lumber and hardware stores. These dowels run 4" to 5" long, are sharpened on both ends in an ordinary pencil sharpener, and are then dyed to match the barrette with regular leather dye. For the woman who prefers wearing two pony tails, you can make up two smaller barrettes, one to be worn on each pony tail.

Thickness is the basic ingredient for selection of leather for barrettes. The best is 12 to 14 ounce cowhide. The leather needs to have enough thickness to resist permanent bending. It's this resistance to permanent bending which provides the natural, spring-like action in holding the hair in place. If barrettes are made from dry leather such as an oak tanned cowhide, I suggest you lubricate the leather with Lexol before trying to bend it to fit the dowel. This initial lubrication will prevent dry leather from cracking. Again, scraps from bottom sandal soles make the best barrettes.

Because barrettes are made from thick leather, they look much better as finished projects if the edges are beveled with either an edge beveler or the curved blade of an X-Acto knife. I also prefer to dye barrette edges a darker shade than the surface, and to burnish the finished edges. This bit of extra attention presents a handsome finished piece.

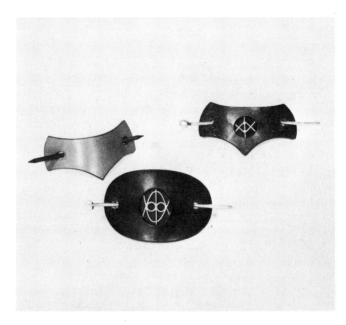

Three hair barrettes, made from 8 ounce cowhide. The barrette on the left incorporates leather with a ⅛" pine dowel sharpened on both ends with a pencil sharpener. The other two barrettes use brass dowels. Courtesy of Justis Taylor, Bennington, Vt. Photo, Larry Hyman.

Three hair barrettes. Made by Tom Tisdell, Cambridge, Mass. Photo, Dave Congalton.

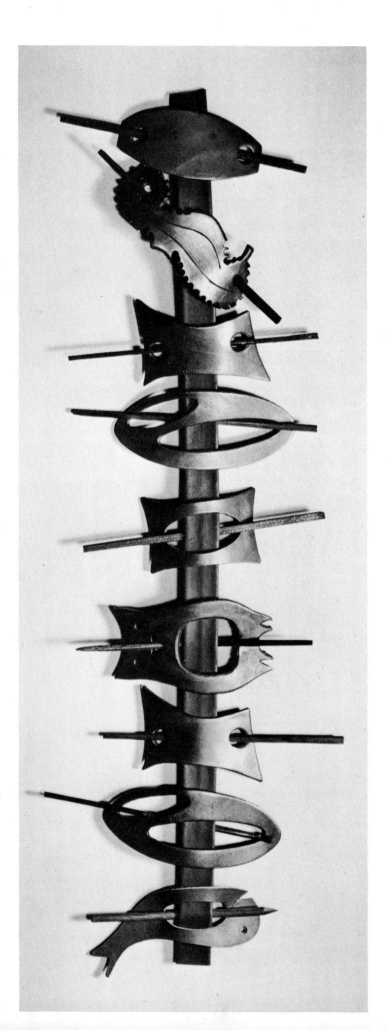

Pendants

Just about any leftover scrap leather is suitable for pendants. Most craftsmen generally begin a pendant with a scrap of something about 6 ounces thick and then build on it by laminating on layers of other textures, colors, and grains. There are literally no rules governing shapes and sizes of pendants. I usually let the shape of the first piece of scrap lead the way to the end design.

The photographs in this section illustrate several styles of pendants and necklace beads. The illustrations indicate the amount of freedom that can be exercised in developing color, texture, thickness, and related materials. I've seen leather pendants which combine old keys, old coins, and even abstract squiggles of dyed rawhide glued to the pendant surface. Leather rawhide lacing is the most common material used to suspend pendants.

One technique used in making pendants is to laminate several layers of thick cowhide together and then reduce it to a solid form by carving it with an X-Acto knife. I've also seen this same technique expanded where the craftsman uses alternate dye colors between layers of lamination. Still another technique in making pendants is to design a reversible pendant with a separate color and image on each side. A reversible pendant has the versatility of two single pendants.

An offshoot of the leather pendant is the leather pin, which is constructed in the same manner, but uses a clasp cemented to the back side so that it can be worn on a coat, sweater, or blouse rather than suspended around the neck. The jewelry findings suppliers listed at the back of the book will be able to supply you with the clasps used in making leather pins.

Hair barrettes. All of these pieces were cut from a die, using a clicker. The holes for the dowel in these types of hair pieces can be cut with either a round drive punch or an oval drive punch. Made by Bort Carleton, Boston, Mass. Photo, Dave Congalton.

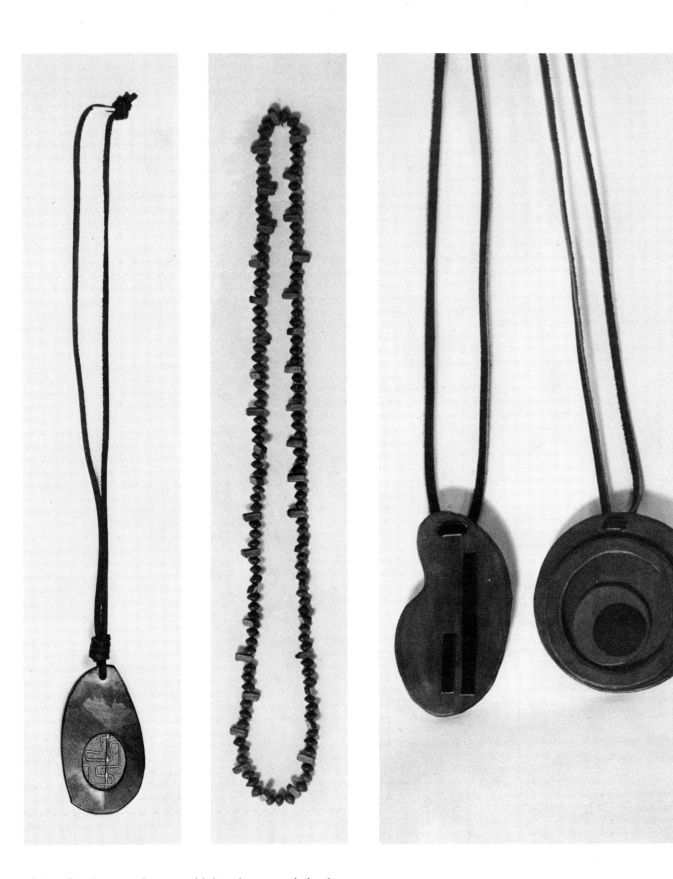

(Left) Leather pendant combining brass and leather. Courtesy of Justis Taylor, Bennington, Vt. Photo, Larry Hyman. (Center) Necklace combining leather beads and sandalwood seeds. Necklace and photo, courtesy of the author. (Right) Two leather pendants made from 12 ounce cowhide; both done as abstract reliefs and using rawhide lacing as a strap. Pendants and photo, courtesy of the author.

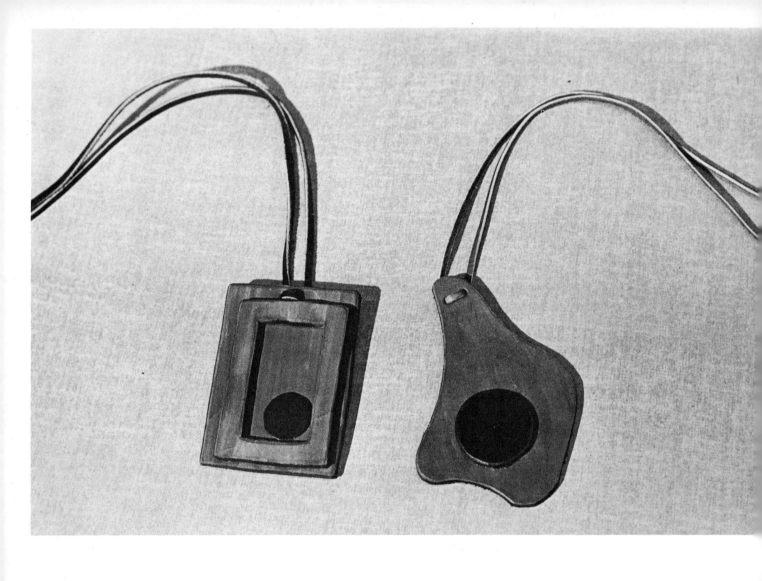

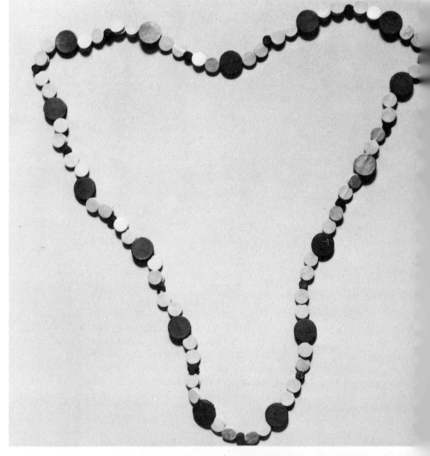

Earrings

Still another use of scrap is to make leather earrings. The photograph illustrates several shapes and styles. These earrings were designed to be worn with pierced ears. Earring loops, clasps, and wires can be ordered through the jewelry findings suppliers listed at the back of the book.

Additional Projects

Before concluding this chapter, I'd like to mention a few other attractive items that can be made out of leather. One is a single–piece, triangular head scarf made from 2 to 3 ounce garment leather with a ½" folded hem along the edges. The hem is either sewn down by machine, or cemented down with leather contact cement. This type of head scarf ties under the chin with two thin strips of the same leather knotted, riveted, or sewn through two of the scarf corners (see Figure 69).

Another popular version of the same head covering is the scarf shaped in a long, thin rectangle. This style serves much more as a headband or hairband than as an actual head covering. It's tied down under the chin in the same manner as the triangular scarf.

Still another leather project is the neckerchief ring that serves as a slide fastening for scarves. This is a simple ring with either a snap or a rivet on the back side. I've also seen a number of craftsmen who have made very attractive finger rings using leather as the band material, and one craftsman who made a very successful pair of eyeglass frames out of leather and then had the glass set by an optometrist. At this point, I'll conclude by referring you back to the list of project ideas at the end of the introductory chapter.

A selection of earrings made from scrap by Justis Taylor, Bennington, Vt. Photo, Larry Hyman.

(Above Left) Two leather pendants made from scrap 12 ounce cowhide; both done as abstract reliefs. Pendants and photo, courtesy of the author.

(Below Left) Leather necklace beads; cut with a round drive punch from scrap leather left over from making sandal soles. The beads are strung on nylon fishline. Courtesy of Ted St. Germain, Nantucket, Mass. Photo, Sy Lippman.

(Below Right) Leather necklace beads; made from 10 to 12 ounce scrap cowhide. These beads were strung on a nylon fishline after being punched out by two sizes of arch punches. Made by the author. Photo, Phil Grey.

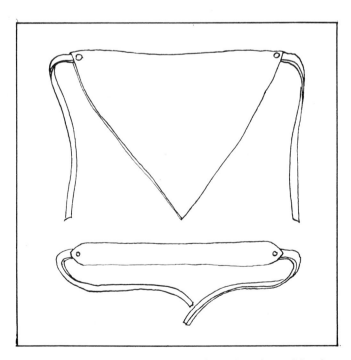

Figure 69. *Two head scarves: a triangular piece of leather hemmed on all sides by machine; and a headband scarf made from a strip of leather hemmed along the edges. Both scarves have matching leather ties.*

CHAPTER TWENTY

Furniture

Leather in furniture design is used either as a veneer, or as a seat material on chairs. Leather furniture design therefore incorporates other materials, such as wood or metal. All of the chairs illustrated in this text use either wood or metal as a structural support for the leather.

In order to construct leather furniture, one must be both a bit of a carpenter–cabinetmaker, as well as a metalsmith. Or, if one prefers not to get involved in the construction of structural supports, it's then necessary to have this work done by someone else. To date, I've not been able to find a single piece of all–leather furniture. I suppose it's possible to design a piece of all–leather furniture, but I have serious doubts that such a design could efficiently support the weight of the average man. The illustrations in this chapter will suggest several methods of developing structural support—from the idea of suspended furniture, to the idea of the sling chair. The point here is that in order to undertake the construction of leather furniture, one must be prepared to either deal personally with the problem of support, or to find someone to construct the support for a fee. The simple tripod saddle stool illustrated on this page is perhaps the easiest kind of object with which to begin experimenting. Details of this stool are offered on page 130.

Tools, Supplies, and Leather

To cut leather for furniture, you'll need either a square point leather knife, a pair of leather shears, or a jig or band saw (depending on how thick the leather is). If you sew the parts together, you'll need an industrial sewing machine. If you prefer sewing by hand, you'll need either an 8-cord polyester dacron thread, latigo goat lacing, or rawhide (depending upon your preference). If you elect not to sew the parts together, they can be held together with heavy–duty rivets. You'll also need a revolving leather punch, a single–slit lacing hole nipper, leather contact cement, a mallet, and dyeing and finishing supplies.

(Left) Leather sling chair; made from saddle leather. The four corners are made with double-thickness pockets that fit onto the metal chair frame. The small stool beside it has three double-thickness corner pockets. Chair and photo, courtesy of Leathercrafter, New York, N.Y.

The thickness of the leather used will depend a great deal upon the design of the given piece of furniture, and the use to which it will be put. If you use leather as a furniture veneer (for example on top of a chest), I suggest you use a smooth grain leather rather than a split. The same is true if you use squares of leather in wall paneling as in the chessboard on page 142.

Leather for chairs, whether webbed or sling–seat, should first of all be curried for minimum stretch. Leather that stretches is unsuitable for chair seats, in that continuous wear will quickly distort the design and shape of the seat. Webbed chair seats will require a weight of from 8 to 14 ounce leather depending upon the given design, and who plans to sit on it. The primary consideration is that the leather be easily flexible if it's to wrap around any type of structural frame. Chair seats can be made from either napped or smooth grain leather, as long as it has an absolute minimum stretch. Leather which is tanned especially for industrial belting is one variety developed with minimum stretch; saddle leather also makes an excellent leather for chair seats.

If you look closely at the suspended chair on page 129 you'll notice how the vertical front straps of the seat have begun to stretch; this stretching threw the balance of the seat off, and caused it to tip forward. This was the first sample chair Mr. Taylor made with that design, and he was able to learn a great deal about how leather stretches from that encounter. His experience is passed along to save you from having to duplicate the lesson.

Leather as Furniture Veneer and Wall Paneling

When using leather as a furniture veneer, for example, on the top of a chest, the leather is normally set so that it rests flush with the rest of the surface. If leather covers only part of the top, it then has to be set by cutting part of the top down to equal the thickness of the leather, or else by building a frame around the leather with the frame thickness equal to the leather thickness. If leather is used as a whole top, or front facing, it should be rounded at the edges, and edge–dressed before it's cemented down.

Some important points to check when cementing leather as a veneer are these: make certain that the wood surface is clean and free of projections and

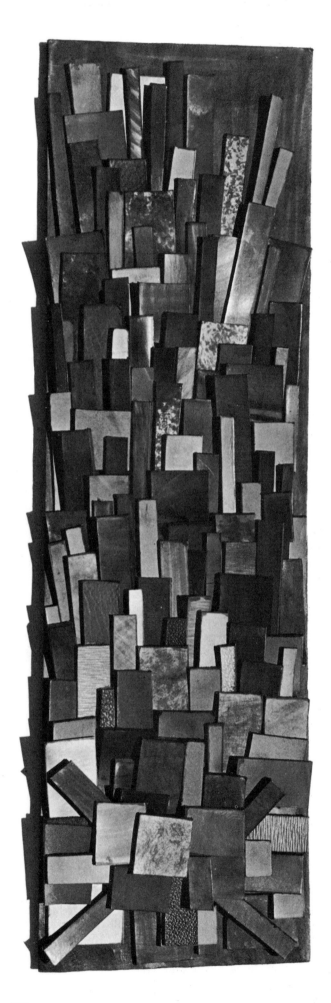

debris, and make certain that the flesh side of the leather is rough textured to gain the maximum strength from the cement bond.

Tops can either be applied in a single piece, or set in sections in the same manner as the chessboard (a sort of mosaic technique). If you're working in square or rectangles of leather, you can add trim by bevelling the leather edges 45 degrees on a jig or band saw table. A contact cement works well as a bonding agent on veneer. The same procedure is also applicable when mounting leather in sections of wall paneling. If you try bonding squares of leather to a wall, you must remove all of the old wallpaper ahead of time so that the leather will be bonded to the actual wall surface. If you bond it over wallpaper, it will more than likely pull away with the paper.

As with the leather relief illustrated on this page, it's possible to develop a whole spectrum of tones and textures when using the piecing, or mosaic, technique on leather veneer. Chest tops and paneling of leather should be cared for regularly with a commercial leather conditioner not only to keep the leather from drying out, but to protect the color from fading.

Suspended Leather Furniture

The hanging chair illustrates the principle of a suspended chair constructed from leather strips. The idea of suspension eliminates the need for a base, but the chair still requires a frame in order to hold its shape. In this instance, the designer has two round, solid brass rods made for both the top and bottom of the vertical strips. The strips and the seat are held in place by wrapping the pieces around the rods and securing them with heavy–duty brass rivets. Suspended seats can be made from solid leather, or woven from leather strips. Each of the strips suspending this chair was finished on the edges in the same manner as one would edge–dress a belt. As mentioned in the photograph caption, Mr. Taylor also plans to use this strip principle to construct a suspended cradle. The same technique could equally be used for a bench, or even for a suspended table, if the consumer didn't mind the idea of its hanging free.

(Left) Leather relief by Larry Simons; made from scrap leather. This all-leather relief is a series of texture and dye build-ups using shades of brown, and gives an idea of what can be done with scrap material left over from your leather projects. Courtesy of the Om Leather and Sandal Shop, Aspen, Colo. Photo, Chuck Askren.

Leather hanging chair, width of seat 42"; made from 14 ounce cowhide (seat), and strips of pre-stretched, curried, 10 ounce cowhide (straps). The handle at the top front of the chair steadies it when you sit down, and can be used to set the chair in motion once you're seated. Made by Justis Taylor, Bennington, Vt. Photo, Larry Hyman.

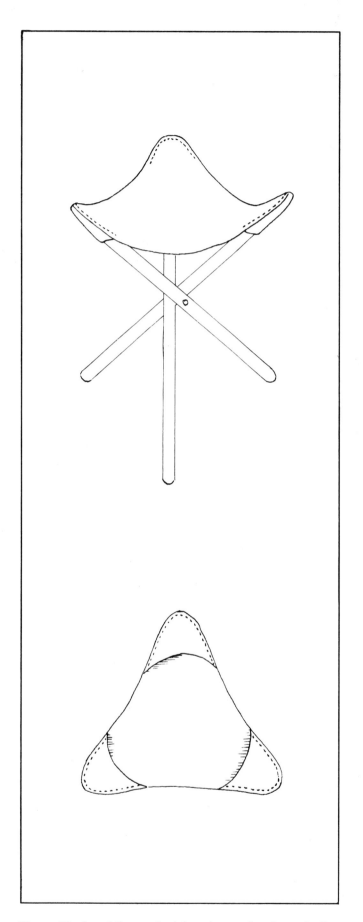

Figure 70. *A saddle stool: (above) completed stool; (be-low) shows underside of seat and the placement of leg pockets.*

Leather Sling Chairs

The photographs in this section illustrate several styles of leather chairs in which the leather is literally suspended within a frame and allowed to hang into shape. The most important consideration in chairs of this type is the location of the seams. As seams will be subjected to great stress, they must be placed where the tension is equalized on all parts of the chair (see the bucket chair). It's also important to place the seam so that the line created by the seam complements the lines in the over–all design. The saddle, sling, and bucket chairs in the photographs are made literally with pockets that fit over the chair frames. The bucket chair is made from four pieces of leather sewn together to form a circle. Seams on these types of chairs can either be sewn on a heavy–duty sewing machine with strong dacron thread, or they can be hand sewn with the thread, lacing, and rawhide mentioned earlier.

Figure 70 illustrates the technique used in making the tripod saddle stool where pockets are hand sewn on the reverse side of the triangular seat. These pockets accomodate the three legs. Legs can be made from either ash or oak handles (sold in hardware stores for brooms, rakes, shovels, etc.), and should be well rounded at both ends to prevent wear on the leather, and on the floor. The three legs are simply joined together with a long bolt and nut. The pockets make the seat removable, and by loosening the nut, the legs can fold together to make the whole thing portable. If you try this stool, I suggest you either make very sure the pocket ends on the stool legs are well rounded, or else plan to buffer them with scrap leather to minimize wear on the leather pockets.

Slip Covers

Just a brief mention should be made of leather as a potential slip cover material. It's possible to cover an upholstered piece of furniture with leather; a smooth grain leather surface, as opposed to leather with a nap, is of course the easiest to care for. Many suppliers sell leather which has been tanned especially for slip coverings; this is a supple leather with a finish which is highly resistant to stains. Usually slip cover leather runs between 1 to 3 ounces thick. Leather slip cover seams are made in the same manner as are other machine–sewn leather seams. The cover should be designed with a minimum number of seams. The procedure for making slip covers out of leather is virtually the same as for making slip covers out of any other fabric. If you intend to make slip covers, I suggest you purchase one of the many available books and pamphlets giving detailed instructions on the subject.

(Above Left) Leather bucket chair, 30" in diameter; made from top-grain cowhide on a steel swivel base. Heavy nylon thread was used to sew the three sections of leather together. Chair and photo, courtesy of Leathercrafter, New York, N.Y.

(Above Right) Leather saddle chair, over-all height 37", width of seat 26½", height of seat from the floor 15"; made from saddle leather. Chair and photo, courtesy of Leathercrafter, New York, N.Y.

(Left) Leather smoker chair, over-all height 32", over-all depth 32", width of seat 26", height of seat from floor 16"; made from saddle leather over a steel frame. Chair and photo, courtesy of Leathercrafter, New York, N.Y.

CHAPTER TWENTY-ONE

Leather as an artist's medium

If you happen to be one of my readers whose mind is set solely upon vacuuming up all and any information on the use of leather in the traditional, "functional" manner, and you can't be bothered with side–track ideas, you might well ask why a book on leather design devotes a full chapter to leather as an artist's medium. You might well argue that leather art is completely non–functional; nobody can wear it, and nobody can get much use from it. Before you pass judgment, however, let me invite you to explore a few ideas.

Sculpture

I honestly don't feel that I'm obliged to justify art as a legitimate avenue of design exploration, but for the reader who finds sculpture in leather a strange concept, I'll attempt to prod some insight. If you let it, exactly the same chemistry that gives you pleasure from the design of a particular pair of sandals, can give you pleasure in response to a non–functional form. What I'm referring to here is visual response. Your response to the design of a given pair of sandals is visual. What your eye takes in is immediately translated into other emotional and sensory responses that generate pleasure, satisfaction, or possibly, disgust. Your response to the visual design of a pair of sandals may have nothing to do with actually wearing those sandals on your feet. It's entirely possible that you're responding to the look of the sandals even though they might feel perfectly miserable on your feet. Those sandals, then, have a visual form existence which is independent of their function. Leather sculpture deals with visual form, the same concept of form as the pleasureable design of a pair of sandals; but in the case of sculpture, the form is an end in itself, and requires no function to justify its existence. This is not a text designed to esthetically justify sculpture; I'm making the bold assumption that my reader will not contest form without function.

In a more practical light, the exploration of leather as a sculptural form forces one to use one's eyes; to be concerned with the shape of an object as it invades space. Experimenting with sculpture, and being con-cerned with pure visual form, can't help but improve the design of functional leather projects. An exposure to pure form without function will develop a visual consciousness that can literally open one's eyes to what design is really about.

Exploring leather sculpture might lead to new discoveries about leather, new concepts of design, and what can be done with these concepts when applied to functional design. Form exploration, especially if you go into the leather business, can provide a delightful and rewarding breather from the routine of making sandals, and can give you a free–flowing outlet for creative energy and new ideas. I might also add that successful sculptural exploration has monetary value, can brighten up the appearance of a leather shop, and can lead to a legitimate off–season by–product. I'd like you to explore this chapter with an open mind and see what challenges you visually, what pricks your own interest.

What Does Leather Offer the Sculptor?

Many sculptors spend a great deal of time and energy hopping from one material to another in search of what they define as a "pure form" material. "Pure form" is a somewhat amorphous term and its definition depends a great deal on who happens to be defining it and what that person has in mind at the time. In general terms, "pure form" means a sculptural material which allows for a minimum in esthetic and technical limitations, or, in other words, a material over which the sculptor can exercise maximum control and in which he can find maximum freedom of expression. I believe that, within this definition, leather is one of the purest of form materials.

What are some of leather's "pure form" advantages to the sculptor? Leather is a natural material as opposed to a synthetic one, and it therefore answers the demands of the sculptor who prefers working only with natural materials. Leather lends itself naturally to organic forms since it's an organic material. Leather is also a sensuous material as opposed to a material such as stone, which is, emotionally, a much colder material. Leather has a texture and a feel, it has a color, a rich, pungent smell, and it enjoys a tradition of being a luxurious material. Also, leather is spontaneous; it responds instantly to form. It's malleable; it's flexible, and can be worked in trial and error experimentation without damage to its core structure; and finally, it's rugged and durable as a material for sculpture.

Hanging Bat, *by Bill Wilson, 30" x 34"; made from buck-skin stretched over an armature, or skeletal structure, of maple twigs. Photo, courtesy of the sculptor.*

Additional advantages of leather as a sculptural material are that it's an intimate material to work with; it develops an intimate conversation, not only with the sculptor–craftsman, but with anyone who can see it as an end form in itself. Leather is also instantly available to work with; it's worked with the hands, and requires nothing such as wheels, masks, or large machines to render it into dimensional form as do so many other sculptural materials. Leather requires no preparation, no mixing of ingredients, a minimum of work space, a minimum investment in tools, no waiting time, and a minimum in cleanup.

To be fair, I should spend just a moment admitting some of the sculptural objections to leather. Many sculptors feel that it lacks sufficient inherent mass for dimensional use; they don't like the idea of having to imply mass. Others feel that leather looks too much like wood; to my mind this is a weak objection, because with the contemporary technical knowledge at hand, just about every sculptural material on the market can be induced to look like something else—wood like metal, or clay like metal are two examples. Still others feel that leather in sheet form is too small in hide size to be used on large environmental pieces. Many of these objections can be overcome with the use of one technique or another; for example, hides can be sewn, laced, cemented, or riveted together to overcome the hide size limitation.

Leather as sculpture is very new, still experimental, and belongs to the present and to the future; it's now only in its infancy. Despite these minor objections, I believe that leather is equal to any other sculptural material currently being used, and I'd like to encourage the reader to get involved in this new dimension.

Tools for Leather Sculpture

The type and variety of tools neded for leather sculpture will, in large measure, depend upon the sculptural technique and the form itself. When using leather as a sculptural skin covering, the leather can be cut and trimmed with a pair of leather shears, but when using thick leather, I suggest the use of either the square point knife, or an X-Acto knife. If you use very thick leather, then you might even need a jig or band saw to cut the initial form. For constructing hollow–core solids, such as the one illustrated in the photograph on page 135, I would suggest the use of a jig saw equipped with a tilting table so that the table can be tipped to a 45 degree angle to cut edge bevels. It's a great deal more accurate to cut edge bevels by machine than to try doing it by hand with a knife; the beveled seams will be much smoother when cut on a jig or band saw. In addition to these cutting tools, you'll need (at least) a revolving punch, leather contact cement, Duco Household Cement, and supplies for dyeing and finishing. Whatever requirements you run into beyond these basic tools will depend entirely upon what you do with the given piece of sculpture.

Leather for Leather Sculpture

Just about any leather in the animal kingdom can be used for sculpture, depending upon the technique used and the physical requirements made upon the leather when using that technique. The only sculptural pieces I've seen thus far while researching this book have been constructed out of cowhide, horsehide, and deerhide. This is not to say that other leathers won't work for sculpture; on the contrary, it's much more the physical properties of the given leather that count than what type of animal leather comes from. As mentioned earlier, leather sculpture is only now in its infancy, and this accounts for the fact that other leathers have not yet been exploited for sculptural effects. Again, for sculptural purposes, the first considerations are technique and tannage; the type of animal skin covering is related only to the special effects one hopes to produce, such as texture and color.

Guidelines for Selecting Leather for Sculpture

Here are a few guidelines for selecting leather as sculptural material. If you use the technique of wetting and bending leather into dimensional form, I recommend thick leather, the thicker the better, at least 10 ounces thick. I also suggest you use leather with a minimum of oil in the tannage. Heavily oiled leather won't retain its shape when wet and bent; the heavy oil saturation tends to spring the leather back into its natural flat plane. Absence of oil, and leather thickness, then, are the primary ingredients to consider when selecting leather on which to use the wetting and bending technique. The sculpture on page 135 entitled *Bird* was made by wetting and bending 12 ounce oak cowhide.

As one additional note, special effects with any of the techniques in this section can be produced by using a wide variety of textures, from smooth to embossed, and from tooled leather to leather with the hair left intact.

For geometric hollow–core solids, I again suggest thickness and dryness as your guidelines in leather selection. Once you've laminated a piece together, you can then apply oils, dyes, and finishes.

When working with kinetic forms, such as the mobile on page 136, I suggest you use thinner leather (4 to 6 ounces) in order to reduce the actual physical weight of the piece. And for coverings, as in *Hanging Bat* (page 132), or *Eagle* (page 137), a thin garment leather works best. What you're after in coverings is to find a leather that's light and pliable. If it doesn't bend easily you'll be in trouble. For incised relief, I suggest anything over 5 ounces thick in order to allow some depth to the surface cuts, and when working with the techniques of collage and applied relief, it makes no difference what kind of leather you use. With these two techniques you're primarily after contrast; here you can use up scrap as was done in the leather relief shown on page 128, and develop a maximum contrast of color, texture, fatliquoring, and thickness.

For laminated and carved leather sculpture, I suggest that you select leather according to maximum thickness and minimum oil tannage. Leather for laminating to carve should be as dry as possible to facilitate the cementing process; cement will adhere better to a light oil tannage than to a heavy oil tannage. Once the pieces have been laminated and the lamination

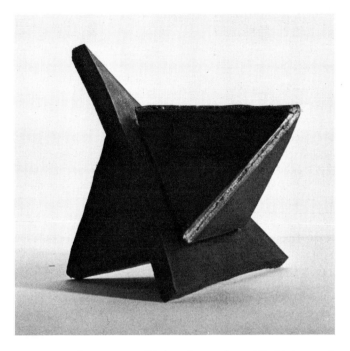

Leather hollow-core solid by the author, 14" high; made from 12 ounce horsehide. The separate pieces of this solid were first cut from a hide, then beveled 45 degrees on the edges, and cemented together. Photo, the author.

Bird, by the author, 8" high x 14" wide; made from wet and bent 12 ounce cowhide. The figure was first cut from a flat plane, the edges were beveled and burnished, then the piece was wet and bent into form. The head is held in place by nylon fishline, and the figure is mounted on two square nails driven through a buckskin-covered piece of plywood. Photo, Robert Estrin.

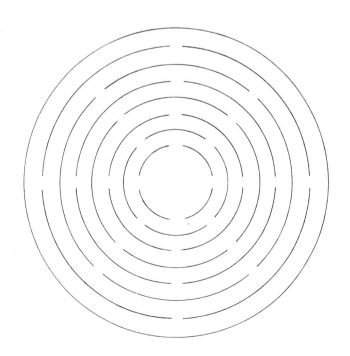

Figure 71. *A pattern for constructing a mobile.*

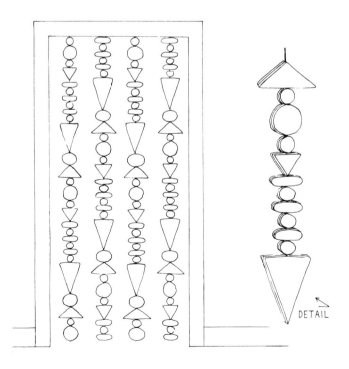

Figure 72. *Leather beads in alternating colors and textures.*

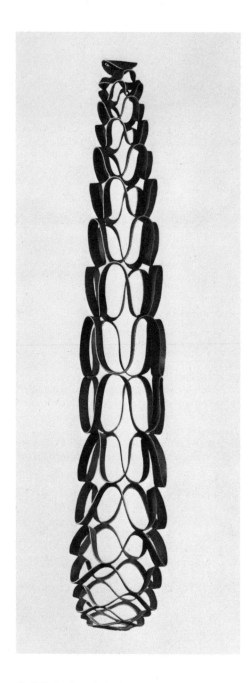

seams are sealed, oil can be applied over the finished piece if you prefer.

Finally, when using leather as an artist's dye canvas, I recommend an unoiled, porous, smooth grain surface. An unoiled leather will do a much better job of soaking up the dye, acrylic, or whatever coloring agent is used.

Complementary Material

In the photos accompanying this chapter, you'll see the use of several complementary materials in combination with leather as bases, appendages, and parts within constructions. There are an endless number of complementary materials that can be used with leather. I've run into sculptors experimenting with stainless steel and leather, trying to develop reflecting stainless surfaces to mirror the leather. I've also run across sculptors experimenting with leather and ceramic, especially stoneware. And then too, I've seen sculptors using glass, sheet copper, iron, burlap, brass, cork, wood, and even hemp with leather. There's literally no limit to the explorations that lie ahead for leather sculpture. And there are no rules for complementary materials. When I first heard of combining stainless steel and leather, I reacted as though these two materials would create visual conflict. Upon seeing the two materials together in the piece, however, I found them to be highly complementary.

Laminated and Carved Leather Sculpture

An example of how layers of leather can be laminated for volume and then reduced to form by carving is illustrated in *Two Figures* (page 137). In this figure, I laminated eleven layers of very dry, 12 ounce horsehide; I then cut the silhouette on a band saw, and finally reduced the piece with an X-Acto knife. Leather carves beautifully, like soft pine and basswood. Goodyear Contact Cement was used to laminate this piece; opposing surfaces were rough–textured with sandpaper before the cement was applied. When laminating to carve, it's essential to create a strong bond. Texturing the two surfaces before cement is applied helps the cement to flow down into the leather core fibers. One can also use a wire brush or coarse steel wool for texturing.

After the layers were placed together, they were pounded flat with a mallet to eliminate the possibility of air pockets. When pounding the final outside laminations, a scrap of leather should be used as a buffer between the outside leather and the mallet head in order to prevent denting the exposed leather. Still another possibility for exploring this type of volume build–up is to dye the leather before lamination and to then laminate in order to deliberately build color tones from layer to layer.

Leather mobile by the author; made from 5 ounce smooth grained cowhide. This mobile is shown hanging in two different positions. It was made from two circles; a series of cuts was made and the circles were cemented opposing each other. The principle here is the same used in making paper patterns. Photo, Robert Estrin.

Leather as a Sculptural Skin Covering

The two pieces, *Hanging Bat* (page 132), and *Eagle* (page 137), illustrate the technique of using leather as a sculptural skin covering. In these pieces, an armature, or skeletal core, was made by lashing maple twigs together with rawhide. Buckskin was then stretched over the core to gain dimensional volume. This technique can be used with just about any material from wood to wire, and the skin covering can be secured by using cement, by lashing it together with rawhide strips, or by sewing.

Leather Hollow–Core Solids

The hollow–core solid on page 135 illustrates how this technique can be used in sculpture. These leather solids were constructed by first cutting out the parts, then beveling the edges 45 degrees on the table of a jig saw, and finally cementing the beveled edges into a solid with contact cement. Still another way of producing geometric solids is to laminate layers of leather into full solids. This technique is similar to that of laminating to carve, except that the pieces are cut to size and aren't reduced.

Opposing Flat Planes to Imply Volume

The geometric leather construction and *Circles* on page 138 are examples of implied sculptural form gained by interlocking opposing flat planes of leather. This is perhaps the simplest technique that can be used with leather in order to imply volume. The feeling of mass is achieved by simply juxtaposing two flat leather planes so that they're placed at a 90 degree angle to one another. Patterns are worked up in advance in such a way that the opposing planes will fit together in mutual support. As with *Circles*, two layers of leather were laminated together—flesh side to flesh side—in order to get smooth surfaces all around.

Wetting and Bending Leather to Imply Volume

Bird (page 135), and the two flower figures on page 138, are examples of the technique of wetting and bending leather into sculptural form. These pieces were made by first cutting the pattern from a flat plane, then soaking the leather with water, and finally bending the leather into the desired shape as one would wet and bend an arch into a sandal sole. After the leather is bent into a new shape (providing thick enough leather is used), it will dry and completely retain its new shape indefinitely. The procedure I've found most successful for wetting is to gradually dampen the leather a little at a time with a sponge until the leather responds to the bends required by the new form. If the leather gets too wet, it will have to be allowed to dry out partially before it's bent. I've also found that if the bend is a bit more pronounced when the leather is wet, it will dry to just about the desired degree; the bend has a tendency to flatten out as it dries, and therefore it's a good policy to make the initial wet bend slightly more pronounced than it will finally be. Another idea is to prop the bend area against a solid surface to hold the exact bend as the leather dries. This stabilizes the bend during the drying process.

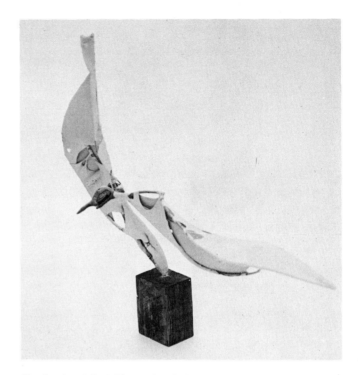

Eagle, *by Bill Wilson; buckskin stretched over an armature of maple twigs. Photo courtesy of the sculptor.*

Two Figures, *by the author, 22″ high; made by laminating eleven layers of horsehide to gain volume. The layers were cemented together with Goodyear Neolite All-Purpose Cement after first being textured with sandpaper to create a better bonding surface. It was reduced and carved with X-Acto knives, and finished with shoe cream. Photo, Robert Estrin.*

Geometric leather construction by the author, 16" high; made from 12 ounce horsehide. This piece was an attempt to build sculptural form from a flat plane, and is a knock-apart. Photo, the author.

Circles, *by the author, 12" high; made from leather, burned cork, and nylon fishline. Four round pieces of 12 ounce cowhide were laminated back to back to form two, double-thickness circles. Slits were then cut in opposite ends of these circles so that they would fit together as opposing planes to imply volume. Photo, Robert Estrin.*

Two flower figures by the author; the figure on the left is 8" high and the figure on the right is 10" high. Both figures were made from 12 ounce cowhide. They were cut from a flat plane, beveled on the edges, burnished, wet, and then bent into dimensional proportions. Both figures were dyed with All-Purpose Rit fabric dye, and finished with saddle soap. Photo, Robert Estrin.

Incised Relief

This technique is similar to stamping and tooling, where cuts are made into the leather surface in order to develop a motif. The process is similar to cutting into linoleum blocks and, in fact, I use linoleum block gouges to work this technique. What you're trying to do here is to remove leather in order to create light and shadow contrast around a central motif. If you do choose to experiment with stamping tools, may I suggest that you try and use them in an original way, or else create your own stamp designs so that the finished piece will not look like the surface of a tooled Texas handbag. There's nothing wrong with using stamping tools on leather if only the craftsman will add a bit of originality to the application.

Applied Relief and Collage

The leather collages on page 140 are examples of applied and collage relief. In most of these pieces, leather was built up over a backing of plywood. This is a wonderful way to make use of leather scraps. The dimensional proportions of these reliefs were built up by cementing layers to a flat surface, one on top of another. Duco Household Cement was used to hold the layers to the backing. This technique is exactly the opposite of incised relief. Here, the surface is being built out and away from the background, while incising the motif is a matter of cutting into the surface.

Leather as Material for Kinetic Form

The mobile on page 136 illustrates a way of producing implied kinetic volume from leather. This mobile was made by simply planning slit cuts on the flat plane of two identical leather circles in such a way that when the slits were opened and pulled apart, the series of slits would create a volume–developing pattern. This is exactly the same technique used in folding, creasing, and cutting paper, only in the case of leather, it can't be folded and cut, but must be cut when flat. Figure 71 illustrates this technique; the two circles were glued at four points along the circumference and then pulled apart to create volume. If you want to learn more about this technique, I suggest you purchase one of the many books available on creating with paper.

Leather as a Dye Canvas

Leather 8 ounces thick and more can be cut to any desired shape and used in the same manner as one would use an artist's canvas. I suggest that leather with a minimum oil tannage be used in order to gain maximum color penetration. Preferably, the leather should also have a smooth surface. Leather used in this way makes an excellent surface for acrylics, regular leather dyes, most enamels, food coloring, vegetable dyes, and even oil paints. Another application I've seen using this technique is to use leather for restaurant menus and indoor boutique shop signs with the hand lettering executed in oils, enamels, or acrylics.

Leather as a Weaving Material

I've seen leather used successfully as strip material in hand and in loom weaving, as in the wall hanging on page 141, where it was combined with strips of wool. In this instance, rawhide lacing can be used, or strips of leather can be cut with either a plough gauge, or a draw gauge. I've also seen the weaving technique used in making leather table place mats from strips, and seen very successful baskets woven from ½″ strips of leather in the same manner as one would weave baskets from reeds, splints, and raffia. Woven strips of leather can also be used as chair seats.

Using Leather Negatives

Another interesting technique is the use of the leather negative. The illustration on page 29 shows a planned leather negative left over after punching out buttons from a piece of 8 ounce cowhide. These negatives can be used just as they are for abstract wall hangings, or they can be cut to fit into frames for room dividers—to be used perhaps along a stairway opening, or mounted in frames as portable room screens. If the hide is cut into a rectangle before it's punched, the negative can then be easily fitted into a frame. I've seen this done with planned leather negatives left over from clicking out sandal soles; the waste negatives, when mounted, or even left in the shape of the hide as a wall hanging, often sell for more than the original cost of the whole hide—the craftsman then profits by a hide full of sandal soles at no cost. A planned negative (in case you're wondering), is a negative in which the pattern to be cut, for example sandal soles, is placed carefully on the hide so as not to break out any negative strands, or cause overlap and spoil the image. It takes only a very few extra minutes to create useable negatives. If you plan to use a clicker for sandal soles, for hair barettes, or for parts of any other projects in leather, then planned negatives are a must.

If you want to experiment, negatives can usually be picked up free from such places as shoe manufacturers who can't be bothered saving them, or who aren't imaginative enough to realize their potential. The aggressive and imaginative craftsman can convert these so–called waste negatives into attractive, valuable wall hangings. One of the most attractive wall reliefs I've ever seen was made from the brilliant colors of the patent leather negatives left over from a company that was clicking out watchbands. These negatives were planned and exactly duplicated on each color of leather used. The relief was made by cementing one layer over another and leaving just enough of an offset on each lamination for the color underneath to show through.

Still another sculptural technique is the construction of leather beads from scrap. The illustrations of beads and pendants in Chapter Nineteen show what can be done with leather beads used in necklaces, and Figure 72 illustrates how large leather discs can be cut and strung as door beads. The necklace beads were cut with an arch punch from scrap leather left over from sculptural pieces and sandal soles. The beads were pierced with a needle and then strung on nylon fishline. This technique is ample proof that with leather, there's no such thing as waste. By taking the time to use scrap, I've very often been paid twice over for the cost of the original hide, and gotten the use of the hide for nothing.

Collage relief by Lois Whitcomb; made from old shoe and belt parts which have been cemented to a wood backing. Photo, Phil Grey.

Leather wall relief by the author, 24" x 16"; made entirely from cowhide. The rings were an attempt to add a changing visual dimension to the relief. Photo, Robert Estrin.

Optical leather wall relief by the author. For this piece, leather was cemented to a backing of plywood and built up to relief proportions. Photo, Robert Estrin.

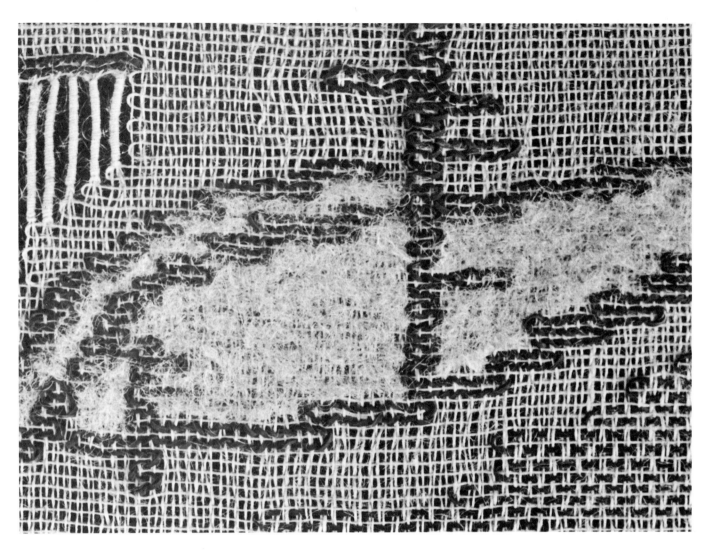

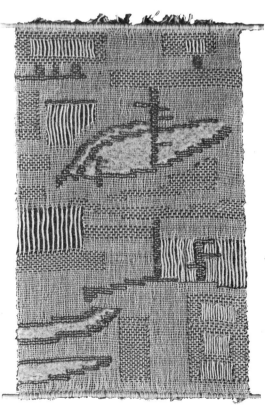

Wall hanging by Klekot; woven on a loom using wool yarn and narrow, dark strips of leather. (See detail above.) Courtesy of the Image Gallery, Stockbridge, Mass. Photo, Clemens Kalischer.

Leather chessboard, 18" x 18" square; made from pieces of 6 ounce cowhide cemented to a wooden backing. The edges of each piece of leather were beveled 45 degrees to provide a clear separation between the squares. Courtesy of the Om Leather and Sandal Shop, Aspen, Colo. Photo, Chuck Askren.

CHAPTER TWENTY-TWO

Additional ideas

Essentially this is an idea chapter—a chapter devoted to suggesting accessory uses for leather beyond those of footwear, garments, handbags, furniture, etc. As we've already seen, there's virtually no limit to what can be made from leather. This chapter then, will present a number of ideas and illustrations to tickle your imagination.

Frames

Leather can be used as a framing material for artwork, photographs, desk blotters, bulletin boards, mirrors, clocks, and even as a casing around phonograph speakers. It can also be used directly as clock face material onto which numbers can be incised, hand–lettered, or glued.

There are two methods of constructing leather frames. The easiest method is simply to laminate thin leather over an already existing flat wooden frame. The second method is to make an all–leather frame by cutting the sides of the frame from 12 to 14 ounce cowhide.

If you use the first method, and laminate leather over an existing wooden frame, I suggest you take one frame apart, reducing it to its four sides before you begin. If you laminate the leather onto each of the four wooden pieces seperately, and then put the frame back together again, you'll increase your accuracy and neatness many times over. I recommend a thin leather under 4 ounces which is supple enough to bend easily around the edges of the existing frame. The most accurate method of cutting your pieces for lamination is to first make a paper pattern for each of the four sides, and then to test this pattern for accuracy before you cut your leather. Once the pattern is accurate, you can then cut out the pieces of leather and bond them to the wood with contact cement. The leather should lap each separate frame edge in one continuous flow. Excess leather can be trimmed off before the frame is reassembled.

If you plan to make a frame of which the four sides are cut from 12 to 14 ounce cowhide, I suggest that you plan ahead and arrange for some type of reinforcement to keep the frame's sides from curling. Unlike wood, leather is pliable, and it must have a reinforced backing if it's expected to hang flat against a wall.

There are many ways to reinforce a frame made with solid leather sides: you can bond wood or metal strips to the back of each of the four frame pieces; you can reinforce the matching corners with short, diagonally placed strips; you can run support strips all the way across from side to side, or from top to bottom once the item to be framed is in place; or you can cover the whole back of the frame with plywood, again after the item to be framed is in place. If the leather frame is to hold a heavy object, such as a mirror, then it's essential to reinforce the frame on the back side for extra strength. Don't allow this reinforcement material to extend flush with the edges of the frame; it should be recessed back from the edges at least ½" or else it will show from the front side.

The procedure for making an all–leather frame is exactly the same as for making a wooden frame. The ends of the four side pieces will either have to be mitered, or angled, to 45 degree cuts, or these same ends can be left flat for a breadboard style frame. On the flesh side of the four separate frame pieces, you'll also have to cut a groove to hold the thickness of whatever fits into the frame. This groove is cut along the inside edges of the frame, and can be cut with a square point leather knife and a steel rule. When the four pieces are ready to be assembled, the corners can be held together with extra pieces of leather, wood, or metal bonded across the back corner seams.

If you plan to frame a single thickness of paper, an artist's print for example, I suggest that first this be bonded to a stiffer material, such as Masonite or plywood, to give the over–all frame additional support.

There are many variations of the all–leather frame. You can laminate several layers of leather together and then carve parts of the frame, the frame can be incised, tooled, stamped, or you can even build up leather layers into a shadowbox frame. And then too, there's a lot that can be done with dyes, and even collage.

Gameboards

The photograph shows a chessboard made by laminating pieces of 6 ounce cowhide to a backing of ½" pine. In this instance, the designer used a leather mosaic technique. As an alternative, he might also have covered the entire board with a thicker piece of smooth grained cowhide, and then tooled on the lines which indicate borders and squares by using an adjustable gouge. Still another idea is to laminate leather over wood and make a cribbage board.

Boxes

Small leather boxes for jewelry, stamps, or even stationery can be made by stacking laminated layers of leather together, one on top of another. This can be done by either cutting the single laminations by hand, or clicking them out with a die.

The procedure for making boxes is very simple; by laminating and stacking layers of leather, one on top of the other, the box becomes solid leather. Boxes can be made in any shape—square, round, rectangular, even flared shapes in which the top flares out and is wider than the bottom.

To make a round box with a 6″ diameter, you would first cut a 6″ circle from a thick piece of 10 to 12 ounce smooth grained cowhide. Next, cut out the center of that circle leaving a border of at least ¾″, and making sure not to cut into the border. What you now have is a round leather ring 6″ in diameter with a center hole 4½″ in diameter. Now cut several of these identical leather rings; the more rings, the higher the box will be. After the rings are cut, rough up the grain side of the leather, except for the top ring, and laminate the rings together with contact cement, making sure that each ring is stacked exactly over the ring below it. Now, cut a solid 6″ circle for the bottom of the box from the same piece of leather; don't cut the center out of this bottom piece. Laminate this circle to the bottom of the stack, placing the grain side facing down. To make certain that the laminations don't pull apart, you can drill a hole up through them from the bottom of the box on both sides of the center opening and then drive in a finishing nail or a dowel, and glue this reinforcement in place. For the top, you can now cut another solid, 6″ leather circle, and then cut a 4″ solid leather circle. Cement the 4″ circle in the exact center on the flesh side of the 6″ circle with the flesh side of the 4″ circle facing down. These two pieces laminated together will now fit over and into the box as a top with a snug lip. The edges of the box can finally be sandpapered and polished on an electric sanding wheel, and then the whole box can be dyed and finished. This procedure can be followed for all shapes and box sizes, and any number of variations can be developed within the technique.

Buttons

Your workshop can provide excellent button material, as handmade, solid leather buttons can be made from pieces of leftover scrap. Button leather should be at least 6 ounces thick. A button can be made by punching out a leather disc with an arch punch, or by cutting the disc out by hand with a knife. Buttons should have a diameter which is at least ⅛″ narrower than the buttonhole. The thread holes in the bottom can be punched out with a revolving leather punch, using the smallest punch tube. Normally, two thread holes in one button are enough. If you want the thread to be recessed into the button surface, cut a narrow, shallow groove into the grain side between the two thread holes. The thread holes should be close together, not over ⅜″ from center to center. To facilitate easy buttoning, I suggest that you taper the

outside edges of all buttons on both the flesh and grain sides. The button should then be dyed, finished, and the outside edges burnished.

When sewing a leather button on, I suggest you leave a thread shank between the button and the garment. A simple way to leave a shank is to place a thin spacer of cardboard or leather between the garment and the button while the button is being sewn in place. This leaves the threads loose after the spacer is removed, and you can then wind the thread around the space between garment and the button at least five or six times to form the shank, and then run the needle and thread back through to the inside of the garment, knot the thread and cut it. This shank device makes the button flexible, and protects the garment fabric from tearing.

Existing flat buttons can also be covered with leather in the same manner as one would cover buttons with other fabrics. If you do cover a button with leather, you'll need a thin, pliable leather under 3 ounces thick.

Leather as a Lampshade Covering

Although leather isn't transparent, it can still be successfully used as a lampshade covering in a situation where lighting requirements don't call for the translucency of a shade; in other words, where the lighting requirements call for direct light as opposed to indirect light. Leather shades should not be considered a novelty item or a conversation piece in the gimmicky sense, but should be used where an accent of leather will blend harmoniously with the decor, especially where leather will complement the material used in the base. I've seen tasteful leather shades used in early American, as well as in contemporary settings.

The simplest procedure is to cement leather over an old shade with existing straight side walls, but you'll first need a paper pattern in order to cut the leather to a perfect fit. A thin, 1 to 2 ounce lining or garment leather works very well for this purpose, providing that the old lampshade has stiff and vertical side walls to support the leather. Many of the embossed grains of lightweight leather make excellent material for lampshades. (See page 12 for an all-leather lamp.)

Leather and Ceramics

The ceramic water jug with leather carrying strap illustrates the affinity between leather and stoneware. This particular water jug was designed to incorporate a leather carrying strap. Still another way to combine leather with ceramic is to use leather as a material for handles on such things as teapots and jars. The almost standard procedure for most potters using detachable handles is to clamp on the cliché, and use ready-made, unimaginative handles made in the Orient. Leather handles are a possibility in replacing these unimaginative, raffia-like handles.

One way of making a leather handle is to wet and bend several pieces of thick leather into the shape of the handle, laminate these pieces together after they're dry, and then carve them into the handle shape

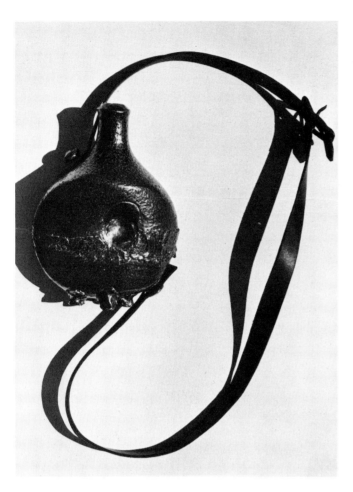

Ceramic water jug with leather carrying strap. This is a successful attempt to combine leather and ceramics. Made by Brad Reed. Photo, Chuck Askren; courtesy of the Om Leather and Sandal Shop.

Leather mug holder; made from 10 ounce, hand-dyed cowhide, and laced with rawhide lacing. The handle and the bottom piece are held in place with brass rivets. The leather was laced together after the glass was in place in order to insure correct fit. Made by Ted St. Germain, Nantucket, Mass. Photo, Sy Lippman.

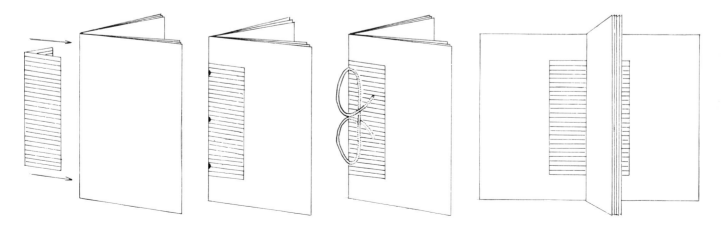

Figure 73. *How to laminate leather to a book cover.*

desired. They can then be burnished smooth and dyed, and finally attached to the pot with strap loops.

Still another way of making a leather handle for ceramic pots is to use the belt-braiding technique illustrated and explained in the chapter, *Belts, Billfolds, Watchbands and Other Small Accessories*. Leather handles are every bit as functionally successful as the raffia handles, and are open to much more originality in design.

Household Accessories in Leather

There are literally hundreds of attractive household accessories that can be made from leather. In this chapter you'll find photographs of several very successful ideas including a rawhide–laced leather mug holder, a glass caddy, a wood tote, a pipe holder, a bottle rack, a pencil caddy, and even a Christmas tree ornament. These detailed photos and their captions indicate how these items were made. This book isn't long enough to include step–by–step instructions on how to make each item. I believe the photos and captions are mostly self–explanatory, and hopefully will serve as a boost to set your own ideas in motion.

In addition to those items pictured, I've also seen such things as attractive leather napkin rings, holders for towel bars, leather wineskins, tobacco pouches, and an endless variety of leather cases to hold anything from common pins to bowling balls. The list at the end of the introductory chapter will suggest even more ideas.

Bookbinding in Leather

This section isn't intended as a substitute text on the craft of bookbinding; it's directed toward introducing you to a number of simple procedural steps by which you can grasp the beginnings of elementary binding with leather. If you want information on how to expand upon these simple techniques, I suggest you consult one of the many detailed texts on the subject, one of which is *Bookbinding for Beginners* by John Corderoy (Watson-Guptill Publications, 1967).

Many suppliers sell leather which has been especially vegetable–tanned for bookbinding. The most important thing required of a workable binding leather is that it be supple, but still have a firm texture. Goatskin or morocco, as well as pigskin, is often used by the professional binder. In the early days of Colonial binding in this country, and before tanning was as technically advanced as it is today, buckskin was very often used in binding. Generally, a thin leather, from 1 to 3 ounces, as long as it's supple, works best for binding. Both smooth grain and napped leather can be used.

In addition to leather, you'll need a good grade of paper for endpapers, plus a supply of tagboard or binder's boards to use as cover board, a pair of leather shears, a bone folder to fold endpapers and book pages, a steel rule, leather contact cement, a razor blade, heavy cotton thread, and a supply of bookbinder's paste. With these basic supplies and tools, you can explore several of the many bookbinding techniques.

The most difficult and time–consuming leather binding technique is that of lapping the cover leather all around the outside edges of the cover board. When this technique is used, the length of turned leather overlap runs between ½″ to ¾″. Using this technique requires that the thickness of the overlap be skived to the thinness of onion skin. This isn't an easy task for a beginner, but it does provide a professional appearance to the binding because the leather then bends around all of the cover board edges rather than remaining raw.

If you're interested in binding a few beginning books in leather, then I suggest that you examine a number of the books in your own library in order to familiarize yourself with the binding techniques used on them. Chances are that you'll find the same technique was used on almost all of the hardbound books which you examine, including the book you're now reading. This is the standard technique used by most binderies.

There are two phases to the binding process: one phase is to prepare the pages so that they can be attached to the cover by means of endpapers, and the second phase is to prepare the cover itself. Before you begin either phase, the book pages should be prepared for the binding process, and should be collated, folded, and trimmed to final size. (For our purpose here, let's assume you'll be rebinding, or simply covering, your own books, and won't need to go into these procedures. For those of you who would like to bind a book from scratch, however, I refer you once again to *Bookbinding for Beginners*.)

The simplest, and perhaps the most common, method of preparing the pages for binding is to either sew, tape, or staple the nest of folded pages to a piece of lightweight cardboard that's folded in half across the outside spine of the nested pages. This piece of cardboard should be about 1″ shorter than the overall height of the pages, and should extend about ¾″ on either side of the pages after it's been folded across the spine. Figure 73 illustrates this. You can sew the cardboard to the pages, with heavy cotton thread and a thin needle. Place the cardboard evenly against the outside of the pages, and begin sewing from the inside of the center fold as indicated in Figure 73. This particular sewing technique (if you follow the diagram) requires only three holes with the string ending up back where it started enabling you to tie a knot on the inside of the center fold.

You're now ready to prepare the cover. There are several styles of cover design; they may be all leather, or they may be leather trimmed. The title can be printed onto a label, and then the label cemented to the cover. There are also many variations of title presentation, from hand lettering, to embossing, even to gold lettering.

The simple cover technique on books that I've found successful is the following. I first cut two cover boards from heavy white tagboard; one for the back cover, and one for the front cover. These cover boards extend ⅛″ beyond both the top and bottom of the pages, and about ⅛″ beyond the width of the pages. If, for example, your pages measure 4″ wide by 8″

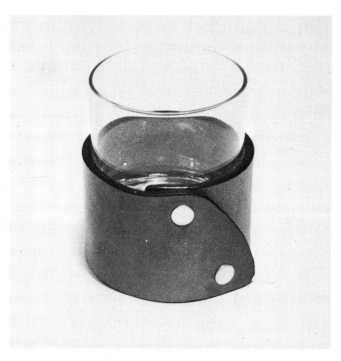

Glass caddy; made from 8 ounce cowhide and secured with two brass rivets. Made by Justis Taylor, Bennington, Vt. Photo, Larry Hyman.

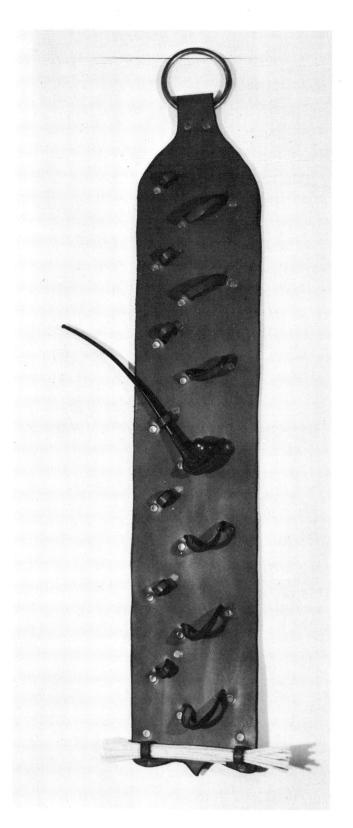

Leather wood tote; made from 8 ounce cowhide. One large brass ring at the top holds the tote to the wall, another ring secures the wood within the tote. Made by Ted St. Germain, Nantucket, Mass. Photo, Sy Lippman.

Leather pipe holder, 22" long; made from 10 ounce cowhide. A brass ring at the top holds the piece to the wall. Made by Ted St. Germain, Nantucket, Mass. Photo, Sy Lippman.

Leather bottle rack, 26" long; made from 10 ounce cowhide. Made by Ted St. Germain, Nantucket, Mass. Photo, Sy Lippman.

high, then your two cover boards should each measure 4⅛" wide by 8¼" to allow for the required overlap. With most books, the cover is slightly larger than the actual page size to protect the pages from damage.

For an all–leather cover, cut out a piece of leather exactly the same height as the cover board, and wide enough to allow for two widths of the cover board plus the width, or thickness, of the package of pages. If the thickness of the pages is ⅜", the rectangle of cover leather should measure 8⅝" wide by 8¼" high. With contact cement, cement the two cover boards to the flesh side of the leather, leaving the ⅜" space between cover boards at the center or eventual spine. When this cover is wrapped around the bundle of pages, it provides a perfect fit with the proper ⅛" overlap on three open sides. If there should be any unevenness between the edge of the leather and the edge of the cover board, this can be trimmed off with a razor blade. With this type of cover design, the leather does not lap the cover board edges, but remains flush with them. If the leather has a firm texture, unlapped edges will still remain perfectly smooth as long as you do a good job of laminating.

The final step in binding (exclusive of title or label) is to secure the bound pages to the cover board by means of endpapers. Endpapers aren't considered pages of the book, but are an integral part of the binding. They serve to secure the pages to the cover, and on turned or lapped edges, the endpapers cover those rough edges with a smooth, even surface.

To secure the pages to the cover, you must first cement the outside piece of page cardboard to the inside of the cover, making certain to place the pages equidistant from both the top and bottom cover board edges. While the binder's paste is still wet, close the book in order to make sure the pages are in exactly the position you want them. Next, take two endpapers twice the size of a single page, fold them in half lengthwise, and with binder's paste, cement the back of one endpaper to the inside of one of the covers. Now do the same with the other cover. When cementing endpapers, it helps to run the edge of a piece of cardboard across the paste to make sure the two surfaces are flat and that all air pockets are eliminated. Your book is now completely bound except for title.

If you prefer turning or lapping the edges of the leather around the cover board, you'll first have to evenly skive the area that folds over until it's as thin as possible. Cut a small square out of each leather corner to avoid leather being folded over leather, and turn these edges, cementing them down to the inside of the cover board. If you have any problems, or are at all unsure of yourself in your first attempt, I suggest you first practice with a piece of paper taking the place of the leather. Use a paper that approximates the thickness of the leather that you'll use. Another safe way of following this procedure is to visually compare the above step–by–step description with a book of your own that was commercially bound. For detailed techniques on lettering, and gold leaf application, I suggest you consult the book, *Bookbinding for Beginners*, mentioned earlier.

Leather pencil caddy, 8" high; made from 10 ounce cowhide. This pencil caddy consists of three separate pieces of leather which were cut on a clicker. The holes were punched out with a round drive punch. Made by Justis Taylor, Bennington, Vt. Photo, Larry Hyman.

Leather Christmas tree ornament, 7" in diameter; made from split cowhide garment scraps. Each separate piece began as a circle and was sewn on a sewing machine in a triangle pattern within the circle. Made by Jolene Dewey. Photo, Larry Hyman.

CHAPTER TWENTY-THREE

Opening a shop and selling your craft

So, what do you do with the fruits of your labor? By now it should be very clear to you that leather is a prolific product material. Like most people, you may begin by giving these products away as gifts; birthday gifts, Christmas gifts, graduation gifts, and even Valentine's Day gifts. But what do you do when you've run out of birthdays?

If your enthusiasm for leather grows, and I hope it will, you may at some point want to think seriously about selling what you make. In researching this book, I've visited well over fifty leather and sandal shops up and down the Atlantic coast, and from Maine to California. Many of the problems inherent in selling leather goods are common to all craftsmen. In this chapter, you'll find a number of suggestions which may prove invaluable to you in making the jump from amateur to professional.

As of this writing, leather is solidly the "in" material across the United States, especially among college-age buyers. The small sandal shop proprietor can well pat himself on the back; very often he's setting styles, rather than following them. The demand for sandals, wide belts, leather skirts, capes, pendants, watchbands, and handbags crafted by hand is on the upswing. A handmade leather garment is a prestige item, and well it should be. And from all the signs, the demand for handcrafted leathergoods can go nowhere but up.

One needs only to stand in a sandal shop for a few hours to discover that it very often becomes a gathering point for style–conscious young people. There seems to be almost a mystical attraction to a leather shop. Even if the consumer can't afford an immediate purchase, he seems to show up with regularity anyway, as though waiting to see what new idea the leather craftsman will come up with. Much of the attraction to leather is caused by the fact that it's a handmade product. A factory leathergoods store, selling the cliché assortment of briefcases, suitcases, and generally uninspiring billfolds, is literally ignored by young people, while right next door the hand craftsman may be bursting his walls with customers.

Yes, you can make a living as a hand leather craftsman! I've met many craftsmen who've supported themselves comfortably, and put as many as four children through college from the profits of a one–man shop. He may not jockey a 400 horsepower machine, live in a wealthy suburb with a summer place in the country, or tote the attaché case of the daily commuter, but he's his own boss, and he's doing what he enjoys most.

Location

If you hope one day to set up shop as a leather craftsman, the location of your shop is of the utmost importance. There's a reason for the concentration of leather and sandal shops around such places as Harvard Square in Cambridge, Hyannis, Provincetown, Marblehead, and Nantucket, Massachusetts; and around cities like Miami Beach, Key West, Washington, D.C., and Greenwich Village and the East Village in New York City. These are the places where the consistent buyers are; these are the places frequented by young people, and by tourists. I've been in many sandal shops literally doing business in the shadow of colleges and universities. If you plan to go into business, there's no profit in expecting the consumer to discover you gathering dust on the prairies of East Watertank, Nebraska. You've got to bring your craft to the consumer, dump it on his doorstep, and set up shop where there's an ever–present source of tourists and young people. You may not like the idea, but location is the first hard and fast rule to profits in the leather business.

Many craftsmen actually follow the consumer; they follow good weather and the people who move with the weather. I've run into a number of small shop owners who operate summer shops in New England, and winter shops in Florida. Ted St. Germain, whose work is illustrated in a number of places in this book, operates a summer shop on Nantucket, and a winter shop in Miami Beach. For Ted to remain on Nantucket in winter would be a lost cause for the pocketbook. One of the delightful advantages of working in leather is that the performance of the craft allows for this kind of mobility. About the largest item to cart around (assuming you have one) is a sewing machine. Most of what's needed to operate a leather shop can easily be fitted into the back seat of a Volkswagen. This idea of mobility might well be something to tuck away as reserve strength in case you start your own shop.

Round Mexican leather handbag, made from two pieces of 6 ounce cowhide laced with a ½" wide strip of the same leather. The bag has a unique design, using only two round circles of leather, plus the lacing and the flap closure. It's shown here against a bed of pine boughs, illustrating the way in which the natural beauty of leather can be enhanced by using an interesting background when displaying it. (For complete construction directions, see page 108.) Courtesy of Shirley Ambridge, Aspen, Colo. Photo, Chuck Askren.

Diversity

For the most part, leather is a seasonal business. If you live in the north, or at least where there is some type of winter, 70% of your sales will take place during the summer, with a brief flurry again around Christmas. Again, you may not like to hear this, but the seasonal imbalance is a fact.

The bulk of business for a small leather craftsman is the making and selling of sandals. Sandals are worn only in warm weather, and this accounts for part of the seasonal aspect of the leather business. If you refuse to make sandals, you may very well encounter some real problems in getting started as an independent shop owner. Perhaps making sandals is the price the leather craftsman pays for his independence. At any rate, sandals are, as I've said before, more often than not the craftsman's bread and butter. The next most popular items are belts, handbags, moc boots, pendants, watchbands, bracelets, and garments, more or less in that order.

The seasonal imbalance of leather sales is part of the reason a few craftsmen follow the weather. But what if you have roots, and don't elect to migrate with the robins? There are a number of very practical things you can do to offset the seasonal imbalance of leather sales.

The most practical move you can make in order to counteract the seasonal nature of leather sales is to diversify. Use your imagination and some of the ideas in this book to test the sales potential of leather used for something other than garment or footwear fabric. If all you produce are seasonal, or limited interest items, then obviously that's all you have to sell. If, on the other hand, you diversify, experiment, and get leather into the home, you'll have discovered a new market. This is why so many craftsmen are making accessory items like room dividers, furniture, door beads, glass holders, wood totes, wine racks, pipe racks, and even Christmas tree ornaments. They're making an effort to even out the seasonal aspect of leather sales.

Mail Order

Many craftsmen have gone into limited mail–order sales in order to develop an off-season business. Christmas offers a tremendous mail–order potential. One suggestion for mail order is to develop a catalog, not only of standard items, but including items that can be used as gifts and in the home. A Christmas catalog should reach the consumer early in November.

If you prepare a catalog, do it tastefully. Invite the consumer, by means of your catalog, into a gallery of your wares. A mimeographed slip of paper is no way to develop a mail–order business. Don't be afraid to spend a little money in preparing tasteful advertising.

If you use photographs, use good ones, and eliminate background clutter. Don't be content with hazy, gray snapshots that require a magnifying glass to see what it is you're trying to sell. If you can draw, then think about working up a number of line drawings of the items you plan to sell, and include these drawings in your catalog. One suggestion is to develop your catalog into something more than a throw-away. Perhaps it can be a reflection of your own peculiar philosophy, a Christmas greeting, or an informative essay on tanning, the physical properties of leather, the historical uses of leather, or something else equally interesting. A catalog developed in this way becomes much more than a catalog; it's something to save, and something to pass along to interested friends. One friend of mine did this so successfully that he was able to actually sell the catalog at a profit.

One problem in developing a mail–order catalog is that it can quickly become obsolete. When prices change, when postage rates increase, or when you want to discontinue an old design and add a new one, your catalog will have outlived its use.

One way to cut down on the expense of completely reissuing a whole new catalog is to design the catalog so that it's a loose-leaf portfolio of unbound pages. I've seen very successful catalogs done this way, in which the catalog cover functioned as an envelope into which the unbound pages were inserted. Each page describes a separate item, and a separate page is included listing prices and postage. If prices go up, or if you want to delete or add a design, you simply have a separate page printed up to replace the outdated one. In this way, a current catalog costs only the price of printing one new page.

Testing Your Designs

If you want to know whether a design works, both functionally and visually, don't be afraid to test it out. Begin by working up a sample, and then pass it around for reaction. Let's take the example of a new handbag design; let a few college coeds look it over, try it on, fiddle with it, and then ask them for honest criticism. If it works, they'll let you know. If it doesn't work, then ask them for suggestions, or ask them to tell you what they find wrong with it in the way of eye appeal, size, or ease of access. Another suggestion is to keep abreast of what other leather craftsmen are doing, what type of things are selling well for them.

Unique Findings

As we've seen, a finding can often spell the difference between an exciting design and a dismal failure. Keep your eyes open for unique findings, one-of-a-kind items that will offer your customer something special, something he can't get anywhere else but from you. I've tested this idea and it works. On a number of occasions I've made up identical handbags, left one plain, and incorporated a unique kind of finding on the other one. I've used brass keys, old key plates, bobbin spindles, and even old harness brass. Without exception, the handbag with the unique finding will disappear first.

Cooperative Buying

A source of supply for leather, leatherwork supplies, and findings can be a problem to a small shop owner. If you're set up in East Watertank, Nebraska, and the nearest source of supply is 300 miles away, you can already anticipate supply problems, delays, lack of variety, and absence of competitive wholesale prices. Setting up shop near the sources of supply has many advantages.

One way to overcome some of the volume buying problems is to get together with other craftsmen and make single, cooperative purchases. Volume buying will open many new doors in the selection of materials. And whenever possible, try and visit your suppliers in person. Keep abreast of new developments in findings, leather, and supplies. You may occasionally run into a supplier who seems to entertain nothing but disgust for the little guy. He burbles and grunts when you show up with your tiny order, and gives you the impression that he's used to dealing in carload lots. As I've suggested in the beginning of the book, try bringing this fellow a *free* handbag for his wife.

Pricing

There *is* a price consistency in handcrafted leather products. Be prepared to discover this consistency. The public is aware of it, and you should be too. In other words, handmade sandals, handbags, belts, etc., are all subject to a price consistency that varies from shop to shop by only a dollar or two. If you're completely in the dark on pricing, then visit a leather shop of quality equal to your own, and compare prices.

At this writing, leather is one of the blue–chip crafts. It's bringing in a sound return for talent, time, and investment; it's one of the few crafts where there's some sensible equation between price and product.

Wholesale

If you chose not to open your own shop, but still want to sell, you'll have to be prepared to sell wholesale. There is an enormous market for wholesaling handcrafted leather designs in gift shops and boutiques, but you'll have to be prepared to accept less for your product. The retailer expects from 30% to 50% in markup over what the item costs him. You'll have to wholesale your wares with this markup in mind, being certain not to price the item out of competition with the sandal shop owner. The leather–buying public does know the going prices for most items. And don't deal in consignment unless you're absolutely forced to; cash in the hand puts meat on the table.

Display

How you display your leather can often make or break a potential sale. Try to avoid clutter. Leather is most advantageously displayed against earthy material such as wood and weathered wood, cork and burned cork, burlap, hemp, and even fish netting. Display is an art in itself and is open to the limits of the imagination.

If you have a display window, you'll have to think about protecting your finished goods from direct sunlight, unless they're only samples. One excellent eye–catcher is to place your work table near enough to the window to attract potential customers from off the street; and leave your door open during the summer. In this age of machinitis, there's nothing more magnetic to a potential customer than to look in a window and see a man working with his hands. As a hand craftsman, you've got to expect to be something of a one–man side show, and you might as well take advantage of it.

Summary

Up until this point, we've mutually survived a long look at leather. This book can't tell you where leather is going, but I think that it's told you honestly at what stage leather is today. The many craftsmen who've helped in preparing this book weren't always leather craftsmen. One was a sailor, another a biologist, another a teacher, and still another, a high school dropout. Some began as apprentices; others began from trying to make themselves a leather vest, or a pair of sandals. You have one advantage over them; they didn't have a book on leather design to read.

It's now time to get off the page, and to get busy! Here's something to think about while you do:

"... Fold up your aprons, craftsmen, cast your tools away, fling off Necessity's firm yoke, for Freedom calls. Freedom, my lads, is neither wine nor a sweet maid, nor goods stacked in vast cellars, no, nor sons in cradles; it's but a scornful, lonely song the wind has taken ..."

The Odyssey, A Modern Sequel
by Nikos Kazantzakis

Seated Man, *by the author, 10" high x 14" wide; made from 12 ounce cowhide and mounted on a base of burned cork. Burned cork is one of many complementary materials which can be combined with leather in order to emphasize its natural qualities. Photo, Robert Estrin.*

Suggested reading list

Better Homes & Gardens Sewing Book, Meredith Press, New York, 1961

Coats & Clark's Sewing Book, Golden Press, New York, 1967

The Complete Book of Tailoring, by Adele P. Margolis, Doubleday & Co., Inc., New York, 1964

How to Sew Leather, Suede, Fur, by Margaret B. Krohn and Phyllis W. Schwebke, The Bruce Publishing Co., Milwaukee, 1966

Leather Braiding, by Bruce Grant, Cornell Maritime Press, Cambridge, Maryland

Leather Craftsmanship, by John W. Waterer, Frederick A. Praeger, Inc., New York, 1968

McCall's Sewing Book, Random House, Inc., New York, 1963

Simplicity Sewing Fashion Fabrics (pamphlet), Simplicity Pattern Co., New York, 1965

Publications of Tandy Leather Co., Fort Worth, Tex.

Braiding and Lacing for Fun (pamphlet)

Figure Carving, by Al Stohlman

How to Carve Leather, by Al Stohlman

How to Lace (pamphlet)

Leather Handbook (pamphlet)

Sewing with Leather (pamphlet)

The Techniques of Making Leather Garments, by Gus Bouquet

Also Recommended:

Leather Facts (pamphlet), The New England Tanners Club, Peabody, Mass.

Omega Hi-Liter Instruction Manual (pamphlet), Omega Leathercraft Products Co., division of Omega Chemical Co., Fort Worth, Tex. and Los Angeles, Calif.

Suppliers' list

Abrasive paper

Abrasive Products, Inc., S. Braintree, Mass. 02184
Behr-Manning, Division of Norton Co., Dept. 6373, Troy, N.Y.
The Carborundum Co., Niagara Falls, N.Y.
Manufacturers Supplies Co., 716 N. 18th St., St. Louis, Mo.
Minnesota Mining & Manufacturing Co., 900 Bush Ave., St. Paul, Minn.

Adhesives and cements

Allied Shoe Machinery Cement Corp., 241 Winter St., Haverhill, Mass.
American Finish & Chemical Co., 1012 Broadway, Chelsea, Mass.
Atlas Trading Corp., 111 Worth St., New York, N.Y.
Barge Cement, Division of National Starch and Chemical Corp., 100 Jacksonville Rd., Towaco, N.J. (makers of Barge's All-Purpose Contact Cement).
Borden Chemical Co., New York, N.Y. (makers of Elmer's Fast Dry Contact Cement, and Elmer's White Woodworking Glue).
Bradstone Rubber and Adhesive Co., 501 Adams Ave., Woodbine, N.J.
Cambridge Chemical Co., Inc., 251-257 Third St., Cambridge, Mass.
Compo Industries, Inc., 125 Roberts Rd., Watham, Mass.
Devcon Corp., Danvers, Mass. (makers of Devcon glues).
Dow Corning Co., Midland, Mich. (makers of clear cements).
Eastman Chemical Products, Inc., Kingsport, Tenn.
Franklin Glue Co., Columbus, Ohio
General Adhesives & Chemical Co., 6100 Centennial Blvd., Nashville, Tenn. 37202
Goodyear Rubber Co., 132 Duane St., New York, N.Y. (makers of Goodyear High Speed Neolite All-Purpose Cement).
H-B Products Co., 462 Court St., Brockton, Mass.
Charles L. Hardke, Inc., 3320 W. Hopkins, Milwaukee, Wisc.
Kepec Chemical Co., P.O. Box 782, Milwaukee, Wisc.
Master Chemical Co., 27 Bradston St., Boston, Mass.
National Chemical & Plastics Co., 1424 Philpot St., Baltimore, Md.
Polymer Chemical Co., 131 Barron Drive, Cincinnati, Ohio
Prime Leather Finishes Co., 205 S. 2nd St., Milwaukee, Wisc.
Slocum Chemical Co., Inc., 1409 Buchanan St., Lynchburg, Va.
Tandy Leather Co. retail stores, distributors of Craftsman All-Purpose Cement
U.B.S. Chemical Co., Division of A.E. Staley Mfg. Co., 491 Main St., Cambridge, Mass.
Union Adhesives Co., Inc., 1591 Hyde Park Ave., Hyde Park, Mass.
United Shoe Machinery Corp., 140 Federal St., Boston, Mass.
U.S. Plywood Corp., 2305 Superior Ave., Kalamazoo, Mich. 49003 (makers of Weldwood Contact Cement).
Wisconsin Latex and Adhesives Co., 321 W. Mill Rd., Milwaukee, Wisc.

Adhesive tape

Minnesota Mining & Manufacturing Co., 900 Bush Ave., St. Paul, Minn.

Aprons and gloves

Berman Leather Co., 103 South St., Boston, Mass.

Arch cushions

Thomas J. Anthoine Co., 561-567 Pleasant St., Lewiston, Me.
Connecticut Artcraft Corp., 21 Ann St., S. Norwalk, Conn.
The B.F. Goodrich Co., 6 Bridge St., Shelton, Conn.

Belt lacing

American Lace Leather Co., P.O. Box 121, Richmond, Va.
California Tanning Co., 1905 Shenandoah Ave., St. Louis. Mo.
National Supply Co., 28 Washington St., Haverhill, Mass.

Benches and tables

Compo Industries, Inc., 125 Roberts Rd., Waltham, Mass.
Master Cutting Table Co., 50 W. 27th St., New York, N.Y.
The Singer Sewing Co., 30 Rockefeller Plaza, New York, N.Y.

Binding and piping

United Stay Co., Inc., 222 Third St., Cambridge, Mass. 02142

Bleach

Fiebling Chemical Co., 516 S. 2nd St., Milwaukee, Wisc.
Master Chemical Co., 27 Bradston St., Boston, Mass.
Tandy Leather Co. retail stores

Brushes

Master Chemical Co., 27 Bradston St., Boston, Mass.
National Shoe Products Corp., 56 Monk St., Stoughton, Mass.
United Shoe Machinery Corp., 140 Federal St., Boston, Mass.
Whitman Shoe Polish Mfg. Co., 531-535 Washington St., Whitman, Mass.

Braid

Louis Ungar Braid Co., Inc., 973 Brook Ave., Bronx, N.Y. 10451

Buckles

Bernard Abrams, Inc., 52 W. 39th St., New York, N.Y.
Allens Mfg. Co., 89 Shipyard St., Providence, R.I.
American Shoe Specialties Co., 318 W. 39th St., New York, N.Y.
Felch-Anderson Co., 248 Toronto Ave., Providence 5, R.I.
General Fashions, Suite 957 Marbridge Bldg., 47 W. 34th St., New York, N.Y.
Handy Ormond Mfg. Co., 50-05 47th Ave., Woodside, N.Y.
Lynn Buckle Mfg. Co., 721 Washington St., Lynn, Mass.
Nailhead Creations, Inc., 20 W. 31st St., New York, N.Y.
North & Judd Mfg. Co., New Britain, Conn.
Precision Buckles, Inc., 231 Georgia Ave., Providence, R.I.
United Shoe Ornament Co., 35 Tripoli St., Cranston, R.I.
E.E. Weller Co., 253 Georgia Ave., Providence, R.I.

Buttons

American Shoe Specialties Co., Inc., 318 W. 39th St., New York, N.Y.
Bowcraft Trimming Co., Inc., 6 W. 32nd St., New York, N.Y.
Liberty Shoe Ornaments, 438 W. 37th St., New York, N.Y.

Chemical dyes

Fiebling Chemical Co., 516 S. 2nd St., Milwaukee, Wisc.
Master Chemical Co., 27 Bradston St., Boston, Mass.
Omega Leathercraft Products Co., Division of Omega Chemical Co., Fort Worth, Tex., and Los Angeles, Calif.
Tandy Leather Co. retail stores
United Shoe Machinery Corp., 140 Federal St., Boston, Mass.
Whitman Shoe Polish Mfg. Co., Inc., 531-535 Washington St., Whitman, Mass.

Cork

Armstrong Cork Co., Lancaster, Pa.
Dodge Cork Co., Inc., Lancaster, Pa.
Spano Shoe Products, Inc., 867-881 E. 52nd St., Brooklyn, N.Y.
Thompson Shoe Products, Inc., 67 Perkins Ave., Brockton, Mass.

Cut soles

Berman Leather Co., 103 South St., Boston, Mass.
Eastern Cut Sole Co., 268-274 Broad St., Lynn, Mass.

Cutting boards

Killam Cutting Block Corp., 35 W. 19th St., New York, N.Y.
Master Cutting Table Co., 50 W. 27th St., New York, N.Y.
Tandy Leather Co. retail stores

Cutting dies

Acme Cutting Die & Machine Co., 512 Boston Turnpike, Shewsbury, Mass.
John J. Adams Die Corp., 10 Nebraska St., Worcester, Mass.
Auburn Die Co., Inc., Auburn, Me.
Boston Cutting Die Co., 50 Freeport St., Dorchester, Mass.
Chicago Die Cutting Corp., 2333 W. Nelson St., Chicago, Ill.
North East Cutting Die Corp., 601 Washington St., Lynn, Mass.
United Die Corp., Danvers, Mass.
United Shoe Machinery Corp., 140 Federal St., Boston, Mass.

Ear wires

E.A. Adams & Sons, Inc., 33 Bassett St., Providence 1, R.I.
Eastern Metal Goods Co., 19 W. 34th St., New York, N.Y.
W.R. Cobb Co., 101 Sabin St., Providence, R.I.
Metal Findings Corp., 152 W. 22nd St., New York, N.Y. 10001
A. & J. Findings Co., 6 W. Bacon St., Plainville, Mass.

Elastic loops

Bowcraft Trimming Co., Inc., 6 W. 32nd St., New York, N.Y.

Eyelets

Approved Apparel Trimmings, Inc., Rm. 402, 267 5th Ave., New York, N.Y.
Atlas Tack Corp., Pleasant St., Fairhaven, Mass.
Bowcraft Trimmings Co., Inc., 6 W. 32nd St., New York, N.Y.
Handy Ormond Mfg. Co., 50-05 47th Ave., Woodside, N.Y.
Stimpson Shoe Eyelets, 70 Franklin Ave., Brooklyn, N.Y. 11205

Felt

National Felt Co., 24 Mechanic St., Easthampton, Mass.

Foam rubber

Chris-Craft Industries, 1980 E. State St., Trenton, N.J. 08619
General Foam Corp., 640 W. 134th St., New York, N.Y.
Shoe Factory Supply Corp., 235-247 Lynch St., Brooklyn, N.Y.

Fur trimmings

Arco Novelty Co., 209 W. 26th St., New York, N.Y.

Handbag findings

Best Mfg. Co., 1101 Atwood Ave., Johnston, R.I.
D. & W. Tool & Findings Co., 52 Salem St., Providence, R.I.
Eastern Findings Corp., 19 W. 34th St., New York, N.Y.
M. & F. Casting Co., 50 Aleppo St., Providence, R.I.
American Jewelry Findings Co., 10 W. 47th St., New York, N.Y.

Heels

Allied Heel Co., Inc., 24 Simmons St., Roxbury, Mass.
Coulson Heel Co., Inc., Hanover, Pa.
New York Heel Co., 1155 Manhattan Ave., Brooklyn, N.Y.
Penn Wood Heel Corp., Akron, Pa.

Knives

Allied Shoe Machinery Corp., 241 Winter St., Haverhill, Mass.
Harrington Cutlery Co., Southbridge, Mass.
New England Knife, Inc., 6 Burton St., Worcester, Mass.
C.S. Osborne Tool Co., Harrison, N.J.
Powers & Reed, 581 Washington St., Lynn, Mass.
Warren Cutlery, Inc., P.O. Box 289, Rhinebeck, N.Y.
X-Acto Precision Tools, Inc., 48-41 Van Dam St., Dept. 25, Long Island City, N.Y.

Laces

American Lace Leather Co., Inc., P.O. Box 121, Richmond 1, Va.
California Tanning Co., 1905 Shenandoah Ave., St. Louis, Mo.
Essex Shoe Supply, Inc., 137 Welles Ave., Dorchester, Mass.
Footwear Products Co., P.O. Box 357, 628 Fairview Ave., Gettysburg, Pa.
Hope Webbing Co., 1005 Main St., Pawtucket, R.I.
Thomas Taylor & Sons, Hudson, Mass.
United Shoe Machinery Corp., 140 Federal St., Boston, Mass.

Last blocks

S.H. Stafford & Sons, Morrisville, Vt.

Last makers' supplies

Compo Industries, Inc., 125 Roberts Rd., Waltham, Mass.
United Shoe Machinery Corp., 140 Federal St., Boston, Mass.

Last remodelers & repairers

The Geo. E. Belcher Co., Stoughton, Mass.
Brockton Last Corp., 4 Capen St., Stoughton, Mass.
Robert Last Corp., 341 Taylor St., Manchester, N.H.
Vulcan Corp., 6 E. 4th St., Cincinnati, Ohio

Lasts

Century Last Co., Inc., 1831 10th St., Portsmouth, Ohio
H. & S. Last Co., 360 Merrimack St., Lawrence, Mass.
Leader Last Co., 35 Congress St., Salem, Mass.
Vulcan Corp., 6 East 4th St., Cincinnati, Ohio

Leather

Alligator
Connecticut Import Export Corp., 1140 Broadway, New York, N.Y.
Disbrook Trading Co., 1123 Broadway, New York, N.Y.
Florida Tanning & Sponge Co., Walton Ave., Tarpon Springs, Fla.
Southern Trading Corp., 404 Park Ave., New York, N.Y. 10016

Antelope
R.G. Leather Co., Inc., 127 Spring St., New York, N.Y.
Risedorph, Inc., 140 W. 8th Ave., Gloversville, N.Y.

✔ *Belt leather*
Adams Tanning Corp., 118 Adams St., Newark, N.J.
A.C. Products Co., 422 Hudson St., New York, N.Y.
Arrow Leather Co., 39 W. 32nd St., New York, N.Y.
Dermaton Leather Co., 291-297 New Jersey Railroad Ave., Newark, N.J.
Farkash, Inc., 114 E. 25th St., New York, N.Y.
National Supply Co., 28 Washington St., Haverhill, Mass.
Berman Leather Co., 103 S. St., Boston, Mass.
Virginia Oak Tannery, Inc., Luray, Va.
Williams Industries, 213 Wilson Ave., Newark, N.J.

Buck
Beggs & Cobb, 179 South St., Boston, Mass.
Button's Buckskins, West Danville, Vt.
Dauer Leather Co., 5 Beekman St., New York, N.Y.
Rueping Co., Fond du Lac, Wisc.
Legallet Tanning Co., 1099 Quesada Ave., San Francisco, Calif.

Buffalo
C. & P. Leather Co., 222 Verona Ave., Newark, N.J.
Essex Tanning Co., 148 River St., Haverhill, Mass.
Renar Leather Co., 68 Spring St., New York, N.Y.

Cabrettas
Crown Leather Finishing Co., 422 N. Perry St., Johnstown, N.Y.
Feuer Leather Corp., 160 Broadway, New York, N.Y.
A.C. Lawrence Leather Co., Peabody, Mass.
Leather's Best, 120 Wall St., New York, N.Y.
R.G. Leather Co., 127 Spring St., New York, N.Y.

Calf
C. A. Andres & Co., 386 Park Ave., New York, N.Y.
Barrett & Co., 49 Vesey St., Newark, N.J.
F. C. Donovan, Riverview Industrial Park, Needham Heights, Mass.
The Ohio Leather Co., Girard, Ohio
R. A. Rubin & Co., 684 Broadway, New York, N.Y.
Louis I. Silverman, Inc., 729 Atlantic Ave., Boston, Mass.
Victory Tanning Corp., 23 Upton St., Peabody, Mass.

Calf suede
Globe Leather Corp., 432 Park Ave., New York, N.Y.
Hunt-Rankin Leather Co., 134 Beach St., Boston, Mass. 02111

Capeskins
Coey Tanning Co., Wartrace, Tenn.
Donnell & Mudge, 151 Canal St., Salem, Mass.
Liberty Dressing Corp., 17-29 Burr St., Gloversville, N.Y.
Steinberg Brothers, 443 Park Ave. S., New York, N.Y.

Colt and horse
John A. Dauer Leather Co., 100 Gold St., New York, N.Y.
John Flynn & Sons, 80 Boston St., Salem, Mass.
Legallet Tanning Co., 1099 Quesada Ave., San Francisco, Calif.
Weil & Eisendrath Co., 2221 Elston Ave., Chicago, Ill.

Cordovan
Horween Leather Co., 2015 Elston Ave., Chicago, Ill.
Steinberg Brothers, 443 Park Ave. S., New York, N.Y.

Embossed grains
Armour Leather Co., 1113 Maryland Ave., Sheboygan, Wisc.
Hallmark Leather Co., 46 N. Central St., Peabody, Mass.
Keystone Leather, 81 Spring St., New York, N.Y.
Superior Tanning, 1244 W. Division St., Chicago, Ill.

Garment leather
Berman Leather Co., 103 South St., Boston, Mass.
Blackhawk Tanners, 1000 W. Bruce St., Milwaukee, Wisc.
Coey Leathers, Wartrace, Tenn.
A. L. Gebhardt & Co., 226 N. Water St., Milwaukee, Wisc.
Independent Leather Corp., 315 S. Main St., Gloversville, N.Y.
Thiele Tanning Co., 123 N. 27th St., Milwaukee, Wisc.

Kangaroo
William Amer Co., 215 Willow St., Philadelphia, Pa.
American Guild of Kangaroo Tanners, 1405 Statler Bldg., Boston, Mass.
Mullins, Towbridge & Co., 210 South St., Boston, Mass.

Ostrich
Dreher Leather Mfg. Corp., 42 Garden Ave., Newark, N.J.

Pigskin
C. & P. Leather Co., 222 Verona Ave., Newark, N.J.
Hallmark Leather Co., 46 N. Central St., Peabody, Mass.
Harvey-Mallis Leather Co., 386 Park Ave. S., New York, N.Y.
Wolverine World-Wide, Inc., Rockford, Mich.

Rawhide
Griess-Pleger Tanning Co., Waukegan, Ill.
National Rawhide Mfg. Co., 1464 W. Webster Ave., Chicago, Ill.

Reptile
Peter Baron & Sons, Inc., 1st and Bergan Sts., Harrison, N.J.
Cedamar International, 24 Commerce St., Newark, N.J.
Hagen Co., 386 Park Ave., New York, N.Y. 10016
Redi-Cut Reptile Co., 60 Warren St., New York, N.Y.

Seal
Dreher Leather Mfg. Corp., 42 Garden St., Newark, N.J.

Shark
Ocean Leather Co., 42 Garden St., Newark, N.J.

Sheepskin
Adams Tanning Corp., 118 Adams St., Newark, N.J.
Homer Bear & Co., 225 W. 34th St., New York, N.Y.
Chicago Tanning Co., 1508 W. Cortland St., Chicago, Ill.
Morris Feldstein & Sons, 215 Water St., Brooklyn, N.Y.
Globe Tanning Corp., 432 Park Ave. S., New York, N.Y.
Sirois Leather, Inc., 73 Lowell St., Peabody, Mass.
Weil & Eisendrath, 2221 N. Elston Ave., Chicago, Ill.

Sole leather
Berman Leather Co., 103 South St., Boston, Mass.
Charles L. Hardtke, 3320 W. Hopkins, Milwaukee, Wisc.
Virginia Oak Tannery, Inc., Luray, Va.
Wisconsin Leather Co., 1830 S. 3rd St., Milwaukee, Wisc.

Woven leathers
Arrow Leather Co., 39 W. 32nd St., New York, N.Y.
Ouimet Welting Co., Brockton, Mass.
Shain & Co., 179 South St., Boston, Mass.

Leather belting

United Shoe Machinery Corp., 140 Federal St., Boston, Mass.

Machinery; clicking

Allied Shoe Machinery Corp., 241 Winter St., Haverhill, Mass.
United Shoe Machinery Corp., 140 Federal St., Boston, Mass.

Machinery; sewing

Allied Shoe Machinery Corp., 241 Winter St., Haverhill, Mass.
Associated Pacific Machine Corp., 1227 S. Olive St., Los Angeles, Calif.
Atlas Shoe & Sewing Machine Co., 240-42 W. 23rd St., New York, N.Y.
Eastern Sewing Machine Co., 120-124 W. 25th St., New York, N.Y.
The Singer Co., 30 Rockefeller Plaza, New York, N.Y.
United Shoe Machinery Corp., 140 Federal St., Boston, Mass.

Machinery; sewing attachments

Willcox & Gibbs, 1040 Ave. of the Americas, New York, N.Y.

Machinery; skiving

Willcox & Gibbs, 1040 Ave. of the Americas, New York, N.Y.

Mallets

C. S. Osborne Co., Harrison, N.J.
Tandy Leather Co. retail stores
United Shoe Machinery Corp., 140 Federal St., Boston, Mass.

Needles

Compo Industries, Inc., 125 Roberts Rd., Waltham, Mass.
International Needle Corp., 1841 Broadway, New York, N.Y.
C. S. Osborne Co., Harrison, N.J.
Tandy Leather Co., retail stores

Organizations

Tanners Council of America, 411 5th Ave., New York, N.Y. 10016
New England Tanners Club, Box 371, Peabody, Mass, 01960

Ornaments

Bowcraft Trimming Co., Inc., 6 W. 32nd St., New York, N.Y. 10001
D'Or, Inc., 37 W. 17th St., New York, N.Y. 10011
Liberty Shoe Ornament Co., 438 W. 37th St., New York, N.Y. 10018
Musi Corp., 253 W. 26th St., New York, N.Y. 10001

Pattern paper

John S. Cheever Co., 44 Farnsworth St., Boston, Mass.
Geo. W. Miller, 280-90 Lafayette St., New York, N.Y.

Patterns

Butterick Patterns, P.O. Box 200, Canal St. Station, New York, N.Y.
McCalls Corp., Pattern Service, 230 Park Ave., New York, N.Y.
Simplicity Pattern Co., Inc., 200 Madison Ave., New York, N.Y.
Vogue Pattern Service, P.O. Box 200, Canal St. Station, New York, N.Y.

Publications

American Shoemaking, 683 Atlantic Ave., Boston, Mass. 02111
Leather & Shoes, 10 High St., Boston, Mass. 02110
Shoe Factory Buyer's Guide, 683 Atlantic Ave., Boston, Mass.
Tandy Leather Co. retail stores
Weekly Bulletin of Leather and Shoe News, 183 Essex St., Boston, Mass.

Punches

C. S. Osborne Co., Harrison, N.J.
Tandy Leather Co. retail stores

Shears and scissors

Compo Industries, Inc., 125 Roberts Rd., Waltham, Mass.
National Supply Co., 28 Washington St., Haverhill, Mass.
C. S. Osborne Co., Harrison, N.J.
Tandy Leather Co. retail stores
Schnitt, Muholos, 521 5th Ave., New York, N.Y.
Westpfal & Co., Inc., 4 E. 32nd St., New York, N.Y. 10016
Wiss Scissors, Newark, N.J.

Supplies; miscellaneous

Anchor Tool & Supply Co., Inc., 12 John St., New York, N.Y. 10038
Boin Arts & Crafts Co., 91 Morris St., Morristown, N.J.
William Dixon, Inc., 32-42 E. Kinney St. Newark, N.J.
A.C. Products Co., 422 Hudson St., New York, N.Y. 10014
Robert J. Golka Co., 400 Warren Ave., Brockton, Mass.
H. K. Kauffman & Sons Saddlery Co., 139-141 E. 24th St., New York, N.Y. 10010
Plymouth Cordage Industries, Inc., 51 Sleeper St., Boston, Mass.
Sax Crafts, 1103 N. 3rd St., Milwaukee, Wisc.

Thread

Advance Silk Thread Corp., Lodi St., Hackensack, N.J.
American Thread Co., 90 Park Ave., New York, N.Y.
Coats & Clark, 430 Park Ave., New York, N.Y.
Fawcett, Inc., 129 South St., Boston, Mass.
Premier Thread Co., Bristol, R.I.
Robinson Thread Co., 19 McKeon Rd., Worcester, Mass.

Zippers

Manhattan Staple Co., 452 W. Broadway, New York, N.Y.
NYNCO, 123 Old Country Rd., Varle Pl., Long Island City, N.Y.
Serval Slide Fasteners, 36 Lawrence St., Flushing, N.Y.
Talon, Inc., 43 E. 51st St., New York, N.Y.

Index

Edited by Margit Malmstrom
Designed by James Craig
Drawings by Sandy Willcox
Composed in nine point Aster by Harry Sweetman
  Typesetting Corp.
Offset by Halliday Lithograph Corp.
Bound by Chas. H. Bohn & Co., Inc.